Twilight of the American State

Twilight of the American State

PIERRE SCHLAG

University of Michigan Press
Ann Arbor

For questions or permissions, please contact um.press.perms@umich.edu

Published in the United States of America by the
University of Michigan Press
Manufactured in the United States of America
Printed on acid-free paper
First published February 2023

A CIP catalog record for this book is available from the British Library.

Library of Congress Cataloging-in-Publication data has been applied for.

ISBN 978-0-472-13338-3 (hardcover : alk. paper)
ISBN 978-0-472-03926-5 (paper : alk. paper)
ISBN 978-0-472-90383-2 (OA)
DOI: https://doi.org/10.3998/mpub.12393244

The University of Michigan Press's open access publishing program is made possible
thanks to additional funding from the University of Michigan Office of the Provost and the
generous support of contributing libraries.

CONTENTS

Digital materials related to this title can be found on the Fulcrum platform via the following citable URL https://doi.org/ 10.3998/mpub.12393244

LIST OF CHARTS

ACKNOWLEDGMENTS

For help in writing this book I am grateful to friends and colleagues Fred Bloom, Erik Gerding, Maria Grahn-Farley, Sharon Jacobs, Sarah Krakoff and Zoran Oklopcic. I have benefited from the great work of my research assistant Daniel Sequeira. I am grateful to my friend David Eason for many discussions about the ideas set down herein. Various chapters of this book were presented at the University of Arizona Law School, the University of Colorado Law School, Sciences Po Law in Paris, and the University of Glasgow School of Law. I thank the participants for their comments and criticisms. I am extremely grateful to my amazing faculty coordinator, Kelly Ilseng, who edited and proofed my work and always anticipated the next steps. I am also grateful to my Dean, James Anaya, who was highly supportive of this project throughout and, of course, to my wife, Elisabeth Hyde.

PREFACE

This is an unusual book for law. It has no conclusion. It issues no recommendations. Instead, it offers itself as a preliminary step: it is an effort at awareness and reconnaissance—a kind of intellectual reckoning with our political-legal conditions. Written not from some presumed pinnacle of knowledge, but from a sense that the epistemic scaffolding has already collapsed.

In America, such thinking is not generally welcome. I am reminded of a leading progressive thinker at Harvard Law School reacting to postmodern thought a few decades ago: "It's demobilizing," this thinker said. I did not write then the obvious response: "I see, so—mobilized, are you?" To which the clear answer was: no, of course, not. No—an answer that would be confirmed repeatedly over the next few decades. A rout.

The legal academy and American intellectual culture were on the wrong tracks then as they are now—carefully applying finishing touches on an edifice of knowledge already hollowed out.

How does one get through?

⟩

Here is a version of the problem succinctly stated. In American intellectual culture, the participants are so eager to find or recommend a solution that they will not tolerate any statement of the problem that does not immediately enable a solution. The perverse consequence of this state of affairs is that American intellectuals (and here legal thinkers are clearly in the lead) will not address any problem for which they cannot offer up a solution.

Pause on that.

In what world is that sensible?

⟩

In the university, the problem is particularly acute. There, not only do we encounter the general culture's distaste for problems that are not immediately resolvable, but we encounter entire disciplines (again law is in the fore-front) organized against any thinking that would require a refashioning of the research agendas or methods of the discipline. Indeed, there are entire disciplines that, as Imre Lakatos observed, are constructed as elaborate defense mechanisms—as intricate ways not to see, not to understand, not to evolve, but to repeat themselves as the same.

How to get through?

When I started teaching (this was 1982) I planned on being as critical as I could, mastering the most serious critiques of law, and then when political circumstances improved (when there was someone in legal officialdom to write for) I would turn. I would write for them.

That didn't happen. Things got worse. A lot worse.

But I did turn—albeit in ways not anticipated. I became more radical in my views of law. I became fascinated with how law and legal thought worked (and didn't). I took to a more descriptive orientation—albeit always informed by an acid critique of the orthodoxy's terms of engagement.

The project seemed more helpful than the legal scholar's typical normative prescriptions—the vast majority of which I viewed as cave-ins to the status quo or missives to the ether. Redundant in the first case and ineffectual in the second.

The political and moral character of law made the prospect of academic escapism implausible. I remained engaged with law, legal thought, and legal institutions. I described many of the pathways of orthodoxy as intellectually, politically, and aesthetically misguided.

Today, I am modified, but unchastened. Most of what I've written in the last forty years still seems right. Shockingly, the vast bulk still seems relevant. Along the way, I got myself to thinking and I hope others as well. A good thing. As my friend Jack Schlegel says, thinking is "the greatest adventure." Yes, and if thinking is not an adventure, it may be doubted that it is thinking at all.

PIERRE SCHLAG
Boulder, Colorado, 2022

I Introduction—Distraction and Catastrophe

We do not know what is happening to us, and this is precisely what is happening to us, not to know what is happening to us.

—JOSÉ ORTEGA Y GASSETT (1922)[1]

Things are not going well. They haven't for some time.

That we Americans have been lied to repeatedly by our leaders as to our identity, our character, our history, our state, and its actions is clear. That those same lies have been used repeatedly in high school, on TV, in speech after speech, to send our sons and daughters to die in useless, immoral, and criminal wars is also beyond dispute. That our elected leaders do not represent the political views of the American people, but rather the wishes of a wealthy minority (a small minority) is also beyond debate. That part of the population expresses and feeds upon a long-standing anger, resentment, revanchism, and militancy that is authoritarian in character, mythological in thought, and ill-disposed in action is also evident.[2] That the U.S. has never adequately atoned nor provided adequate reparations for slavery, genocide, and their legacies is incontestable.

I start from this vantage—one succinctly captured by George Packer on the arrival of the COVID pandemic. He writes:

> When the virus came here, it found a country with serious underlying conditions, and it exploited them ruthlessly. Chronic ills—a corrupt political class, a sclerotic bureaucracy, a heartless economy, a divided and distracted public—had gone untreated for years. We had learned to live, uncomfortably, with the symptoms. . . .
>
> The crisis demanded a response that was swift, rational, and collective. The United States reacted instead like . . . a country with shoddy infrastructure and a dysfunctional government whose leaders were too corrupt or stupid to head off mass suffering.[3]

Dead on. In what follows, I hope to contribute to an understanding of how we arrived at this dread moment. I aim to tell only a part of the story. I teach law and so I will speak to what I know. This book then will be about law—albeit law in the grandest sense, a big picture view. There will thus be no coverage of the judicial or regulatory decisions issuing daily from the capitals of officialdom, nor will there be much discussion of the doctrinal exegesis or court-watching that dominates the work of legal scholars. I have no desire to engage in that conversation. Nor do I think its overwhelming dominance in law schools is very helpful. Whatever the Holmesian "path of law" may be, it is not likely glimpsed bit by bit, step by step from the pages of *U.S. Reports* or the columns of the *New York Times*.

Right off, I need to be very clear that law (even in its big picture sense) is not the only story, nor even the most important story, to be told about our contemporary condition. The question, how did all this happen, could yield many kinds of answers issuing from many different provenances. Certainly, a good number of failures variously categorized as economic, social, technological, and cultural have prepared the way for our predicaments. I wish to affirm the importance and the salience of those stories.

Many of these stories have already been told (and told very well). I wish to offer something of a supplement—a story that may well seem idiosyncratic to many. This is a story about law, legalism, and the various iterations of the American state as seen from that perspective. In one sense, this is a narrow view: law and legalism are but a partial take on the state and the social and economic forces that shape national trajectories. In another sense, though, what follows is a very broad take. Again this book is about law in the grandest sense, a big picture view.

I do not wish to exaggerate the role of law, but the idea that law, legalism, lawyers, judges, and law schools have played a part, even a significant part, in the disorders afflicting the country should surprise no one. Whether law is dominant or derivative in the organization of social and economic life (a matter of some debate) it lays out much of the conceptual architecture through which we name, map, and navigate everyday realities and make our way through the world. In time, much of that conceptual architecture becomes so routinized, so normalized, so backgrounded that we fail to even notice it. But law—it is. And effective too. And all the more so for not being noticed.

Indeed, many of the features of our daily lives owe their existence at least in part to law. Corporations, employees, HMOs, insurance, plumbers, electricians—these identities are all in part constructs of law. Even material features of our everyday world are in part constructions of law: strip malls (zoning), the arrangement of federal buildings in D.C. (separation of powers), internet service and cyber-bullying (section 230), condominiums (property law), and gig economies (contracts). To be clear, the idea here is not that law is somehow an origin, nor that it is autonomous, nor even relatively autonomous. Whether law is derivative or not of other forces or interests (e.g., the social, the economic) is separate from the question of what law contributes to the design and solidification of the conceptual architecture within which these other forces are expressed, given shape, vindicated, formalized, and entrenched (as well as thwarted, excluded, and derailed).

Here we explore four iterations of the American state: liberal democratic, administered, neoliberal, and dissociative. What will matter in the discussion that follows is not the state. Certainly, this is in no way state theory. In fact, the expression "state" does not have much content here. (More on this in Notes on Method.) The real bite of the work here lies in the four iterations of the state. All these iterations emerged successively and reached their zenith at different times. Each iteration in the series displaces the previous ones, but never completely. Each of the four iterations survives in the contemporary moment—in various relations of antagonism and symbiosis. Each iteration of the state, and all of them together, are pervaded by conflicts and contradictions, which are routinely denied and evaded, bringing about the compromise of each iteration and enabling the next to emerge. The iterations are, in different moments and from different perspectives, objective or subjective, passive or active, stable or mutable. By the time we reach the last iteration, the dissociative state, we have, to put it bluntly, quite a mess on our hands.

In an important sense, this is a story of how we arrived at this dissociative state. Insofar as this is a big picture story, it goes against the grain. It deviates sharply with the way we Americans typically talk about democracy, law, and politics. Ours is a pragmatic, event-focused, fact-saturated, down to earth orientation. Our talking heads are not intellectuals. They are almost always specialized experts—people who are extremely knowledgeable about matters within their particular jurisdiction. Their great virtue is competence (not insight), specialization (not breadth).

This is not the only way to do things. The French are not like this. Their intellectuals are high theory. Of course, sometimes *too* high: they'll write entire books deducing the American character on the basis of their one-week road trips to Las Vegas, Yosemite, and some random diner in Barstow. I would want to tell the French: "You know, you guys ought to do a little empirical homework before you start theorizing. Yes, I know you live in *Paris* and all that, but that is not a free pass to deduce the world. Really—it just isn't."

What would I say to Americans? "Listen, I have an idea. How about you guys get out of your fact-focused journalistic stories, your great men biographies, and your available data sets once in a while? Really. Get some perspective, climb out of the silos. Yes, I know, you like facts, events, and details, but the thing is, silo-knowledge doesn't generalize easily. Scaling up is a real problem. And no matter how many silo-knowledges you put together, in the end it's still not going to add up to a whole. Really—it just isn't." Just take a walk around your university: each department's discipline seems to be built on core assumptions that form the highly contested subject matter of the discipline next door. And so on, all around campus.

As I see it, Americans could stand to be a bit more French (just as the French could stand to be a bit more American). I mention all this because, being an American (in America) I am going to be leaning hard French in this book. In fact, that will be one of the ongoing themes—that where American law and legal thought is concerned, Americans are way too exceptionalist and way too enthralled with their historical events, personages, texts, and the details of their highly mythologized constitutional history.

Meanwhile, before delving into the various iterations of the state, there are some extremely annoying popular distractions to dispatch. They are a hindrance to the project here. They are going to be put aside. As decisively and expeditiously as possible. Now is the time to do it. On the upside, if we succeed here and now, we won't have to dwell on these distractions again in the rest of the book.

So here's a huge one—bright, shiny, neon orange, and lethal.

The Trump Show

Remarkably, as this book goes to press, the Trump Show endures. That show triggered a serious ongoing national derangement in Trump's supporters and in his opponents as well. One of the curious aspects of this derangement is that as consummate narcissist, Trump was an amazing success. He managed to draw extraordinary attention to himself as a man of great import. His ego and its needs became the center of national attention.

Remarkable as well—and a profound source of a national identity crisis—is that a man so bereft of any admirable qualities and indeed so deeply steeped in their opposites could be so venerated and even loved by so many. The man is vindictive, vulgar, selfish, misogynistic, racist, cognitively compromised, poorly educated, incurious, prone to narcissistic rages, mendacious, and sadistic. So what's to like here? Is this now the personification of America? Is this is who we are?

Well, in a sense, yes—apparently, this is a very large part of who we are.

It is impossible to write about America in this moment without recognizing the import of this derangement. One aim in this section then is to put the Trump Show and its spin-offs in their place. Another aim is to learn how to turn away from that broad array of Establishment institutions, practices, and personnel (the media, the polls, Congress, the Supreme Court, the endless stream of expert TV talking heads, the blogs, and so on) that unwittingly helped create the Trump Show and sustain the Trump Nation. An intellectual turn away from all this is not easily accomplished. So bear with me—just one section on the Trump Show (not even an entire chapter) and then no more.

Here goes.

On November 8, 2016, Donald J. Trump was elected president of the United States. Trump's electoral triumph was almost entirely unexpected by the pollsters, the political commentariat, the academic cognoscenti, and the *bien pensant* of the political world. Perhaps most perplexing was that Trump's outlandishness was not the clownish joke depicted in the media, but rather a major ingredient of his electoral success. When Trump assumed office, his idiosyncratic behavior—a mix of sociopathy, whining self-regard, and bullying—continued, indeed, intensified. It was presidency by outrage, government by mendacity—a political carnival of buffoonery, incompetence, and vulgarity. The world, it seemed, had been turned upside down. Asylum seekers were branded as criminals while neo-Nazis could be "very fine people." And yet through it all, Trump held fast to the loyalty of his base. The Trump Nation neither rejected nor abandoned him, but seemed almost to relish his crude outré behavior. "Yeah, he's a thug. But he's our thug." It was almost as if his being a thug was a touchstone of his authenticity.[4] "See—he tells the truth. We know because he lies all the time. So, you see? He's truthful: he doesn't pretend he's not lying."

Meanwhile, the political carnival was documented in meticulous fact- and factoid-driven 24/7 detail in the media. This entire carnival—Trump, his acolytes, his media sponsors, his media critics—this was the "Trump Show." It is what happens when entertainment substitutes for politics (reality TV) and politics substitutes for governance (the permanent campaign). This, as will be seen later, is a manifestation of the dissociative state—a state that has lost its organizing *raison d'être* and is thus barely a state at all—largely defenseless against colonization. How did the U.S. get there?

Anyone attempting to understand the epic fails in the rise of Donald J.

Trump must contend with the realization that the very institutions typi-cally relied upon to provide answers and edification—namely, the media, academia, expertise—have revealed themselves to be questionable sources. How so? Well, many of these institutions and the knowledges they propound (including law) almost completely failed to recognize the risks posed by the Trump Show and the Trump Nation. They failed to recognize Trump's capac-ity to awaken, nurture, and channel a dormant ethos of anger, despair, and revolt across much of the U.S.

Thus it is that the very institutions and knowledges usually relied upon to tell us what is happening revealed themselves to be severely compromised as sources of truth and insight. Not because, as Trump claimed, they are agents of "fake media." (They are not.) Instead, the main problem has been more the converse: CNN, MSNBC, the *New York Times*, the *Washington Post*, the *L.A. Times*, and the sundry contributions of the high-end blogosphere revealed themselves to be unwittingly captive to the rhythms, aesthetics, and forms of the Trump Show. They allowed themselves—simply by doing their jobs (as they saw things)—to become in a limited but important sense part of the Trump Show as they charted meticulously his impulsive deviations from conventional templates of history, law, and the norms of presidential prac-tice. The media left the audience mired in a world of Trumpish facticity—the media's habitual focus on facts, events, and details were almost perfect for an unwaveringly day-by-day transactional Trump. Perhaps many (most?) of the media personalities were, as mentioned above, just doing their jobs. Maybe, but there is also a more cynical explanation. They needed to hate Trump: it had become their business model.

Hence, the accidental brilliance of the Trump Show itself: the media and the commentators were all primed to feature his daily vulgarity and nightly ugliness. It was contagious. We had all been conscripted to serving time on some presidential version of his show, *The Apprentice*. We even became habit-uated to social media as a normal vehicle for the announcement of national policy. It became baseline-normal.

Lacking the theoretical apparatus, business model, or inclination to dis-tance themselves from the Trump Show, the media and the political com-mentariat devoted itself to producing an augmented reality version of the Trump Show: what the Establishment transmitted was truthful, but what it truthfully transmitted was the reality of a surface world—fractionated, atom-ized, chaotic, and staccato. The political equivalent of one car crash after another. Now, to be sure, that world *does* exist. It is not "unreal." It is, however, a world of superficiality that, if taken too seriously, eclipses deeper, more edifying stories about what is happening. And ironically, there *are* deeper and more urgent stories to be told (including stories about how and why our world has come to be seen and experienced as relentlessly fractionated, atomized, chaotic, unreliable, and staccato).

This book, in describing the unraveling of the American state across the centuries, is an attempt to tell one such story. These are historical times once again. The moment of postmodern ennui, which in the '80s and '90s diagnosed a cultural and intellectual stagnation, has passed. Today, history has awakened again, and with malign affect. We face "interesting times" again as the Chinese curse has it. And so we must learn to think *big picture* once again.

So now that we've bracketed the Trump Show, its many shiny objects and all its media refractions, the best way we can, let's transition quickly to what can be called, for the sake of nomenclature, "The Current Disorder." This disorder is far broader, deeper, more ancient, more pervasive, more pluralized, and very likely longer lasting than the flailing of the Trump Show.

The Current Disorder

The transition begins here—by turning attention away from Trump to the epic fails of sundry American institutions in forestalling his election in 2016.

Now, of course, it might be said that, in a *formal* sense, the institutions did not fail at all in 2016: Trump's opponents in the Republican primary lost fair and square. Trump was to some degree vetted. Voting worked. The electoral college worked. The Constitution was not abandoned. The losing Democratic candidate conceded. She was not prosecuted.

Nonetheless, this was a simulacrum of democracy. Democracy as mere form—detached from any robust self-conception. Having neglected for decades the prerequisites for democracy (education, political education, limits on the systems of citizen manipulation), 2016 was a game show of an election—a shallow entertainment spectacle with intensity and passion transformed into hatred and disdain. It was a Chardonnay vs. Budweiser election staged as burlesque.

How did this happen? The short story: we had many different malfunctions, originating at different times, each failing at different speeds, some from long ago and far away, but all of them converging in a perfect storm of institutional failures—their force memorialized in a historic vote on one Tuesday night in November 2016. On that night, the U.S. elected a person manifestly unfit for the presidency. And apparently none of our institutions—

investigative, informational, educational, intellectual, civic, political, cultural, legal—was able to prevent this from happening.

Of course, perhaps this is exactly what democracy means. Maybe.

In the moment after the election, in the wake of this historic defeat for a great many of the Establishment institutions, it was not unreasonable to hope that they would do a lot of self-examination and reckoning. After all, it was the media that helped elect Trump by giving him free airtime and print space for his outlandish campaign spectacle. It was the press that largely (not entirely) failed to uncover and showcase the alarming pattern of fraudulent behavior by Trump prior to the election. It was the Republicans whose candidates were unable to mount an effective primary challenge to Trump. It was the Democratic Party that greased the pathway for a candidate who, at the time, was under FBI investigation, and who was for entirely predictable reasons (there were many) unable to capitalize on Trump's unfitness. It was the elite law schools, responsible for training not only the Supreme Court justices but also a good number of presidents, members of Congress, and political-legal leaders, that somehow failed to impart to their students an understanding of the political fundamentals of constitutional democracy and thus helped paved the way for cascades of structural corruption.

And yet, despite these glaring failures, very little institutional self-reflection and reckoning has taken place. It did not happen.

One reason for the absence of self-reflection and reckoning is that the very discourses, the very institutions, the very personnel that dominate in diagnosing our predicament are the very same that so dramatically wished to absolve themselves of responsibility for the Trump Show. Indeed, on the threshold of their defeat (and ever since) one thing was clear to these Establishment institutions: "It's wasn't us. It wasn't our discourses. It's not what we did. We were not responsible for any of this. The responsibility lies elsewhere. It was FBI director Comey. It was Russia. It was a fluke. It was whatever reprieves us of any need to examine our discourses, our politics, our knowledges, so as to allow a smooth return to the status quo ante unchastened and unmodified."

Notice that there was a kernel of truth in these Establishment claims externalizing responsibility: where an election turned on roughly 100,000 votes (it did), there is a strong likelihood that the actions of Director Comey and Russia did affect the outcome. True. But what this answer missed, and what rendered it disingenuous in the extreme, is that this election should never (ever) have been close. That was especially true since the primary claim of the Democratic Party candidate, Hillary Clinton, to the presidency of the

United States was competence. That was pretty much her only real claim to the presidency. Not vision. Not ideology. Not stellar achievements. Competence. President Obama virtually said so: he endorsed her because, as he said, there has never been anybody more qualified than Hillary Clinton to serve as president of the United States of America. Well—competence didn't seem to pan out.

Among the things that the establishment institutions failed to recognize (the Bernie Sanders contingent excepted) is that for decades the center-left and the left failed to deliver to their ostensible constituencies. They dropped the working class. They abandoned the poor. They sacrificed the middle class. And so, just as in the rest of world where the center-left and the far left failed to deliver (where so-called socialists became de facto neoliberals), many within these constituencies turned hard right.

The lack of reckoning by the institutions was unfortunate. It was unfortunate not simply because Establishment institutions failed to own up to their epic failures, but because this was a moment in which a deeper interrogation of American institutions including the state might have been possible.

Then comes the 2020 presidential election. On the brink of that election, in the midst of the COVID-19 pandemic, many American citizens no doubt longed for a return to the *status quo ante*. This desire was as understandable as it was naïve. For one thing, there was no *status quo ante* to return to. There was no going back in political-legal terms. Trump had awakened the Trump Nation—an irreducible part of the American body politic that remains angry, resentful, revanchist, and militant. Trump's 45 percent nation will not easily be reassimilated into a civil political discourse or behavior. Numerous metaphorical bridges have been burned and sundry boundaries breached. Floor after floor of decency and tolerance have been demolished. It was one thing to support Trump in the 2016 election—it was quite another to support him in 2020. And it is still another to endorse his lies of a stolen election.

Reckoning did not happen.

I mention all this because this book is a start on such a project. I will be doing what I believe everybody else ought to have been doing—namely, looking hard and long at their own institutions. Being a law professor, I propose a candid look at the Current Disorder in terms of the various iterations of the American state as constructed by law and legal institutions.

As the approach here is idiosyncratic, there is an appendix at the end—Notes on Method. Now for the itinerary.

The first four chapters describe four iterations of the American state, to wit:

The Liberal Democratic State
The Administered State
The Neoliberal State
The Dissociative State

These iterations present conflicts and contradictions both within and among each other. These conflicts and contradictions are arguably survivable. By contrast, the failure to take cognizance of the conflicts and contradictions poses a much greater challenge. Why? Well, it is through these unstable conflicts and contradictions that various forces (sometimes salutary, sometimes ambivalent, sometimes malign) are enabled to modify the character and identity of the state. To ignore or deny these conflicts and contradictions is thus to overlook the ways in which the iterations of the state might be modified—reformed or supplanted. More than that, the denial mechanisms (in psychology, denial is a primitive defense) will perforce have spill-over effects. Denial does not simply eclipse its target—what is to be denied—but it overshoots. It erases context and entourage as well. At the limit, denial becomes a mode of life. Or more topically here—a mode of law. What then happens to law when denial mechanisms take hold? Or worse: when the denial mechanisms become the law? Enfeeblement follows. Rather than address the regulated objects, the law qua denial becomes a way for legal professionals to protect themselves from the recognition that their law *neither is nor does what it claims.*

The various iterations of the state have different legitimation myths, governance mechanisms, aesthetic structures, substantive aspirations. Each of these iterations is internally challenged by its own conflicts and contradictions.[5] The conflicts and contradictions are not simply internal to each iteration. Indeed, the various iterations of the state are also in conflict (as well as in symbiosis) with each other. Sometimes, the various aspects of the iterations align in this context or that. Sometimes they don't.

The logic of metamorphosis that drives the rise of various iterations of the American state is the failure of a prior state to address real or perceived problems. The failure to address the problems is most often a failure of *awareness and reconnaissance*, which in turn leads to a *legitimation deficit* (state promises left unfulfilled) or a *governance crisis* (social coordination thwarted) or both. This matters because legitimation and governance are key functions that constitutional democracies must perform and satisfy.

Specifically:

Legitimation: In order to succeed, a constitutional democracy must legitimate itself to the people (or some minimum subset thereof). The state offers a number of "goods" to its people—defense from others, prosperity, domestic tranquility, opportunity, and so on. Whatever the people feel they are entitled to receive from the state must somehow be delivered (or appear to be delivered). Few things destabilize a state so well as a failure to meet expectations. In conventional accounts, failure to meet expectations would induce various behaviors noxious to the state: revolt, corruption, bypass, alienation, anomie (and the like). Once the state achieves a degenerative condition (the neoliberal state) the onset of apathy, atomization, alienation, and anomie among the populace perversely serves to stabilize the state in its ongoing decline. The role of legitimation is taken up by stupefaction.

Governance: In order to succeed, a constitutional democracy must also exercise effective governance. That is to say, it must have a way to both apprehend and address problems necessary for effective rule. In a liberal democracy—a political offspring of the Enlightenment—this implies the exercise of reason of some sort (as opposed to resorting to fiat, faith, tradition, intuition, action, and so on) as a mode to apprehend problems and challenges and to formulate responses. It also, of course, implies some measure of other virtues of governance: efficacy, transparency, and more.

Both legitimation and governance require action. But they also require the venues of awareness and reconnaissance to ascertain whether and when such actions are not working. Obviously, some feedbacks in constitutional democracies are fairly brute (e.g., citizen protests, riots, revolts). Others are fairly tame (e.g., op-eds, books, complaints). And some are in between (e.g., lawsuits, electoral challenges). More on this later.

So, for now, a brief look at the four iterations:

The Liberal Democratic State: By design, the liberal democratic state sought to recognize a sphere of life separate and distinct from the state—notably what Adam Smith and Karl Marx described as "civil society" (the market, the family, religion, and so on). The idea is that in civil society, the state is to have as little role or effect as possible so as to preserve the liberty of the *individual liberal subject*. The conceptual and practical challenge at the heart of the liberal democratic state lies in using law to ensure that law does not intrude on the liberties legally guaranteed to actors in civil society. Framed this way, it is an impossible challenge: at some point the state *must* intrude on civil society to preserve the social and economic conditions from deterioration and to enable as well as delimit the very liberties this state was designed to protect. It is unavoidable. In this regard, the best that the liberal democratic state can do is strive not to intrude "too much" on civil society (a problematic project). As the conceptual challenge for the liberal democratic state becomes more acute, a reciprocal or spiraling process ensues: the conceptual difficulty exacerbates practical and historic contradictions just as the latter increase the poignancy and stakes of the conceptual difficulty.

For many liberal democratic states, those conditions reached a crisis point at the beginning of the twentieth century. At that point, the subjugation and impoverishment of the working and middle classes precipitated political and economic crises, threatening liberal democracies in the U.S. and other countries. The ensuing challenges across the industrialized world brought about major transformations of the liberal democratic state. What is key here is to appreciate that the failure of the liberal democratic state to recognize (and thus address) the dire conditions in civil society was not an accident, but an outgrowth of *its legal design, its legal structure.* Put another way, what the liberal democratic state advertised as its virtues (the protection of liberties) were simultaneously its vices (political-legal indifference to the depredations of civil society). The two—virtue and vice—were intertwined, indivisible absent the morphing of liberal democratic state into something else.

Why should this matter to us in the present moment? The reason is simple. If the liberal democratic state still rules (and to some degree it certainly does) the pattern will repeat itself: disturbances in civil society will not be perceived. If perceived, not addressed. And if addressed, not remedied. (At least, not by this iteration unmodified.)

By way of illustration, we can speak of three major ongoing challenges that have rocked civil society in the U.S. for which the liberal democratic state has had no solution. The first might be the construction of American civil society on the backs of slave labor and the ensuing radical subordination of Blacks throughout American history. While the egalitarian norms of the Reconstruction amendments were put in place in 1860-1870, they did not begin to have bite in according full citizenship to Blacks in the South until a century later. Most of the American South remained governed until the 1970s by authoritarian states engaged in corrupt police state practices that terrorized and disenfranchised Black people. So while it is true that there "have been improvements," it is also undeniable that the liberal democratic state largely failed to subdue forces of racial subordination that continue to rule. Equally relevant is that, for a large part of the country (the South, though not just), the long American political experience has not been democracy, but rather authoritarianism. To understand the American state, we need to recall the history not just of the victims but also of the perpetrators. For nearly a century, the latter were trained and schooled not in democracy, but in authoritarianism.

The second challenge to the liberal democratic state was the immiseration and, later, the de-skilling of the working class.[6] The liberal democratic state was incapable of addressing immiseration problems, which were not alleviated in the U.S. until the rise of the administered state and, ultimately, the compelled production of World War II. With the 1970s and the return of competition on the world stage, followed by globalization, the economic degradation of the working classes resumed. Again, the liberal democratic state showed itself lacking both the motivation and means to do much about it.

A third challenge, the most recent (and perhaps most virulent) for liberal democracy, was the stunning failure of its institutions (state and civil society) to rationally address the vast social and cultural changes wrought by the advent of cyber technology—most notably the internet. One reason is that the advent of cyber technology was an intense reorganization and restructuring of civil society in ways that silently colonized (and perhaps largely destroyed) the reality of liberal democracy's most prized political-legal ideas: the liberal individual subject, individual rights, individual autonomy, self-direction, privacy, and so on. It was a rout. There are many ways in which this rout might be demonstrated, but one can get a glimpse of it in the failed efforts of cyber-law experts to devise schemes to control the advent of cyber technology. The reason is simple: they focused on traditional liberal democratic rights perspectives that seek nobly (but often ineffectually and incoherently) to protect *the victim* ("individual privacy"). What they largely failed to recognize was the awesome power of *cyber logic* and its devastating actions for liberal democracy: to wit, the 24/7 surveillance, manipulation, and intimidation of the populace.

With the advent of cyber technology, "We the people" have been reduced by multiple 24/7 big data surveillance and aggregated personality profile algorithms to individual potential consuming units. In that capacity we are delivered en masse to sellers, advertisers, foreign governments, and political organizations that will pursue manipulative agendas aimed at undisclosed ends. There is no control group. The algorithms run by themselves. The options on the screen read "Decline" or "Accept"—a choice almost always exercised by clicking "Accept" without reading what has just been "accepted."

The Administered State: Going back to the immiseration of the working class at the beginning of the twentieth century, the liberal democratic state was then in full crisis. Some nations, like Russia, Germany, Italy, and Spain, turned to communism or fascism. Other countries, like France, became an unstable mess. Still other countries, like the U.S., instituted an administrative state. Most jurists and legal scholars in the U.S. associate the administrative state with the dramatic rise of the federal and state regulatory agencies during the early twentieth century, especially during Franklin Delano Roosevelt's New Deal. These agencies (and those created at the state level) clearly operate with, within, and under a different set of laws and are still clearly present on the legal scene as recognizably distinct institutions with different personnel and offices.

While this institutional taxonomic concept called "the administrative state" is useful for some purposes, in this book we will talk about a broader formation: *the administered state*—which extends *far beyond* the agencies of the federal and state governments. The administered state refers to the transformation of law into administration. The latter infiltrates all institutional fora—the judicial, executive, legislative, administrative, and even the institutions of civil society such as firms and private organizations.

The relations between the liberal democratic and the administered state are both symbiotic and antagonistic. Because the egalitarian aspect of the liberal democratic state is an important part of its basic structure,[7] that state is in some ways consonant with social democracy and social welfare. But at the same time, the liberal democratic state is not consonant with the administered state if we understand the latter as the concerted deployment of *political-legal institutions that closely monitor, adjust, and fine-tune* the affairs of civil society to realize the imperatives of social democracy and social welfare.[8] Thus, by way of example, the Code of Federal Regulations may well be the product of legitimate liberal democratic processes, but that does not mean that the regulations are themselves consonant with liberal democratic governance. On the contrary, that sort of "hands-on civil society" welfarism (as opposed to a *merely* redistributive egalitarian welfarism) is fundamentally in tension with the "hands-off civil society" structure of the liberal democratic state. The general point here is that within liberal democracy, liberty norms can accommodate egalitarian norms—so long as the latter are not realized or enforced through the administered state mechanisms of close supervision and intricate legal adjustment of civil society.

As mentioned, the administered state is in part an outgrowth of the administrative state. It is easy to see how the transformation happened: as the administrative state propagated, its modes of reasoning, positive regulatory law, and perspectives could not help but migrate into judicial processes, executive decision-making, and legislative drafting. To put it differently, in the very course of recognizing and evaluating the actions of the administrative state, courts unavoidably allowed administrative discourse into their own. Hence, the administrative state contributes to the rise of the administered state. And both states have their intellectual genesis in a common source: the functionalism, consequentialist reasoning, and policy analysis of legal realism and sociological jurisprudence of the 1920s and 1930s.

The advent of the administered state has entailed displacing liberal democratic inhibitions against ostensible interference with civil society in favor of a more "hands-on approach" to civil society's affairs. This advent has also entailed trying to establish new governance mechanisms and new legitimation schemes. Like the liberal democratic state, the administered state is beset by a fundamental challenge. Having made the deliberate decision to intrude into civil society in the pursuit of various goals and objectives deemed to be in the "public interest," the administered state must struggle both conceptually and practically to identify and honor this public interest ideal in a way that coincides with the practical needs and wants of actors in civil society. Over time, this turns out to be a daunting challenge: ultimately the public interest devolves into various formulas and mechanisms for the aggregation of private interests. Vexingly, the realization one day dawns—courtesy of feminist jurisprudence, critical legal studies, as well as law and economics— that the conceptualizations of the public interest are but different versions of private interests restated in universalized form and accordingly elevated to "the public interest."[9] In short, we have the projection of concrete experience into a purportedly neutral universal form. At that point, a veritable thicket of nagging problems surface: Which (neutral?) aggregation principle and what (neutral?) metrics should rule? Cost-benefit analysis, votes, utility, willingness to pay, politics—just what precisely?

At that point, not only are the liberal democratic state and the administered state afflicted with certain internal difficulties, but they also encounter each other as their reciprocal opposition. This is a point that has been variously explored by a good number of leading legal scholars including Bruce Ackerman, Duncan Kennedy, Jon Michaels, and Ed Rubin.[10] The competing logics and objectives of the two states—the preservation of individual liberty or the enhancement of welfare, the "hands-off" or "hands-on" civil society orientations—yield a conflict that has been long-standing, is well-rehearsed, and is deeply entrenched in the American political-legal register.

But while this conflict is recognized (at least among legal professionals), its implications have not been fully assimilated. Indeed, rather than experiencing the conflict as a moment of contradiction and *possible* irrationality in the organization of the state, most legal professionals just take it as a given—a rift of minor irritation.[11] They are thus able to argue for an administered state hands-on (welfare-maximizing) scheme in one moment and to argue for a liberal democratic hands-off (liberty-preserving) scheme in the next without experiencing any sense of dissonance or intellectual embarrassment. Not only do they feel no particular difficulty in switching grounds in this way, but they are also seemingly untroubled by the syncretic, highly contextualized manner in which they perform their ad hoc pick and choose.[12]

To say at this point that this conflict has led to an *arrested dialectic*—one that doesn't go anywhere—seems clear. For nearly a century, the law of the liberal democratic and the administered state have oscillated back and forth across this divide, restating themselves as largely the same, albeit in ever more intricate, multilayered and hybridized ways. There is no sign of any synthesis in sight.[13] Many legal scholars have tried. All have failed. The sense of stasis—of political-legal disputes that go nowhere—is palpable.

The Neoliberal State: It is amid this arrested dialectic that a third iteration of the state emerges—the neoliberal state. Here, too, we will explore an idiosyncratic version. Suffice to say that the neoliberalism described here is not the usual upgrade of liberalism often found in the legal literature. Nor is it the Hayekian or Pèlerin Society vision, nor the Thatcher-Reagan version, nor even the German ordo-liberal version, but something quite different—the appropriation and submission of state, culture, intellect, and cognition to the epistemic and financial imperatives of marketization and market actors.[14] In some sense, the genesis of this iteration of the state is quite different from the prior two. While the liberal democratic and the administered state can be described as "intellectual projects"—states by design with commendable (even if contestable) intellectual pedigrees and ambitions—the neoliberal state described *here* has an altogether different genesis. In some sense, that is because the neoliberal state is an effect—in fact, *a derivative effect*—of actions taken by powerful market actors and market forces acting not so much to build a new political order as to increase their own wealth and power by insinuating themselves, their interests, and their idioms into this or that aspect of state governance. Neoliberalism is a kind of entrepreneurial state—not just in the sense that the state has become entrepreneurial (although that too is true as well), but rather in the sense that entrepreneurs have taken hold of many aspects of the state and morphed it piece by piece into an assortment of profit centers.

Neoliberalism is thus an iteration of the state that emerges as a result of various powerful market actors in civil society taking advantage of the stalled governance wrought by the endless oscillations of the liberal democratic and the administered state. Viewed from their individual perspective, the progenitors of the neoliberal state are behaving rationally in response to opportunities and stimuli.[15] Rent-seeking, regulatory arbitrage, capture, even a certain degree of legalized corruption—these are all things that rational firms do (indeed, as we will see, *must do*) in order to survive. Viewed in terms of political-legal governance, the entire pattern looks opportunistic in both the moral and biological sense of the term. If one wants to truly to understand how and why neoliberalism happens, it is important to keep the micro (the individual) and the macro (the collective) perspectives distinct: what is rational in the former may well be irrational in the latter.

Deploying the rhetoric of the free market—"entrepreneurship," "growth," "disruptive innovation," and so on—neoliberalism is the completion in deed and thought of the fractioning of the public interest already begun in the administered state.[16] The public interest is redefined as the sum of (some) private interests. Neoliberalism is thus the inversion of the liberal democratic state (where law and politics are supposed to rule). Instead, law and politics are now explicitly demoted as archaic, clumsy, rigid discourses to be exploited for financial gain. Neoliberalism celebrates other approaches: it vaunts the flexibility, efficiency, and innovation of various market actors as they refashion the state in their own image, idioms, and modes of management. The neoliberal state is the colonization of all sectors of both state and civil society (e.g., culture, education, military, media) by the agendas, ideals, and idioms of the market (economics) and private market actors (business). Indeed, it is characteristic of neoliberalism to elide any distinction between economics and business as well as markets and firms. Thus it is that, without abandoning the mythic appeal of Adam Smith's celebration of the invisible hand and decentralized competition, the neoliberal state nonetheless institutes and entrenches altogether different market-forms:

the military industrial complex
the prison industrial complex
the health industrial complex
the food industrial complex
the education industrial complex, and soon:
the anything industrial complex

Like its predecessors, the neoliberal state is beset by a major structural contradiction: it is an *actively and virulently self-cannibalizing state*. Whereas the liberal democratic state effectively undermines itself by renouncing control over aspects of social life on which it depends (civil society) and whereas the administered state keeps losing track of its polestar (the public interest), the neoliberal state quite literally consumes the conditions of its own existence (community and law).

The Dissociative State: In the contemporary moment, all three iterations—liberal democratic, administered, and neoliberal—coexist, registering their logics and effects on and within each other to form the "dissociative state." What is left in the dissociative state is a kind of Potemkin state—a state going through the motions of what it has reduced to formalisms of political-legal institutions (e.g., voting). Having lost any sense of role or mission, the dissociative state wanders on haphazardly—a political-legal zombie engaged in erratic acts of force clothed in residual illusions of grandeur. Perhaps nothing better illustrates this syndrome than the astonishing record of serial failure and killings wrought by the U.S. military on foreign peoples and the American people as well.

Our extended collective failures to recognize and thus address the dissonance among these states and our willingness (particularly among legal professionals) to pretend to a political-legal coherence that is compromised have left us with no sense that the political-legal register provides a rational or defensible social steering mechanism. In the dissociative state, those who claim to follow and honor law have only the thinnest shared account of what this "law" might be. It is thus not clear at all what "law" it is they are honoring other than the unrationalized dictates of legal officialdom (whatever these may be).

These are the overarching internal dynamics that have led the four iterations of the state to experience both legitimation and governance deficits. In hindsight, it is also possible to think about the transitions to the new states in terms of external shocks such as wars and depressions. The importance of such shocks cannot be denied. At the same time, external shocks are prominently the kinds of things that a resilient state guards against and should be prepared to address. More to the point perhaps is that such shocks are only "external" to the degree that the state has not precipitated those shocks, which is to say that many of these "external shocks" (e.g., war and depression) are not external at all.

Whether external or not, the rise of new iterations of the state is often presaged and prompted by crisis. For instance, *the liberal democratic state* emerges in the United States (France as well) as the result of popular revolt against decadent and predatory monarchies. Later, *the administered state* arises in response to serious economic crises wrought by capitalist institutions let loose in the liberal democratic state: the Depression, labor strife, and the rise of totalitarianism abroad. *The neoliberal state* arises as the release of a kind of capitalism-unbound in response to the fall of the Soviet empire. Contrary to Francis Fukuyama's thesis at the time, this was not a weak Hegelian triumph of democracy, but rather the unleashing of the U.S. from international restraint, as its global reality principle, the Soviet Union, was dismantled. As for *the dissociative state*, it coincides with the rise of the algorithmic society, and if one needs a date certain—the onslaught of the Great Recession in 2008. The dissociative state fittingly leaves the largely innocent victims to pay the bills while those who created the economic havoc are rewarded for their recklessness with bailouts and bonuses. The dissociative state thus represents the moment where whatever shared collective political, economic, ethical, and prudential compass the U.S might once have had seems almost beyond retrieval.

In the dissociative state, the conflicts within and among the states produce the grounds for the possible emergence of more serious pathologies— the dark specters (elaborated below). What this evolution/devolution of the American state portends is a populace facing social and economic stress and a culture racked by anomie, alienation, atomization, apathy, anger, and despair. What large parts of this populace see and experience is a state that, in so many ways, simply has not delivered relative to expectations and that can easily appear unable to govern.[17]

What Now?

Yes. What happens now? To the degree that the dissociative state is already slouching toward a failing state, it would not be out of the question to see a turn toward the authoritarian temptation. How would this occur? Consider that if the neoliberal and the dissociative states are currently "what democracy looks like," then it cannot be surprising that for many people "democracy" elicits no great attachment. Consider that in popular parlance, the neoliberal state translates into structural corruption and the dissociative state into pervasive incompetence. If that is what democracy looks like, then really—what's to like? When political-legal action is blocked, and when this blockage is successfully ascribed to democracy, authoritarianism looms large as a possible response. Authoritarianism meanwhile is unlikely to announce itself as such: instead, it will claim to be a restoration of national integrity, the maintenance of law and order, a battle against corruption, a return to the way things used to be. Most disturbing would be the embrace of authoritarianism along with the resurgence of fascist mythology. This would not be fascism in the economic or political sense (an interwar phenomenon linked to the prospect of proletarian revolution) but rather the adoption of fascist myths, about the volk, the intellectuals, the betrayal of the nation, and so on. (Later on all this.)

Moving on from the authoritarian temptation, *The Contest of Diagnoses* is an attempt to reflect on all of the foregoing from a broader perspective.

The thwarting of awareness and reconnaissance is the basic through line of the book. Awareness and reconnaissance depend upon moments of both *inception* and *reception*. On the inception side, the state must create and maintain the pathways, sites, and means through which the people and various groups can voice desires and dissatisfaction. On the reception side, the people and various groups must motivate themselves to use these pathways, sites, and means to become sources of inception in turn. At that point, the state must be capable of reception. It must be able to understand and register whatever message the people and various groups are issuing. In turn, the state must have the motivation and capacities to reflect on its own activity and initiate action to remedy the situation.

In this reflexive process, law, legal institutions, legal education, and legal professionals play key roles in creating and maintaining awareness and reconnaissance. The roles played by awareness and reconnaissance will be exemplified throughout this book. Still, a few prefatory points might help. Law's role in facilitating awareness and reconnaissance is obvious at the level of lawsuits, elections, protests, books, blogs, newspapers, and so on. Law helps create the public events, such as lawsuits, trials, and hearings, that enable the press and the people to recognize what is happening. This aspect of law was dramatically exemplified with the George W. Bush administration's attempts to fight terrorism in the dark—rendition, the imprisonment of suspects incommunicado, and the performance of torture behind closed doors. The press and the people didn't learn what was going on until later. For a time, it was as if nothing had happened. This was an instance of a clear thwarting of awareness and reconnaissance. When failures of awareness and reconnaissance intensify and proliferate, new iterations of the state arise to address or exploit real or perceived problems.[18]

So, yes—awareness and reconnaissance thwarted is a main theme here. But why and how does such thwarting occur? This last chapter strives to enlarge the scope of inquiry by canvassing just a few of the more interesting diagnoses. The idea is that the identification of the four iterations and their interactions affords some basis for further reflection. To be discussed:

Culture-wide Decadence
Macro Blockage and the Proliferation of the Micro
The Dark Specters
Misapprehending Social Coordination

The diagnosis of a culture-wide decadence holds that the discomfiture of the American state is but a manifestation of a greater culture-wide phenomenon. Yes—the political-legal has degenerated. But there is nothing special here: so has nearly everything else. Or so the argument goes. This is perhaps the bleakest of the diagnoses.

A second diagnosis ascribes our sorry state to an untethered proliferation of micro-law and a blockage of macro-law. The hypertrophy of the micro has become so institutionally and cognitively entrenched that only adjustments at the micro level (a court case, an ad hoc statutory program, a domain-specific regulatory regime) remain plausible vehicles for change. Meanwhile, should any greater structural changes be in the offing, they are immediately referred and channeled to the micro-institutions and micro-discourses of courts, legislatures, and administrative agencies . . . where they are likely ruthlessly trimmed or shut down entirely. Similarly, should macro challenges or problems arise, there is simply no channel, no obvious way to respond at the same level of scale. Stated this way, the problem is far broader than the recent acknowledgments that the U.S. Constitution (specifically the amendment process of Article V and the hardwired geopolitical aspects) is a real impediment to actions by "the people."[19] It certainly is. But while the paralyzing role of the Constitution is severe, the problem is broader than the Constitution or constitutional discourse. The macro has been shut down at every level of law.

Interestingly, regarding the micro/macro dichotomy, law is very different from economics. The latter divides the discipline into macroeconomics and microeconomics. In law, we are all micro. We have no macro-law nor indeed any institutions or practices that would correspond to that idea. One obvious reason is that the state stands in opposition to that. Why? Because a key constitutive idea of the state is precisely its presumption *that it is itself* the existential expression of the macro level. The idea that a state would tolerate frequent destabilizing macro-level contestation would seem antithetical to the idea of the state itself.

One aspect of macro blockage and the proliferation of the micro is the closure of the political. Arguably the state has evolved into what Herbert Marcuse prophetically described in *One-Dimensional Man*.[20] The realm of the political—understood here as contests over what collective forms of life should be created, maintained, or discarded[21]—has been almost entirely displaced by a politics that is exclusively dedicated to how material goods, wealth, status, and power should be distributed among different social groups. As for the politics of meaning, by contrast, it has been exiled to contextualized disputes over symbolic politics. We have, it seems, taken a kind of perverse turn—where politics now means having many concrete enemies and a few abstract friends. Solidarity is thin, enmity is abiding, and weaponization is the order of the day. Given that sort of politics, whoever wins (winning being an improbable outcome) is extremely unlikely to produce anything good.

From progressive to conservative, contemporary political philosophers and legal professionals have tailored their thinking to track the existing state and the productions of legal officialdom. Organized politics rules while the political is on holiday. At this point, one could even ask whether "politics is political?" and moreover produce a pretty good brief showing that it is not. It is as if Margaret Thatcher were right—she of the closeting proclamation: "there is no alternative."[22]

A third diagnosis (less scopic than the others) is the notion that the iterations of the state have each been beset by certain dark specters that have created both governance and legitimation deficits. In the present moment, we have some dark specters dancing on the near horizons:

    policy disasters
    loss of trust
    increasing inequality
    political polarization
    structural corruption
    cultural nihilism
    permanent war

A fourth diagnosis is the misapprehension of social coordination mechanisms. For a long time, American jurists and legal scholars have presumed with confidence, gravitas, and a great deal of ritual that law rules. Even today judicial opinions often end with the not so modest line, "It is so ordered," as if the mere uttering of the phrase could make things so. Today, that is a serious misapprehension: this is no longer (if it ever was) the way law is fundamentally related to or distinguished from other modes of social coordination. Instead, what we have is a contest of modes of social coordination: law, politics, markets, technology, military, police, architecture, and more. Each of these can appropriate, subordinate, contest, destroy, join, and support any of the others. Each of these has different vices and virtues. Each strives to create and entrench social realities in its own image—all the better to facilitate a "re-uptake" of these social realities and thus enhance its own dominance. What requires inquiry, then, are the various relations and insularities of the state (as both actualities and illusions) to these other modes of social coordination. If the iterations of the state fail, it is in part because they all have misapprehended the contexts in which they are operating. They have misunderstood the significance of competing forms of social coordination.

There was a time, when the saying was "keep the lawyers out of the room." This was among other things an unwitting testimonial to the power of law and lawyers. Today? It is arguable that the lawyers do not have to be kept out of the room at all—because they have become, for the most part, subservient to the clients. The role of lawyers regarding democracy and the fate of the downtrodden has frequently been ambiguous and ambivalent. We face today the unhappy prospect that the power of jurists and legal scholars to produce emancipatory forms of life has dwindled to virtually nothing while their capacity to freeze politics at the direction and in the interests of the wealthy and the powerful remains.

II   The Liberal Democratic State

In order for a nascent people to appreciate sound political maxims and follow the fundamental rules of statecraft, the effect would have to become the cause; the social spirit, which should be the product of the way in which the country was founded would have to preside over the founding itself; and, before the creation of the laws, men would have to be what they should become by means of those same laws.

—JEAN-JACQUES ROUSSEAU, *THE SOCIAL CONTRACT* (BOOK 2, CHAPTER 7)

The emergence of the liberal democratic state from the ruins of monarchy, feudalism, and theocracy was a remarkable achievement. The political ideals associated with liberal democracy—notably human dignity, rights of political participation, equality, and respect for individual autonomy—were nothing short of inspired and revolutionary.

But high ideals are not everything. Liberal democracy, even by its own lights, has always suffered from certain gaps between its aspirational ideals and the lived everyday experience of its subjects. This gap between ideal and actualities is hardly unique to liberal democracy. On the contrary, it is to be expected of any political-legal regime. What differs among political-legal regimes and thus what matters here are the kinds of responses characteristically offered to address such gaps. The partisans of liberal democracy—its historians, philosophers, legal scholars, and jurists—have taken note of these gaps in a number of characteristic ways and have offered several classic responses worthy of mention.

The Necessitarian realpolitik response. One response to the gaps has been to appeal to the inexorable resistance of collective life to political perfection. The liberal democratic state operates within a field of economic scarcity, cognitive limitations, and the admittedly crude tools of governance. Because the liberal democratic state is by design a limited state, it can only do so much to address the gaps. This realpolitik response has some appeal to jurists. Legal scholars are understandably less enthusiastic. The punchline in this response is always the same and all too easily achieved: liberal democracy *is* what it *is* and between the first "is" and second, there is not much room for academic work. That doesn't make the realpolitik response wrong, but it does make it flat. It evokes the complaint Hegel directed at stoicism: it is "wearisome."[1]

The Progressive response. A much more prevalent response is to situate the gaps between actuality and ideal on a redemptive timeline, thus allowing reforms to make the future better than the past. The gaps are seen as contingent and temporary lapses between a flawed actuality and the promise of desired ideals.[2] The execution of sound normative prescriptions is supposed to bridge the gap. In the classrooms of American law schools, this Whiggish presumption about the power of normative reason has a tenacious hold on the imagination. American legal scholarship is subject to a stylized demand that it produce normative prescriptions to improve or perfect (existing) law. Perhaps the greatest challenge for this scholarship is that there is no singular abiding relation between the words on the page and actualities in the world. The verb "should" can only bear so much weight.

The Reduction to the steady state. A third response (perhaps the least appealing of the three) lies not in trying to adjust the actuality to the ideals, but rather the reverse. In other words, as in the implacable logic of neoliberalism, the ideals are redefined and reconceptualized to match the flawed actualities. As Karl Marx, Friedrich Nietzsche, and Jacques Derrida each showed (albeit in very different ways and to very different ends) the ideal is but a romanticized projection of the actual onto some imagined ideal plane. From there, with a bit of reflection, it becomes obvious that adjusting the ideal to conform to the actual, as so many of our contemporary jurists and legal scholars routinely do, is not much harder than compressing an accordion. Indeed, this is one of the abiding normativity critiques aimed at the progressive response above.

More radical critics, both left and right, have been less forgiving of shortfalls. For radical critics, the gap between the theory and the practice of the liberal democratic state is less a contingent lapse than an integral aspect of the state's design. Many of the radical critics routinely view the gaps as the structural outgrowth of liberal democracy's fundamental determination to leave civil society to be ruled by the logic of capitalism (this is a characteristic critique on the far left) or the displacement of a traditional order by an unwarranted faith in reason and modernity (this is a characteristic stance on the far right).

This chapter borrows from both partisans and critics of the liberal democratic state in giving shape to the inquiry. For those interested, the appendix (Notes on Method) describes in greater detail the approach taken here.

For those who would rather get to the actual discussion, we are almost there. Nonetheless, please indulge me in a few very quick points on the approach—if only to sketch out the path ahead.

Following the partisans of the liberal democratic state, we will strive to understand the liberal democratic state *on its own terms*—that is, in light of what it is ostensibly striving to do, to accomplish, and to avoid. Specifically, the approach used here is one elaborated by the German political theorist F. E. Ankersmit. He suggests that if we wish to understand a state—its character, possibilities, and limitations—we must try to appreciate the kind of problems it was designed to address and resolve.[3] Ankersmit's approach establishes a charitable premise—one that is admittedly steeped in a certain philosophical idealism. And it does not eschew a short-circuit: the possibility that the problems to be addressed by a state are articulated in truncated ways, thereby rendering resolution and success easier.[4] The accordion again. Nonetheless, Ankersmit's approach seems like a plausible way to begin an inquiry.[5]

From the critics, we will draw upon their efforts to identify the *conflicts* and *contradictions* inherent in the liberal democratic state and the inadequacy of *responses* thereto. We will strive to state the contradictions and their more dire implications as forthrightly as possible in order to describe how the liberal democratic state apprehends and attempts to resolve, defuse, or deny these contradictions.

Some critics of liberal democracy (perhaps taking cues from Hegel and Marx) often present contradictions as fated to be overcome. Perhaps that is right if we are talking about logical contradictions, but logical contradictions are virtually never what critical theorists mean: instead, in the critical lexicon, contradiction almost always refers to a variety of conditions (none of which require *logical* contradictions). Indeed, the idea that political, economic, or social forces could somehow be sharpened sufficiently to be caught in internal "logical contradictions" seems bizarre. Such forces would first have to be reduced to propositions, but economic, social, or political formations *are not* propositions.

Moreover, even if they were propositions (which they are not), achieving the kind of conceptual determinacy or specificity that would enable the appearance of a logical contradiction seems quixotic at best.[6] In the critical lexicons, contradiction thus means something else. At various levels of intensity, contradiction can mean tension, opposition, conflict, incompatibility. This refusal to reduce political, economic, and social forces to theses (in the manner of some analytical philosophers) is not a weakness, but a strength. Where political, economic, and social life are concerned, this refusal is not an "absence of rigor," but rigor itself. Indeed, the reduction of political, economic, or social phenomena to "theses" ready for manipulation on the page or the screen is itself a failure to observe rigorously the character of the object under inquiry.

One implication of the foregoing is that the emergence of contradictions in a political, economic, or social force is not necessarily fatal. It does not *automatically* signal a stage of impossibility or unintelligibility. What may well be fatal, however, are the ways in which the contradictions are apprehended and articulated (*or not*) and the ways in which they are understood and addressed (*or not*).

Note here that there is nothing terribly surprising about the presence of contradictions in liberal democracy. On the contrary, as one partisan put it:

> Democracy is rife with these sorts of occasionally discordant yet indivisible dualities: it always has to balance freedom and equality, conflict and consensus, inclusion and exclusion, coercion and choice, spontaneity and structure, expertise and mass opinion, the local and the global, and the present and the future. There can be no unambiguous resolution on one or the other side of the binary.[7]

Indeed, in both its means and ends, liberal democracy is committed to delivering a wide array of conflicting goods. That the simultaneous pursuit of these goods should result in contradictions—sometimes even entire discordant discourses—should surprise no one.

Moreover, as will be seen, the truly biting aspect of critical theory vis-à-vis liberal democracy is not the internal contradiction per se, but rather that the political-legal strategies of liberal democracy to manage the contradictions turn out to be inadequate. If there is any surprise in all this, it is in liberal democracy's tendency to deny and even suppress its major constitutive contradictions. While the denial and suppression of such constitutive contradictions may help the liberal democratic state present itself as strong, stable, and integrated, the attendant obfuscation is a departure from and a distortion of the character of liberal democracy itself—its commitments to reason and to democracy.

The commitments to reason and democracy require, as a predicate condition, a self-understanding of liberal democracy's governance mechanisms—what these mechanisms are and what they do. Obfuscation, on first impression, would thus seem to be contrary to liberal democratic practice and theory—unless we are satisfied by a highly chastened conception of liberal democracy consisting of a merely formal recognitions of the vote, the rule of law, and the like. This would be liberal democracy as scaffolding—even authoritarian states could comply with such formal requirements. If liberal democracy is to hold any appeal, there will be no getting away then from a more robust vision of both liberalism and democracy. But that in turn, requires that liberal democracy enable and maintain robust channels of awareness and reconnaissance.

One would thus expect liberal democracy, in order to perfect and realize its political-legal character, to cultivate the channels and methods of *awareness* and *reconnaissance*. This is not simply a question of individual capacities and competencies, nor simply of educational levels, nor even just of research and reporting. It is also a question of having the *governance mechanisms* and *conceptual schemes* in place that register what is happening in the political, the economic, and the social. It is a question of gaining and providing feedback. If these mechanisms and schemes are given over to obfuscation, that will not help much.

Indeed, the denial and suppression of conflict and contradiction—their withdrawal from popular and professional awareness—deprives the liberal democratic state of feedback and learning. To the extent that the gaps—the absences—are significant, the liberal democratic state will fail to fully understand and control its own identity and evolution.[8] Some of these transformations are bound to be beneficent and others not.

Most troubling is the possibility that, as a result of this shortfall, liberal democracy is open to morphing from within into one or more of its ostensible political-legal antagonists (e.g., authoritarianism). This *morphing from within* is not an avenue of inquiry that partisans of liberal democracy have been keen on pursuing. On the contrary, as soon as illiberalism and authoritarianism emerge on the political-legal scene, they are almost immediately apprehended and represented as emanating from some designated "outside"—some source or origin external to liberal democracy itself. Indeed, among the philosophers of liberal democracy, the latter features only as an opponent to authoritarianism, never its crucible. In a very important sense, the idea that liberal democracy might contain within its own ideational and material architecture the seeds of authoritarianism is rarely pursued.

These are all fairly harsh observations about liberal democracy. But it is the observation, not the harshness, that is the point. None of the arguments about failings, shortfalls, blind spots, and the like are offered as *criticism* of liberal democracy. To be sure, they could be used as predicates for criticism, but criticism is not the point here. Rather, the point is to identify and understand those shortfalls that leave liberal democracy susceptible to transformation or displacement by forces both benign and malign.

More narrowly, the effort is to try to understand and articulate the pathways of liberal democracy's own undoing—a kind of "critique" in the old-fashioned sense of the term, an inquiry into the conditions of possibility. Here, we would be trying to articulate the structural conditions of possibility for the liberal democratic state's own undoing.

We now turn to a deeper exploration of liberal democracy in terms of its achievements and failings.

The Emergence of the Liberal Democratic State

The "liberal democratic state" emerged through violent revolutions, many of them culminating in constitutions setting forth the broad outlines of liberal democracy. Here, the constitutions stemming from the French and American Revolutions can serve as the chief historical markers and key articulations of the liberal democratic state. The liberal democratic state decisively cast off theology and monarchy as explicit legitimations of the state; it dissolved lord-vassal relations as the key form of political governance; and it sought to put an end to the religious wars by removing the state from theological disputes (hence, secularism in France and freedom of religion in the U.S.).

This history is well known and so we turn immediately to the political-legal story. Begin then with Thomas Hobbes, that dark political thinker, who wrote on the brink of the liberal democratic idea. What Hobbes bequeathed to his liberal successors was one hell of a political-legal problem: while a Leviathan state is to be preferred to a state of nature in order to safeguard humans from the violence they might inflict on each other (so argued Hobbes), who or what will ensure that the Leviathan state does not itself become a source of violence against its subjects (a question for his successors)? This would soon become a key liberal democratic problem,[9] particularly salient and enduring in the U.S. It is a problematic that shapes the identity and character of the liberal democratic state.

However, fear of tyranny is not the only concern motivating the design of the liberal democratic state. There is also a more optimistic, aspirational, and utopian side that informs the design—namely, the dream of individual freedom and self-realization. This is a political-legal idea, and like all fundamental political-legal ideas, it has its roots in a kind of ontological predicate about the identity or character of human life. To explore the connection between the two, we turn to Immanuel Kant's short essay, "What Is Enlightenment?"

This essay, published in 1784, reveals succinctly the connection between the Enlightenment and the politics of the liberal democratic state.[10] Responding to the query, "What Is Enlightenment?," Kant offered the following answer:

> Enlightenment is man's emergence from his self-imposed immaturity. Immaturity is the inability to use one's own understanding without the guidance of another. Self-incurred is this inability if its cause lies not in lack of understanding but in the lack of resolution and the courage to use it without another's guidance. *Sapere aude*. Have the courage to use your own understanding, is therefore the motto of the enlightenment.[11]

Today, this can sound a bit trite—a creaky version of charges routinely issued at graduation ceremonies, but if one can imagine reading Kant's essay in 1784, this must have been a moment. The idea that human beings have *the capacity* and, even more, both *the right* and *the obligation* to think for themselves was revolutionary. Indeed, no sooner had Kant said this than he recognized just how difficult it would be for most humans to live up to this aspiration. The task at hand was nothing less than to awaken from a long feudal slumber.

How then does this right and obligation to think for one's self turn into a political-legal idea? Kant argues that the passage out of immaturity into enlightenment requires freedom—namely, freedom of thought and speech, freedom of the scholar to make public use of reason. Here we have an intimation of the construct of the liberal individual subject. This particular subject is the ontological predicate that motivates the demand and desire for a certain political-legal order (the necessity of certain freedoms). Kant's relation to democracy was complicated (at best), but there is no doubt that he was a liberal.

There is thus a utopian aspect to the celebration of the classic liberal democratic liberties—freedom of speech, conscience, religion, and property. The utopian vision is that the individual subject will be *left free in civil society* to pursue his and (much later) *her* own chosen goals or form of life. The claim is that this freedom will not only allow choice and self-determination but also a good measure of self-realization.[12] As Frank Michelman, the famous constitutional theorist, aptly puts it, "Liberals are those who affirm the existential primacy of individuals, the surpassing value to them of freedom, and the primordial claim of everyone to the same concern and respect."[13]

Beyond fear and aspiration, both of which motivate and shape the design of the liberal democratic state, there is also a prudential political aspect to the canonization of the liberal freedoms. Indeed, the affirmation of the liberal individual subject as a key aspect of the political-legal ontology of the liberal democratic vision arguably serves two *prudential strategic functions*. Here, we move beyond Kant.

First, the canonization of the liberal individual subject serves to put the classic historical "antagonists" of the Enlightenment—tradition, religion, theocracy, feudalism, and monarchy—on the defensive. Prior to the Enlightenment, these "antagonists" laid claim to govern not just the state, but civil society. By placing the liberal individual subject at the heart of its politics, the liberal democratic state offers its citizens a non-negligible political prize: individual freedom. This political promise offers citizens nothing less than the possibility of enjoying those activities and pursuits previously denied by tradition, religion, feudalism, theocracy, and monarchy. In terms of securing popular allegiance, this is not nothing.

The second prudential aspect to the celebration and canonization of the liberal individual subject lies in mobilizing a cultural force in civil society that serves as a counterweight to religion and the religious wars from which the liberal democratic states sought to extricate themselves. The liberal freedoms create in civil society a number of serious competitors to religion. Indeed, liberalism recognizes liberal individual subjects who have interests (both ideal and material) that compete with and are sometimes antithetical to those of the various religious orders. The political theory of liberal democracy is not just that the state frees itself from religion and thereby removes itself as a prize to be captured by this or that religion. It also sets up in civil society an abstract political being (the liberal individual subject) who will seek to enjoy and protect his freedom, thereby effectively serving as a check on religious orders and theocratic ambitions.

The attempt to secure the people from tyranny as well as the utopian project of protecting the liberal individual subject coincide with the major design features of the liberal democratic state. Democracy ostensibly secures the people against tyranny. Liberalism ostensibly protects the freedom of the liberal individual subject. Both concerns yield the division of state and civil society. As a caution, this is merely a description of how the ideas fit together. It is neither history nor genealogy.

All of this leaves the liberal democratic state with two fundamental dualities that define its identity and character: liberalism and democracy as well as state and civil society.

Liberalism and Democracy

Frank Michelman describes the American constitutional commitments to liberalism and democracy as follows:

> I take American constitutionalism—as manifest in academic constitutional theory, in the professional practice of lawyers and judges, and in the ordinary political self-understanding of Americans at large—to rest on two premises regarding political freedom: first, that the American people are politically free insomuch as they are *governed by themselves collectively*, and, second, that the American people are politically free insomuch as they are *governed by laws and not men* [*sic*].[14]

This presents, of course, a conundrum—and as Michelman explains in a later article: "The people are *sovereign* and yet sovereignty is to be governed by *law*. 'We the People' are the constituent power, but the people can only express themselves through the constituted form of constitutional law."[15]

Liberalism and Its Conundra

U.S. jurists and legal scholars have generally eschewed direct confrontation with the dilemma of the constituent power/constituted form conundrum. Perhaps this is an effect of flying lower to the juridical ground. Or perhaps it is a legacy of *Marbury v. Madison*, which failed to consider the depth of the conundrum by subsuming the problem within the parochial particulars of the U.S. Constitution. Whatever the reason, "judicial review" and "the countermajoritarian difficulty" became the thing.

Having thus largely avoided addressing the difficulties posed by the conundrum, U.S. jurists and legal scholars have been able to indulge the view that liberalism and democracy are largely symbiotic. In the main, each is ultimately supportive of each other. Such assertions of symbiosis are not wrong. But symbiosis does not preclude nor erase opposition. Democracy is inhibited by liberalism, just as liberalism is curtailed by democracy. In this section, it is not the symbiosis that is of concern, but rather opposition.

One way of beginning to think about the opposition between liberalism and democracy is to recognize that the character of a democracy is less often defined by the "democracy" term than by the limiting adjective necessarily attached:

Liberal democracy
Social democracy
Representative democracy
Direct democracy
Bourgeois democracy
Proletarian democracy
Pluralist democracy

There is, in short, no democracy in general—no democracy in the air. As if to confirm the point, the proponents of various kinds of democracies often treat competing forms of democracy as undemocratic. Thus, the specific character of a particular democracy often lies in its limitations. The character of a democracy also lies in part in the ascertainment of the identity of "the people." Rule by "the people" is nearly always an etymological and a conceptual given, but the identification of who or what "the people" are turns out to be vexingly elusive.

The identification of "the people" is itself haunted by a conundrum: on the one hand, a full legal determination of "the people" (for instance, by jurists or a legal scholars) is arguably a negation of rule by the people: it deprives the people of articulating and determining their own identity. On the other hand, the absence of any legal determination of the people would make it difficult to ascertain in many instances that it is truly the demos, the people, who are ruling. Between the two (determination and fluidity) it is not apparent that there is any copacetic solution. This is not to say that all solutions are as good as any other.

In a liberal democracy, the identity of the demos, the people, will rest on the character of the limitations, enablements, and protocols through which

(1) "the people" are somehow conceptualized (i.e., legally, geopolitically?)
(2) "the will" of said people is ascertained (i.e., by vote, acclamation, consensus, consent?)
(3) "representation" is constructed (i.e., by interest, region, occupation?)

Here, the thought of Carl Schmitt allows greater precision. As we will be dealing at some length with Carl Schmitt, it is important to recognize that Schmitt was a Nazi, a major jurist of the Third Reich, a supporter of right-wing dictatorship, and a virulent anti-Semite. Nonetheless, Schmitt had a number of telling criticisms of liberalism and liberal forms of democracy. Some of these criticisms might be considered as repurposed abstractions from the works of Marx and Vladimir Lenin. But Schmitt also developed his own thought. Much of his thinking has had a significant influence on political, legal and economic theorists of both right and left throughout the twentieth century. The events of the twenty-first century have made his thinking relevant again. Still, make no mistake: if one adopts *all the key themes* of Schmitt's work, they conduce straightforwardly to Nazism. As David Dyzenhaus, a noted commentator on Schmitt's work, has observed, given Schmitt's writings, he had, by the time the Nazis rose to power, deprived himself of all theoretical grounds to object to Nazism.[16]

One of the ways of thinking about liberal democracy is, as suggested above, to think about how various terms are conceptualized: "the people," "the people's will," and "representation." Washed in Holmesian "cynical acid" (always a crucial analytical step in understanding political-legal phenomena), it must be recognized that *all* democracies, if they are to have any form at all, contain *a dictatorial moment*. This *does not mean* that all dictatorial moments are the same *nor* that their political and moral value are equivalent. It does mean, odd as it may seem to some people, that liberal democracy does not escape the dictatorial moment. Indeed, the very effort to give specific content to the three parameters above (the people, the people's will, and representation) inexorably enacts, from some nontrivial perspective, an infringement on the power of "the people" to self-identify as "the people" and to rule according to what they would determine to be "their will." The fact that these restrictions on self-identification by "the people" and "their will" may well be necessary to any modern democracy seems self-evident. But self-evidence does not address, much less answer, the problem just identified.

A little elaboration is required. Liberal democracy institutes a particular form of representation and limits on the authority of that representation. In other words, the kind of democracy instituted in liberal democracy is not just any democracy, but *this kind of democracy*. This is what Carl Schmitt effectively describes as *a dictatorial moment*—the nonnegotiable institution and entrenchment of a particular form of democracy that is itself designed to resist further transformation into some other democratic (or nondemocratic) form. It is perhaps a bit shocking to partisans of democracy to hear that liberal democracy has a *dictatorial* moment, but that makes the observation neither wrong nor necessarily fatal: where we are talking about a political-legal register that presents as a state (democratic or not) we are to an inescapable degree in a world of force, fiat, and coercion. As Robert Cover once darkly suggested, the court does not *talk* a criminal convict into jail.[17]

If the dictatorial moment is unavoidable in any state, it would surely help from an analytical and evaluative perspective to recognize and consider this dictatorial moment in liberal democracy. Examining the dictatorial moment in liberal democracy would be the equivalent of Robert Lee Hale's demand that in recognizing "liberties," jurists and legal scholars examine the situation not just in terms of the freedom granted but also on the restrictions imposed. Among the reasons commending this approach is that it enables jurists and legal scholars to recognize that bestowing liberties is not just an augmentation of freedom, but its curtailment as well. In the same sense, understanding that democracy has a dictatorial moment directs attention to the *specific* dictatorial aspect of *this* democracy versus *that* one. Again, not all dictatorial moments are the same. Nor are they equally problematic.

In terms of the U.S. Constitution, this analytical approach is particularly salient given the authoritarian history of the U.S. Constitution—its embrace within its very structure of chattel slavery (Black slaves) and the political subordination of ethnic groups (Indians), gender identity (women), and social classes (indigents and vagrants). The point here is that the inevitable moment of dictatorialism in democracy has a specific and sweeping historical and political-legal salience in the United States. With regard to *this* constitution, the examination of its dictatorial and authoritarian moments is not some abstract philosophical exercise—it is a delving into a violent authoritarian history written in blood and thus posing thorny problems of juridical and political philosophy.

Constitutional theorists as a group have yet to plumb the full depth of the dictatorial moment. One obvious reason is that they almost always get their law from the official legal materials—the latter, of course, are seldom inclined to disclose the downsides of their own political-legal project. As a general matter, when the tools of analysis are simply taken from the tools of legitimation one cannot really expect much in the way of illuminating insights.

There are other, perhaps more fundamental, reasons the dictatorial moment escapes inquiry. One of the intellectual derailments lies in the generalized framing of the issue of constitutional constraint and enablement in terms of the people's "consent." Characteristic of this approach is to pose the fundamental problem as one having to do with reconciling "past consent" (the founding) with "present consent" (the views of the existing generations).[18]

What this focus of attention leaves underexamined is this notion of "consent." Again, we are typically referred to the particulars of the U.S. Constitution, its successful ratification, and so on—as if this disposed of the problem of consent . . . and with this disposal, all related matters as well. The problem is that consent as a concept doesn't quite get to the crux of the dictatorial moment or to related concerns about latent authoritarianism. It's true that authoritarianism will often entail the absence of consent, but to make consent the crucial issue is to institute a rather shallow conversation. It's not as if our main complaint with authoritarianism is lack of consent. Does authoritarianism become significantly less problematic if there is consent?

In addition to the truncation of inquiry through the idea of "consent," there is another major vehicle used in ways that derail any serious reckoning with the dictatorial and authoritarian aspects. The dictatorial and authoritarian moments are often transformed and processed (sometimes at great scholarly length) through explorations of judicial review, the counter-majoritarian difficulty, the intertemporal difficulty, and interpretive methodology. The through line on all these subject headings is that they help avoid any deep recognition of the ways in which the U.S. Constitution constrains or even thwarts liberal democracy. It is only if one starts from a deeper, richer, and potentially more disturbing articulation of the conundra of liberalism and democracy that one can make any serious headway. As a general matter, that has not happened much in the U.S.—even if there is now some nascent belated understanding of the problem.

Given such sustained structural denial, intervention arguably seems indicated. Indeed, when we finally get down to putting this modern state on the couch, as Paul Kahn humorously suggests, "we find a social organism that is simultaneously deeply in fear of its own death (the existential crisis) and in deep denial of the fact that it is willing to do anything at all to put off that death (liberal theory)."[19]

The de facto response from American constitutional theorists to Paul Kahn would likely be a more nuanced version of the following: "No, neither we nor our state require therapy. On the contrary, we here all agree we don't have any problems that we can't resolve. We are extremely careful in this regard: the only problems we recognize are those we can solve."[20] This is the closing of the American constitutional mind.

This closure becomes all the more apparent if we turn to the specifics of the constitutional disputes about the legitimacy of judicial review (law over democracy?), the counter-majoritarian difficulty (displacement of democracy?), and the intertemporal difficulty (temporal tyranny?). Now, as a caution, none of these topics pose trivial questions, but they do inaugurate a narrow discussion insofar as they bring the parochial peculiarities of the U.S. Constitution into play. The authoritative or quasi-authoritative invocation of that particular text muddies the waters as the various parties waffle in their arguments between law and philosophy, legality and legitimacy, authority and reason, legal idealizations and realpolitik, past consent and present consent, this constitution and constitutionalism. The enterprise, even as it announces itself as theoretical, turns out to be surprisingly shallow and oddly unmoored—enabling all suitably credentialed participants to wander without any restraint in their arrangement and rearrangement of the dualities just mentioned.

For now, we will bracket all these conventional conversations about judicial review, the counter-majoriticism difficulty, the intertemporal difficulty, and interpretive methodology. Instead, we will try to situate these conventional conversations in a deeper understanding and appreciation of the dilemmas of liberal democracy. For this a European formulation of the question is more enlightening. The European formulation will allow a reinvigoration of the great conflicts and contradictions that have both vexed as well as energized the liberal democratic state.[21] One of these contradictions is framed as the tension mentioned earlier between *constituent power* and *constituted form*.

This tension between constituent power and constituted form in a democracy brings us to the problem of the identity of the *demos*. In a democracy, it is the *people* who are to rule. So, who are "the people" who are to rule? And how do we know "the people" when we see, hear, or feel them? Jean-Jacques Rousseau gave us an early version of the question in the form of a paradox: the people do not exist before they are constituted as "the people" through a constituting (legal) form, and yet such a (legal) form perforce impinges upon and inhibits the self-determination of the people's own identity and action in the adoption and observance of the constituted form.[22] Does the former survive the impositions, impingements, and regulations of the latter throughout historical time? If so, in what ways, through what channels, on what grounds, to what ends?

The failure of U.S. jurists and legal scholars to address this paradox *forthrightly* can lead, of course, to a certain skepticism or doubt about the character and legitimacy of the constituted (legal) form. How then is the paradox resolved in the U.S.? The short answer: not in any copacetic way. The political-legal problem endures as a daunting one. And the various serious answers that have been attempted do not provide much reassurance.

Moreover, it turns out that Rousseau's paradox is *generative*: all sorts of thorny collateral questions can spring from his paradox. For instance, when we talk about "the people," are we talking about a social-historical category (the *folk*) or are we talking about a political-legal category (the *citizens*)? Either answer opens the door to highly questionable politics.

If we are talking about the former, the *folk*, how do we know who they are, who speaks for them, what they mean when they speak, and whether they truly are a people at all?[23] Furthermore, what is the source of their legitimacy and their claim to the land? And what is their entitlement to exclude putative others from the category of "the folk?" The canonization of "the *folk*" as the people is at best problematic—and given sufficient intensity, it becomes murderous. Down this path lies the end point of Nazism.

If, in contrast, it is citizens recognized by the constituted form that creates the *people*, just what legitimized inclusion, exclusion, or consent? There too, we see that resort to the constituted form in the U.S. (law, the Constitution) has yielded all sorts of horrendous actions leading to the legal endorsement of slavery, genocide, exclusion, subordination, and more.

In sum, the de facto answers that have been given to who counts as "the people" have been occasionally admirable, but also ghastly. Even if no one has very good answers, these are hardly questions to ignore and bury.

And what of the constituted form? Who or what identifies its form and substance? Its meaning and imperatives? Just *who* is sovereign? And how can this sovereign (or sovereigns plural?) possibly avoid the vicious circularity of self-authorization? Here, it helps to move from Rousseau to Derrida (via strong showings from John L. Austin and Walter Benjamin) in order to confront the full throes of the unavoidable circularity. Indeed, consider Derrida's articulation of the paradox of political foundations:

> A "successful" revolution, the "successful foundation of a State (in somewhat the same sense that one speaks of a "'felicitous' performative speech act") will produce *après coup* what it was destined in advance to produce, namely, proper interpretative models to read in return, to give sense, necessity and above all legitimacy to the violence that has produced, among others, the interpretative model in question, that is, the discourse of its self-legitimation.[24]

There can be no surprise then that the problems posed by the paradoxes of constituent power and constituted form have not been resolved in any satisfactory manner. This is not necessarily damning or fatal in itself. But the obscurantist and deflective treatment of the problem by American jurists and legal scholars might well be.

Two aspects of this failure are worth addressing.

One aspect we have already discussed—the rather impoverished vehicles of the judicial review, counter-majoritarian difficulty, intertemporal difficulty, and interpretive methodology that conflate the *general problem* inherent in liberal democratic constitutionalism with the *specific problematics* of the U.S.

Constitution. To put it simply: you cannot answer questions of political philosophy with positive law.

Another problem (which may well be more daunting) is that the failure to apprehend the challenge in terms of the generalized tension between constituent power and constituted form allows or leads us to overlook a rather startling development. It's one thing to have conceptual or political difficulties identifying who "the people" might be, but what would be truly problematic is if "the people" have slowly disappeared to be replaced by *a mere population currently in residence*—with no centering identity, no political solidarity, no common concrete cultural ties; a kind of anomic and alienated collection of humans ready for capture by a politics of the worst kind, including the siren call of authoritarian politics and fascist mythologies.

Consider the two problematic aspects in reverse order.

The Disappearance of "the People"

One of the reasons that "the People" have not been heard from in a long time in the U.S. is that "the people," as such, have largely left the scene. In part, they may have been subdued by legal impediments (think about the draconian strictures on constitutional amendments and conventions).[25] But there is much more to it than that: it may well be that the people have sustained a cultural, political, and technological assault on their identity. "The people," as agents of democracy, have arguably been degraded into *mere populations* with no robust group identity.[26] The upshot is that even as the technical mechanics of democracy remain (e.g., elections, voting, representation), the vehicles or channels of self-generated political will-formation have largely vanished. Without the possibility to engage in their own will-formation, the votes of these anemic populations become subject to manipulation by all manner of forces (e.g., money, demagoguery, political fantasy, mendacity) that preclude the rise of anything that could be called "the will of the people."

This argument remains speculative and problematic, but there is a good reason for that: the very idea of "the people" as the agent or constituent power in democracy remains itself somewhat elusive—underdetermined. There is no easy conceptual or political-legal way around that last difficulty. At the same time, however, we should not allow this conceptual and political difficulty to serve as an excuse to ignore *the disappearance of "the people."* It would seem kind of perverse in political-legal thought to admit that we confront a serious problem and then, in virtually the same breadth, declare that we should not consider it.

The U.S. might be viewed as emblematic in this regard: what few ties "the people" share currently—and this is perhaps why their ties are so ephemeral, so shallow, and so easily manipulated by political actors, lobbyists, advertisers, and so on—are Facebook, Twitter, Amazon, and Walmart. To put it trenchantly, "the people" have become bio-extensions of unseen 24/7 algorithms of unknown provenance—not only virtual cyborgs, but lonely ones at that. All that is left are individuals who are "bowling alone"—even when they are together. Fodder for fascism.

Carl Schmitt, in an historical moment not wholly unlike ours, insisted on the inertia of "the people." In an execrable 1933 tract (where he fully embraced Nazism), Schmitt argued that the people could only perform its political mission if guided by "a movement" (which he then promptly identified as Nazism).[27] He described "the people" as inert and requiring guidance and direction from a movement (again, Nazism). Here, Schmitt seems to have been taking a page from Lenin's insistence on a need for a "vanguard party"— Lenin had similarly concluded that the universal class (the proletariat) would never develop revolutionary consciousness on its own and thus needed to be led by a vanguard party (the Communist Party).

Since the time of Schmitt and Lenin, the degradation and dissipation of putatively competent political agents conscious of their historical role and responsibilities has proceeded apace. The description of mass culture that José Ortega y Gasset cautioned against and the "one-dimensional man," so presciently profiled by Herbert Marcuse, emerge now as prophetic. Today, "the people" in the U.S. and elsewhere are in the thrall of politics as entertainment.[28] Much of it is a malign entertainment—triggering the glee of resentment-desublimation on one side and outrage-release on the other.

Liberalism Untethered

Attacking liberalism, Schmitt begins his constitutional treatise (an early writing) with a declaration that the Rechtsstaat is based on "the rule of law." No sooner does he make this assertion than he starts to create trouble:

> The bourgeois Rechtsstaat is based on the "rule of law." To this extent, it is a statutory state. But the statute must retain a connection with the principles of the Rechtsstaat and of bourgeois freedom, if the Rechtsstaat is to remain in place. If everything that some person or an assembly dictates is without distinction law, then every absolute monarchy is also a Rechtsstaat, for in it the "law" rules, specifically the will of the king.[29]

Here, Schmitt is saying that a formal positivist approach to law—to wit, a tracing of every legal act back to a succession of higher authorizing legal norms to ensure an appropriate legal pedigree and provenance—cannot suffice to guarantee a liberal state. Presenting his argument in a *reductio ad absurdum*, he notes that even monarchies and sovereign dictatorships can satisfy that simple demand. Indeed, if there is to be any meaning to the idea of a Rechtsstaat, it can only be because there are certain substantive qualities related to the rule of law, liberal freedoms, and the like that delineate a commitment to the Rechtsstaat. There must be *more* to the rule of law if it is to have bite. From here, Schmitt begins to ascribe content to the idea of rule of law until we get to what he calls "the liberal concept of law." This liberal concept of law, according to Schmitt, is expressed in "the rejection of the rule of persons," the "reasonableness and justice" of laws, and a certain commitment to the "generality" of norms.[30] It includes a commitment to norms with "certain qualities, a legal (an appropriate, reasonable) rule of a general character."[31]

But, as Schmitt notes, there is, alongside this liberal concept of law, another concept of law that is also relevant to the Rechtsstaat. Schmitt calls it "the political concept of law" and he understands it as "concrete will and command and an act of sovereignty."[32] Put in terms more familiar to a contemporary U.S. audience, law is both a *norm* (a rule, a principle, a legal proposition, or the like) and *a decision* (an act of political will).[33] In a democracy, the political concept of law is the will of the people (just as in a monarchy, it would be the will of the king).

As mentioned, committed liberals are not blind to this political concept of law. But liberalism, as Schmitt sees it, nonetheless requires the suppression of this political concept of law. Why? Because if the liberal concept of law is to be maintained, it is necessary, as Schmitt puts it, "to suppress the political concept of law, in order to establish a 'sovereignty of the law' in the place of a concrete existing sovereignty."[34] Put more simply, for the "rule of law" to be realized, it must be *the law that rules*—as opposed to some act of will or sovereignty that escapes determination by law. If it is necessary to add an act of will for law to rule, this will must be obscured—shrouded in flattering (even if nearly empty) forms. Thus, for Schmitt, committed liberals are required to constantly shirk an uncomfortable bit of knowledge—not only that some agent must decide *what the law is*, but that this moment of decision must be what Schmitt calls "an act of sovereignty" or "the political concept of law." Here, to draw on a modern image, the liberal might be analogized as someone who is constantly being asked to look at a duck/rabbit picture and to see only the "liberal concept of law duck" and never the "political concept of law rabbit."

Importantly, for Schmitt, the liberal problem occasioned by this need for evasion is *not* so much the prospect of a lapse into bad faith or dirty hands.[35] The difficulty for Schmitt is that, insofar as liberals wish to suppress the political concept of law, they leave open the identity of the sovereign. In other words, they leave "open the question of *which political will* makes the appropriate norm into a positively valid command." For Schmitt, the problem is that this "must lead to *concealments and fictions*, with every instance of conflict posing anew the problem of sovereignty."[36]

And, now, we can move from Schmitt's argument to a disturbing implication: to the degree that Schmitt's analysis is considered convincing, law itself is at risk of internalizing bad faith and dirty hands in the construction or elaboration of its sundry pedestrian legal doctrines and political-legal concepts. Moreover, legal actors (and this would be where law school fails) can be derailed and distracted from recognition of any of this. In turn, the more legal actors are deprived of awareness of these aspects of law—either as a result of jural artifice or outright ignorance—the more likely the problems of bad faith and dirty hands will become *institutionalized* in the discourse of law itself.

There are limits, of course, on how much bad faith and dirty hands a state can sustain without self-impairment. This is particularly the case for a state committed to the virtues of liberal democracy. Indeed, when bad faith and dirty hands become pervasive, there lies the rather cheerless prospect of a full-on political-legal degeneration. This is a stage where even the "symbols of government" (to borrow from Thurman Arnold) lose their power. Even further down the line, we can arrive at a kind of *postcynical world* in which cynicism itself has been rendered impossible because there is no one left to fool. The words of law become requisite incantations to be uttered as vehicles to send the prisoner to jail or the tenant out on the street. One thinks here of Franz Kafka's jurisprudence as portrayed in *The Trial*.[37]

It is not merely decision that is at stake, but, correspondingly, sovereignty and its exercise. In this regard, liberalism cannot do without the political concept of law. At the same time, it is *law that is political*—and that will not do. It is the liberal (apolitical) concept of law that must rule. There thus arises a necessity for self-disguise or self-delusion so that decisions can appear to emerge seamlessly from law itself as opposed to some lawless political source. The problem, to paraphrase Schmitt, is that the same indeterminacies, undecidabilities, and contradictions in law keep threatening to emerge anew as new cases and political-legal struggles arise. It's not that they arise frequently, but rather that they can arise at any moment.

A liberal state places limits on the exercise of sovereignty. But in every case, acts of unspecified sovereignty are required to render decisions. There is nothing that the *liberal concept of law* alone can do to resolve in advance the always concrete problem (and here we find Schmitt's famous "state of exception") of exercising sovereignty, power, and force.

As Schmitt points out, not all conditions warranting a state of exception can be anticipated in advance. However, for Schmitt, there is more to it than that. Fundamentally, the liberal democratic state wishes not to specify in advance where sovereignty lies. Indeed, in the U.S., this is often presented (and not entirely wrongly) as the "genius" of the U.S. Constitution. In constructing the separation of powers by giving each governmental branch swords and shields and a mix of independent and dependent powers, the Constitution constructs a framework in which the political-legal drama of any contested issues and dire decisions must be played out in struggles among the various actors (legislative, executive, and judicial) in public, and, in the last instance if necessary, by appeal to "the people." Schmitt, not surprisingly, focuses on the dark side of this set-up. He views this underspecification as liberalism's aversion to decision. In his view, liberalism fundamentally wishes not to decide.

This argument also forms the basis for Schmitt's critique of parliamentarism—which he derides as an endless debating society, wary of actual decision-making and given over to the (petty) pursuit of advantage over economic or material interests. So it turns out that liberal democracy in its liberal conception of law and in the establishment of bourgeois democracy does have a politics after all: the politics of suppressing politics. Regardless of whether Schmitt is right here, his idea gets an understandable, even if ironic, confirmation in the postwar years when the partisans of liberal democracy created institutions (e.g., the United Nations, the International Monetary Fund, the European Economic Community) aimed at precluding the reemergence of the disastrous "heroic" and "nationalist" politics of the first half of the twentieth century. These postwar institutions aimed to promote a postideological, interconnected, transnational world in which nation-states and their populations would focus on ostensibly depoliticized bread and butter issues—in politics, but also in their daily lives. (In the wake of World War II, this was a good idea—one which worked well, until it morphed, and helped lay the grounds for reactionary nationalism.)

In his broadsides against liberalism, it is unclear, as many have noted, whether Schmitt was more concerned that liberalism in its weakness would lead to an anemic state (fated to go down) or whether, instead, he was more concerned that liberalism might succeed (and thereby extinguish the political). Or perhaps he thought that regardless of what would happen, it would be a lose/lose scenario.

Schmitt's anti-liberalism is, as mentioned, implacable. His views carry on over to impugn the kind of democracy associated with liberalism.

From Liberalism to Illiberalism

In Schmitt's account, the degeneration of the liberal democratic state occurs as the liberty claims of the liberal individual subject vis-à-vis the state morph into social and economic group associations that make material demands upon the state, resulting in an unseemly competition over the distribution of material goods. It is worth quoting Schmitt at length because this diagnosis is echoed on the right (Friedrich Hayek, Ayn Rand, James Buchanan).

> The necessity of regulation and legislation then results from the fact that these rights do not remain in the sphere of private relations. Instead, they contain social catalysts, which include the free expression of opinion, free-dom of speech and of press, freedom of worship, free assembly, and freedom of association and of collaboration. As soon as the freedom of collaboration leads to coalitions, or associations, that struggle against one another and stand opposed to one another with specific, social instruments of power like strikes or lockouts, the boundary of the political is reached and an individualistic type of basic and liberty right is no longer present. The right to form coalitions, right to strike, right to work stoppage are not liberty rights in the sense of the liberal Rechtsstaat. When a social group gains such opportunities for struggle, whether through express constitutional provisions or through acquiescence in the practice, the basic presupposition of the liberal Rechtsstaat simply no longer applies, and "freedom" still does not mean the individual's opportunity for action, which is in principle unlimited. *On the contrary, it means the unhin-dered exploitation of social power through social organizations.*[38]

In short, for Schmitt, the liberal democratic state cannot remain liberal: the privileging of liberties for the liberal individual subject leads ineluctably, according to Schmitt, to the creation of social groupings that seek to maintain and expand those liberties tendentiously by making specific material demands on the legislature. In turn, this means the expansion and exploitation of social and economic power to the detriment of the political.[39] In the text previously mentioned, Schmitt does provide a lucid passage on this metamorphosis. The passage takes us *from* the nineteenth-century liberal democratic state's solic-

itude for the liberal individual subject *through* the latter's *sub rosa* displacement by what we now call interest group politics, government capture, all the
way to the contemporary U.S. variant of neoliberalism.

The basic rights and freedoms of the statal and constitutional system of liberal democracy as such are essentially rights of the private individual person.
Solely on those grounds may they be considered "political. . . ." The liberal
statal and constitutional structure thus reckons *with a simple and direct* confrontation *between the state and the private individual.* Only starting from this
confrontation, it is a natural and sensible attempt to erect a whole edifice out
of the protective legal means and institutions, in order to protect the helpless
and defenseless, poor and isolated individual person from the powerful Leviathan, the "state." Most of the legal safeguards of the so-called legal state
have sense only with regard to the protection of the poor individual. It justifies
thereby that the protection against the state will always be shaped by justice
and will result increasingly into the ruling of a court judicially independent of
the state.

But all this becomes quite absurd as soon as *strong collective formations
or organizations* occupy the non-statal and apolitical sphere of freedom, and
those non-statal (but by no means political) "auto-organizations" will on the
one hand compress the individual persons ever tighter and more forcefully,
and on the other, challenge the state under various legal titles (such as people,
society, free citizenry, productive proletariat, public opinion). Then the political powers take cover in every conceivable way behind the rampart for safeguarding the individual freedom of apolitical individual persons in need of
protection. Non-statal but, as already said, entirely political formations then
dominate both the will of the state (by way of legislation) and also (through
societal constraint and the force of the "purely private law") the individual
person whom they mediate. These become the true and real vehicles of the
political decisions, and wielders of the statal instruments of power, but they
will master it from the non-"public" individual sphere, free of state and constitution, and in this way, evade any political risk and responsibility. In the state
constitution of the liberal-democratic legal state, they can legally never appear
what they are in the political and the social reality, because the liberal binary
schema has no place for them. Every attempt to insert them makes the liberal-
democratic state and its system burst. Consequently, if such formations succeed in seizing the positions and the means of state power by way of the political parties dominated by them—and that is the typical development—then
they look after *their* interests in the name of the state authority and of the law.

They enjoy all the advantages of the state power without relinquishing the advantages of the sphere of freedom, politically irresponsible and uncontrolled, because ostensibly apolitical.[40]

Thus, not only does liberalism harbor within itself a certain intrinsic tendency toward illiberalism (via the opportunistic exploitation of individual rights by groups seeking material gains), but democracy harbors a tendency toward the anti-democratic as well.

If we take seriously Schmitt's challenges to liberal democracy, then the liberal democratic state must address these challenges in ways that maintain the character of the liberal democratic state (keep it from morphing into some illiberal and anti-democratic version of itself). The first step, and here we depart radically from Schmitt, would be to take cognizance of and to articulate these challenges . . . albeit in ways that nonetheless avoid impairing the sovereign state—the proverbial failed or failing state syndrome.[41]

The negotiation of this dilemma helps explain why Paul Kahn puts liberal democracy on the couch. There is a profound sense in which it might be said that liberal democracy is in fundamental ways incompatible with its existence as a sovereign state. It is constantly and repeatedly being asked to negotiate *state sovereignty* with *liberal democracy* and it responds by formulating domesticated versions of the issue while denying the underlying problematic.

The U.S. Constitution—Sacred and Prosaic

Among many American jurists and legal scholars, the Constitution of the United States is routinely identified with liberal democracy. This identification is typically qualified by a recognition that the Constitution may not be entirely up to speed in vindicating the virtues of liberal democracy. Nonetheless, the Constitution is generally taken as a pretty good approximation—sufficiently so that American constitutional scholars slide almost effortlessly from the Constitution to liberal democracy and vice versa. In one sense, jurists, legal scholars, and the lay public are so accustomed to this easy equation, that it has come to seem unremarkable.

But it is remarkable.

Suppose we start with the Constitution end of things. Consider that constitutional analysis could refer to the interpretation or exegesis of *this* Constitution—a parsing of its textual meaning, its various clauses, its structure, its concrete aspirations, and the like. At the same time, constitutional analysis could also lead to the political philosophy of liberal democracy, to the problem of constituent power and constituted form, to the problematics of constitutionalism generally, and so on. Those are two different paths. Either one might be interesting in its own right.

In American constitutional scholarship, the fascinating thing is that *this* Constitution and political philosophy are often conjoined. They are not treated as the same, of course, but they are widely seen by many jurists and legal scholars as continuous. One of the resulting oddities is that the United States is one place on earth where the problems of liberal democratic political philosophy can apparently be addressed and even resolved by reference to an authoritative text—the U.S. Constitution.

Two things are important in the seamless conjunction. The first, already mentioned, is that in moving from the volatile and unresolved tensions of constituent power and constituted form to the more prosaic concerns over judicial review and the like, there is a domestication of the problem. The second, to which we now turn, is that the move from the grand conundra of liberal democracy to the exegesis of the U.S. Constitution helps prepare the way for a virulent constitutional legalism.

This second point requires a bit of elaboration and perhaps an example or two. So now, we move more slowly to show how constitutional exegesis works to domesticate the great conundra of constituent power and constituted form.

Begin with a brief summary of judicial review, the counter-majoritarian difficulty, and the intertemporal difficulty. The problem of judicial review concerns the following question: How can the judiciary (a coequal branch of the U.S. government) have the authority to review and potentially set aside the actions of other coequal branches of government (the Congress and the executive branch)? The counter-majoritarian difficulty is a variation on the same problem: What is the constitutional justification for setting aside the majoritarian decisions of the (more) democratic branches of government? As stated by the acknowledged author of the counter-majoritarian difficulty, Alexander Bickel:

> [W]hen the Supreme Court declares unconstitutional a legislative act or the action of an elected executive, it thwarts the will of representatives of the actual people of the here and now; it exercises control, not in behalf of the prevailing majority, but against it.... [This] is the reason the charge can be made that judicial review is undemocratic.[42]

The characteristic presumptive default setting up the problem is that absent a constitutional justification, democracy, understood as majority rule, should prevail. This kind of setup is, of course, a bit tendentious. The problematic is asymmetrical right from the start—as if constitutional counter-majoritarianism were so extraordinary that, of course, it had to be subordinate to democracy. Moreover, as explained by Barry Friedman, the dramatic setup rests on highly questionable baselines that are contestable both empirically and theoretically. As Friedman puts it:

> There is every reason to believe the counter-majoritarian problem is a less-than-accurate way of characterizing the practice of judicial review. As numerous scholars have observed, both halves of the supposed difficulty are subject to theoretical and empirical challenge. On the one hand, there is every reason to doubt that what we think of as majoritarian politics is designed to, could, should, or does register majoritarian preferences. Thus, judicial review regularly is compared to some imaginary baseline that does not exist. On the other hand, judicial review is a long-established part of our governmental structure. It yields remarkably majoritarian results, and is a process that is different from majoritarian politics but nonetheless responsive to it.[43]

Nonetheless, the counter-majoritarian difficulty and the associated judicial review problem have gripped entire generations of constitutional law scholars.

A more interesting, challenging, and enduring inquiry is the *intertemporal difficulty*.[44] The intertemporal difficulty asks what justifies observance of the majoritarian preferences of one generation (e.g., the founders) over the majoritarian preferences of present generations (e.g., us)? Or vice versa. Still, though it is more interesting, the intertemporal difficulty, as conventionally framed, does not escape the problems of its two antecedents. The classic resolution deployed for all three difficulties can be summarized in two fundamental steps:

First Step: constitutional thinkers in the United States will take
    cognizance of the conundra of constituent power and constituted
    form under the much more pedestrian constitutional headings
    of "the problem of judicial review," or the "counter-majoritarian
    difficulty," or the "intertemporal difficulty."
Second Step: once apprehended within these frames and their attendant
    idioms, resolution of the conflict is immediately relegated to the
    text of the "U.S. Constitution." From there, the conversation evolves

into protracted, highly elaborated disputes under headings like "constitutional interpretation," "fidelity to the Constitution," "judicial restraint," and the like.

This is the classic technique to answer all three difficulties: for instance, what justifies judicial deviation from the basic democratic norm of majoritarian rule? Answer: the U.S. Constitution itself—or more accurately, the Constitution according to my theory, my interpretation, my understanding. In other words, the great dramas of judicial review, the counter-majoritarian difficulty, or the intertemporal difficulty are resolved, often at great lengths, by a kind of rhetorical transmutation showing that under certain conditions (i.e., *my* theory, *my* interpretation, *my* understanding of the Constitution) the problem goes away.[45] That is to say, for all the drama, what we have is arguably a feint: the problem was never really there to begin with. Or at least not with any great force—certainly none that would require the grandeur that has so often attended the dramas of judicial review, counter-majoritarianism or the intertemporal difficulty.

It bears noting that this move of resort to "my understanding of the Constitution" has a long-standing pedigree: it is exactly the same move that Chief Justice Marshall made somewhat mechanically in *Marbury v. Madison*.

Presented again, in two more abbreviated steps this time:

1. *Question*: How do we resolve tensions between law and democracy?
2. *Answer*: We look at the law to see what it says about the relation between law and democracy.

Is this satisfying? Of course not.[46] It is nonetheless a widely shared approach—one that might well have been avoided had the problem been stated initially as pertaining to constitutionalism generally (as opposed to *this* constitution).

But in its legalist fixation on "*this constitution*," the widely shared American approach begs the question. (Remember we are still on the couch.) In referring the resolution of the theoretical issue to an authoritative legal text (the U.S. Constitution), this move works precisely to the extent that one forgets that the tension between law and democracy has just been relegated one-sidedly to the legal exegesis of a putatively authoritative text (the U.S. Constitution). What many American legal commentators fail to notice is that this resort to the meaning (*the authority move*) or interpretation (*the exegesis move*) of the U.S. Constitution is not so much a resolution as a brazen change of topic. Granted, the Constitution is authoritative in U.S. legal circles (legality). But that does not ipso facto accord the Constitution any competence to resolve problems of political philosophy (legitimacy). And liberal democratic law, unless it is a charade, must answer to both legality and legitimacy.

How is it that this is overlooked? There seems to be among legal scholars a misunderstanding of the problem. Specifically, the challenge posed is not simply a *legalist* one of drawing lines, but the much more daunting problem of *legitimately* resolving the conflict between the constituent power and the constituted form in ways that respect appropriate commitments (whatever these may be) to both. On that score, it makes no sense to say that the tension between constituent power and constituted form is to be resolved by appealing to the authority of the constituted form (i.e., the U.S. Constitution). One might as well say the opposite. Indeed, tension between two conflicting sources of legitimacy cannot be resolved in advance simply by giving a priori superiority to just one of these sources: the constituted form or the constituent power. This, to be blunt, is no solution at all.

If we can recognize that the shift here from a *political-legal conundrum* to its ostensible resolution in an *authoritative text* is an error (a "category mistake"), we are poised to recognize that this is not just any error, but an extremely important error. It is a foundational error. How so? Well, it is this error that serves as the foundation enabling a great deal of U.S. constitutional theory to get off the ground in the first place. It is this foundational error that enables constitutional law scholars to believe that they can resolve the law-democracy tension through the elaboration of law. If constitutional law scholars could refrain from making this initial mistake, they would be compelled to recall that the Constitution is to be read as both law and politics. The Constitution is an expression that, in its self-authorization, recognizes the legitimacy of both the constituent power (the people) and the constituted form (the constitution). Just as the first does not have the last word, neither does the second. To be sure, some American jurists and legal scholars are capable of entertaining this possibility, but most are still on the couch. Indeed, there are a great many, even famous, legal theorists who give up on the conundra of liberal democracy, believing them to be already resolved such that all attention can be devoted to the elaboration and interpretation of *this* Constitution. It is in this way that questions of legitimacy are subsumed into issues of legality and thereby extinguished. In some sense, this is to be expected from jurists and legal scholars, but it is nonetheless still disappointing.

There is a parallel in popular understandings of the U.S. Constitution. Consider that the U.S. Constitution is the ultimate destination where political-legal arguments go to die—frequently abruptly so. If someone in a dispute says, "You can't do that—it's unconstitutional," in the U.S., there are only two plausible responses: "no, it's not and here's why," or "right, so let's think about doing it this way instead." As Arthur Leff once noted, the Constitution in the United States is a kind of god substitute—the ultimate political-legal "conversation-ender."[47] In that spare sentence, "You can't do that—it's unconstitutional," lies the popular submission of democracy to law.

There is something even more interesting going on here. Insofar as legal scholars remain somewhat shallow[48] surrounding the discussion of the legitimacy of the U.S. Constitution, the question of legitimacy among the populace has been allowed to devolve into an oddly simple-minded mythology. Among the populace, it is widely believed that the Constitution is entitled to rule because it is an inspired document (hints of theology), or because the founders were an exceptional generation (patriarchy unleashed), or because it is who we are (the ubiquitous and mystical ruler/ruled identification). In short, absent cogent legitimation stories, the Constitution has become an almost sacred mythological object that even theologians might envy.

This is not all to the good. All this "Founding Fathers know best" stuff, this crypto-theology, this cloud of quasi-religious veneration, this monarch-manqué fixation is fundamentally infantilizing.[49] If they are the "Founding Fathers," then who are we—other than their children? What does this consoling quasi-authoritarian mythology have to do with any sort of mature effort at self-government? This point is not offered here as some gratuitous cultural criticism: this infantile constitutional mythology is profoundly anti-democratic.

There is an additional problem: Given that the Founding Fathers are dead, who will speak for them? Who will give voice to their vision, their creation, their law? The Founding Fathers are in need of an oracle. And they have one: the U.S. Supreme Court. And with that comes a *coup de force*—the transmutation of the sacred into the prosaic. What does the Constitution beget when it comes into the hands of the justices? It becomes—what else?—an acute doctrinal legalism.

This *coup de force* is worthy of some consideration. For even if the Constitution is a plausible object of mythological veneration, legalism surely is not. Yet nonetheless this magisterial Constitution is conscripted by jurists and legal scholars to yield excruciatingly technical four-part tests of multi-level doctrine.

In the U.S. Supreme Court, myth is thus conscripted to serve a vigorous legalism. Legalism, in turn, is drafted into the service of freezing the relations between law and democracy—as well as other dualities: state and civil society, liberty and equality. Behold the pretty picture: on the one hand, the sacred character of the Constitution authorizes and legitimates a tenacious legalism that effectively freezes the great conflicts and contradictions (law and democracy, state and civil society) and strips them of their generative power. On the other hand, the tenacious legalism that has replaced the great conflicts and contradictions has put their loss, their disappearance out of view.

State and Civil Society

The duality of liberalism and democracy (its symbioses and oppositions) is very much wrought up with the state and civil society duality. The relation of the dualities is both interesting and complex.

From the standpoint of liberal democracy, the state and civil society duality is essentially a *classification scheme* that allows separation of roles, functions, and authorities to two different spheres. Disagreement can be had (within limits) about whether some social and economic responsibilities should be, or are, allocated to the state or instead to civil society. Internecine disputes can be had, for instance, between liberal welfarism and laissez-faire. The distinction between state and civil society can thus be shifted to some degree. It's also possible for the distinction to be fuzzy, not fully determined, amenable to some modification. But what is not negotiable in a liberal democratic state is the idea and the reality of a separation. The separation is a defining feature of liberal democracy—both in a historical and a philosophical sense. It is existential: one can no more have a liberal democratic state without the separation of state and civil society than one can have a monarchy without a king or queen.

From Liberal Democracy to the State and Civil Society Separation

The relations of liberal democracy to the state and civil society separation are more interesting and complicated than might seem at first. Liberal democracy characteristically provides for democratic rule within limited government according to rule of law norms that articulate ground rules for a broad "free market" economy.[50] This, as it turns out, will entail the separation of state and civil society.

While, in many ways, the liberal democratic state has been displaced in the U.S. and in other advanced democracies by an accretion of subsequent iterations of the state, it nonetheless survives in modified form.[51] The continuation of liberal democracy is obvious in the United States, where the U.S. Constitution continues to play a major role in defining the fundamental political-legal character of the state as a liberal democracy.[52] On one side state and on the other civil society.[53.]

The liberal democratic state is by design a limited state. That identity effectuates a deeply entrenched division between state (government, officialdom, law) and civil society (market, family, private institutions). While both "spheres"[54] are subject to the actions of law and politics, the state's power over and within the two spheres is, by constitutional design, quite different. The state itself is subject to the norms of democracy, liberalism, and rule of law. The agents, agencies, and subdivisions of the state must act in accordance with these norms. In their dealings with each other, however, the persons, parties, and institutions comprising civil society—so-called private parties— need not observe those commitments. Indeed, they are arguably protected from having to adhere to those norms.

This means that state power and obligations vis-à-vis persons in civil society are a different matter than the powers and obligations of persons in civil society vis-à-vis each other.[55] Insofar as the two sets of laws are designed in both their constitutive and regulatory aspects to apply to different actors (those of state or civil society) or to the same actors but in different capacities, it is crucial to maintain cogent operational distinctions between the two.

The import of the state/civil society distinction is reflected in a series of ubiquitous distinctions that traverse U.S. law (constitutional, statutory, regulatory, and common). These homologous distinctions are very familiar to legal professionals:

State[56]	Civil Society[57]
public	private
official	non-official
government	market
public sector	private sector
collective	individual
public good	private good
legislation	private ordering

The power of the liberal democratic state to alter or reorganize the entitlements and disablements of persons in civil society is significantly restrained.

In the U.S., the Constitution plays a huge role in this regard. Typically, those restraints on the state are conceptualized as legal provisions that express, activate, and enforce a constellation of interrelated notions:

> limited government
> specified individual rights
> constraints on powers
> the rule of law
> the dignity of persons[58]

A moment's pause enables the recognition that these general political-legal restraints on the state engage both the duality of liberalism and democracy, as well as the duality of state and civil society. In one capacity, the restraints limit democracy. Simultaneously, they protect civil society from the state.

In the liberal democratic state, the limitedness of the state is tied to another important feature—to wit, *the sovereignty of the individual liberal subject*. Whether conceptualized in terms of the "will theory" or the "interest theory," this sovereignty of the individual liberal subject extends so far as to make the individual responsible for his or her own views, tastes, predilections, actions, welfare, and so on.[59] In liberal democracy, this is the general default view attended by certain narrow exceptions such as disability, infirmity, coercion.

Generally, however, in light of the canonization of the sovereign liberal individual subject, the key role of the state is to protect individual liberty so far as possible. Liberals are quite conscious that this liberty will not extend indefinitely, insofar as liberty X bestowed on A may well conflict as a social or economic matter with liberty Y bestowed on B. This understanding leads to the classic question: should the state then recognize (or not) that A or B (or both) have some sort of duty to refrain from interfering with the other's liberty? It is one of the enduring philosophical problematics of liberal thought to inquire into just how far legal recognition and protection of the two liberties ought to go. Many solutions, both conservative and progressive, have been offered. In his 1971 book, *A Theory of Justice*, the philosopher John Rawls, for instance, famously declared his "first principle" to be that all individuals ought to have the greatest liberty compatible with an equal liberty for all—after which other "secondary goods," such as wealth, income, and the means of self-respect should be distributed in such a way as to maximize the conditions of the least advantaged.[60]

The philosophical resolutions, such as the Rawlsian solution, run into a shared problem that they virtually never address: it remains somewhat unclear how one is to translate the Olympian *macro-imperatives of political philosophy* to the more practical *micro-juridical task* of fashioning legal doctrine.[61] Between the Olympian heights of liberal political philosophy (the macro) and the pedestrian everyday world of legal doctrine and legal cases (the micro), there are no obvious theoretical ways to *scale down*. The connections are too numerous, interactive, complex, and underdetermined. Moreover, in terms of actual practice, homeostasis is in the offing. It is as if (and this is a clear problem for jurists and legal scholars trying to deploy Rawls's Theory of Justice) we were trying to apply macro-principles to micro-issues. The intention to apply macro consideration to micro-decisions is occasionally there. But actually succeeding is a different story. And seldom do political philosophers bother with questions of implementation. (They don't know enough law) and rarely do jurists or legal scholars bother with philosophy. (They know too much law).

Nonetheless, the general orientation of the liberal democratic state remains clear at the aspirational level: wide areas of choice and action are supposed to be left to the sovereign liberal individual subject to do as he or she wishes. Indeed, this protection of individual liberty is, from the perspective of the liberal democratic state, among its principal distinguishing raisons d'être.[62]

The limitedness of the state, as well as the idea of the sovereign individual subject, are (within the liberal worldview) two sides of the same coin. As seen from a liberal perspective, the primary threat to individual liberty comes from accretion of excessive power in the state. In the U.S., the constitutional preoccupation with this particular dilemma (quite evident in the Federalist Papers) is easy to understand from the perspective of the founding generation: monarchy was the problem, and accordingly limited, partitioned, and dispersed government was the solution. The constitutional organization of the state had to be designed in such a way as to constrain the power of the state (hence, the checks and balances, federalism, separation of powers, and individual rights).[63]

As for the possibility of a corresponding oppression by private parties within civil society, that was not, and still is not, viewed by the partisans of liberal democracy as a problem of the same gravity. It was not (and still is not) considered deserving of the same legal recognition or treatment. Hence, private oppression is *generally* not thought to have a constitutional status. In U.S. constitutional law, the most famous exception is the Thirteenth Amendment, which prohibits slavery.

It is in part this discrepancy or difference in the treatment of public and private oppression that enabled Marx to launch his fierce critique of the liberal democratic state exemplified in the oft-quoted passage from "On the Jewish Question" where he described life in the "political state" as heavenly and communal as contrasted with life in civil society where individuals degrade themselves and treat each other as means.[64] This famous charge is a critical reference to *the deliberate self-disabling aspect* of the liberal democratic state mentioned earlier: the limited character of sovereignty in the liberal democratic state and its constitutional self-inhibition from exercising powers to correct legal relations in civil society that permit private oppression, manipulation, and exploitation.[65]

Why does the liberal democratic state disable itself in this way? Well, as mentioned above, for the liberal democratic state, this private oppression *is simply not* of the same order of magnitude or concern as the prospect of public oppression. In addition, for liberal thinkers, some inhibition on restructuring civil society is crucial to *liberal* democracy. This is what the liberal protection of liberty means! Whether we are speaking of John Locke, Adam Smith, Friedrich Hayek, or more contemporary liberal thinkers, the freedom of the individual liberal subject is key. This is viewed as requiring noninterference by the political-legal in civil society.

In effectuating the state and civil society separation, not only must the two classifications be sufficiently cogent and operational to allow allocation of responsibilities, functions, and roles to both sides, but there is a need to protect the classification scheme from erosion. This means that if the state and civil society *classification* becomes *oppositional* (which it does), mutual interference must somehow be kept in check. Why? Well, if there is opposition between the two, then the failure to restrain the actors, forces, and interests on one side of the separation poses a threat to the other side. For instance, if the state is left unrestrained, the state might conscript the activities of civil society for its own advantages and aggrandizement. Down this path lies the road to (an illiberal) authoritarianism that may or may not evolve into totalitarianism. On the other side, if civil society is not restrained, some of its more powerful actors could colonize the state and use it as a vehicle for private advantage. Down this path lies (an illiberal) state of corruption. The advanced structural version of this state of corruption is, as will be seen, neoliberalism.

For partisans of liberal democracy, the containment of this illiberal potential (authoritarianism and corruption) is kept in check through boundary maintenance (an observance of the distinction, line, border, boundary perimeter, reach, and scope) of state vis-à-vis civil society. It is the role of law, legalism, and legal institutions to effectuate and enforce this containment.

This will be difficult.

At the analytical level, it cannot be done.

The Hard-Line Separation and Its Impossibility

The hard line between state and civil society was always impossible—conceptually and materially. It could be approximated and even affirmed in philosophical treatises, judicial opinions, and popular opinion (and it was). But it could never be faithfully actualized. At best, the "hard line" could only be honored in the breach. And this is so for several reasons.

First, civil society depended upon various bodies of law (property, contract, tort, criminal) in order to conduct its business. The law would be necessary in its facilitative, prohibitory, and enforcement aspects. This need for a law of civil society (e.g., "private law") threatens to expose the "hands-off civil society" as already breached. To be sure, it was possible to argue that to the degree the law *simply mirrored, borrowed, or codified* the customs, practices, and institutions of civil society, law was not taking an active role in shaping civil society. The law was merely recognizing what was already there. One finds flavors of this line of reasoning in legal process, legal pragmatism, and normative law and economics—all of which demand that law accord a great deal of deference to things as they are. The only trouble, as many have noted, is that the way things are turns out to be what law has already made them to be.

The second reason the liberal democratic state could not maintain its hard-line distinction between state and civil society is that it apparently could not restrain itself (in matters of family, sex, health, and so on) from enforcing its (bourgeois) moral norms. This, too, would be an intrusion into civil society. So, we are already dealing with a hard-line distinction and separation that has been breached (perhaps not significantly, but breached nonetheless).

Still, ways were found to define all these laws, rights, duties, and powers so that their infringement on civil society seemed minimal, exceptional, and relatively inconsequential.[66] We will address this soon, but notice already that the "minimal, exceptional, and inconsequential" intrusion on civil society described above succeeds in establishing at least *the appearance* of a modest juridification of civil society—a juridification that will provide the "legal hooks" to facilitate further acts of jural modification, fine-tuning, and reform.

In the nineteenth and part of the twentieth centuries, these sort of intrusions by law into civil society were framed and viewed as minimal, exceptional, and relatively inconsequential to the separation of state and civil society. In part, these intrusions were seen as selective deviations from an otherwise secure and governing distinction between state and civil society.

However, in more modern forms of analyses (both Marxist and liberal democratic), this insistence on a hard line is typically viewed as an analytical error. But the mere fact that the hard line is an *analytical* error did not (and still does not) preclude its *social* actualization. This should not surprise: nothing precludes an analytical error or an illusion from gaining a toehold, becoming a widespread social formation sufficiently entrenched that, despite its erroneous character, it is nonetheless extremely difficult to change or expunge. Social construction has no steadfast allegiance to truth and neither does law.

Suppose now that the separation of state and civil society has *largely* taken hold. What are the implications? One implication, as argued below, is that in leaving civil society alone, the liberal democratic state disables itself from taking political-legal cognizance of *challenges and problems* emanating from civil society. And as mentioned, this is not an accident, but by design: ideally whatever happens in civil society is supposed to stay in civil society.[67]

Cognizance and Juridification

Even if the account just given is right, a question nonetheless remains: If the liberal democratic state is a state by design, why is it constructed so that it seeks *to avoid taking cognizance of* challenges and problems in civil society? This question has bite because it is precisely those challenges and problems that will pose an existential risk to the liberal democratic state. Why then not take political-legal recognition? Isn't it possible for the liberal-democratic state to take cognizance of challenges and problems while nonetheless restraining itself from acting upon them?

Well, no—in a deep sense, it is not.

To allow the political-legal recognition of challenges and problems in civil society is to put the state on the path to addressing those problems and conflicts and, thus, to put the state on the path to self-transformation toward some more controlling, more intrusive, more juridical, and possibly even an illiberal state. It may not be obvious why or how this would happen, but think about it this way: *for the political-legal register to take cognizance of a challenge or problem is tantamount to juridifying the challenge or problem.* How so? Well, the liberal democratic state does not "know" of a challenge or a problem unless or until it is juridified—brought within the reach of the liberal democratic political-legal register. To "know" in the political-legal register of liberal democracy *is* to juridify—to apprehend the problem or challenge in *legalist categories* and to locate it somewhere in the various *juridical grammars* of law. The challenge or problem may, of course, be well known to the press, to the commentariat, even to the functionaries of the state, but that is not the same as the political-legal recognition of the challenge or problem.

That last point might seem counterintuitive: Aren't the courts and legislatures devoted at times to addressing "new" problems not yet juridified? Well, yes—but the problems and challenges addressed are selected by the legalist categories and juridical grammars in place: if the problems and challenges are not or cannot be "seen" from that vantage, they escape recognition in the political-legal register. (Things will change to a significant degree, later on, with the advent of the administered state.)

Meanwhile, once a challenge or problem is apprehended and represented in legal categories and juridical grammars, the resulting articulations ipso facto enter into the legal lexicon and its networks. And ipso facto, those articulations become themselves immediately susceptible to circulation throughout the various political-legal frames and moves of the relevant legal conceptual architectures.[68]

This is a fancy way of saying that once an issue becomes legally cognizable, it becomes potentially legally actionable (justiciability concerns, civil procedure, evidence, and remedial law may well have something to say about this). To put it more bluntly, law is a network whose categories and grammars are already actualized as power, and not just because its agents or personnel choose to exercise law as power. And not just because the "outcomes" of law application (e.g., verdicts, rulings) are exercises of power. More fundamentally, it is because law is constructed as an elaborate conceptual and institutional network that bestows *performative force* on statements and articulations (in J. L. Austin's sense of the term "performative").[69] The point is perhaps most obvious in trials. In such legal fora, law will make words and statements do things through their very articulation—regardless and sometimes in derogation of what the speaker may have intended. The courtroom is a *performatively saturated network* where every statement is at risk of being construed for its legal meaning and significance. Indeed, statements made "innocently" are often immediately slotted as "a concession," "an admission," "a grounds for impeachment," and so on. Many things said in the courtroom are, of course, neither significant nor consequential, but what renders them significant or consequential is that very often they are made to register as and thus activate *this* or *that* by the apparatus of law in place—an apparatus fraught with and held together by networks that bestow performative force.

There is thus a deep sense in which if law is to refrain from doing (or not doing) X, it must refrain from knowing X in any political-legal sense. As Duncan Kennedy and Frank Michelman observed long ago, "law abhors a vacuum."[70] And as they argued, once an interest becomes juridified—specifically articulated as a legal interest—it is damned hard to drive it out of the political-legal register.[71] A specifically recognized legal interest can be reallocated, subdivided, unbundled, rebundled, modified, and the like. However, for the legal interest to be extirpated from the conceptual-institutional architecture of law—that is an entirely different matter. Desuetude over the long run is always a possibility, but that is the long run. All sorts of things are possible in the long run.

This raises some related questions: If the liberal democratic state inhibits itself from taking cognizance of matters in civil society, how does it fend off potentially self-defeating self-transformation? How does liberal democratic law regulate civil society without taking "knowledge" of what needs or threats are percolating in civil society? Just how can this be accomplished? Can the self-admonition of the liberal democratic state *to try* to keep its "hands-off civil society" be translated into law?

This looks like an incipient paradox in the making. Interestingly, however, in the heyday of the liberal democratic state (the nineteenth century), there was a kind of answer. Jurists and legal scholars actually did find a way (illusory and flawed though it may have been) to grant legal protections to individuals in ways that might have been seen *as largely free* of law itself. The technique was to use common law, statutes, and constitutional provisions in ways that would *not overly intrude* into civil society, but that would nonetheless protect individual autonomy, freedom, and the choices of the liberal individual subject. Of course, the question resurfaces: Just how can this be accomplished? Just how does one have a contract law or a property law, for instance, that is not itself law?

Framed this way, of course, it seems impossible. And yet throughout the nineteenth and early twentieth centuries, there developed in American law the semblance of a solution. Indeed, partisans of the liberal democratic state famously sought to treat certain domains of social and economic life as "*outside of law*." Again, this was an illusory and flawed solution, but apparently, it was good enough for many jurists, legal scholars, and politicians.

The notion that there are domains such as the "free market" that are "outside of law" was very much consonant with the liberal democratic idea of "hands-off civil society."[72] Among those matters that are still today occasionally treated as "outside of law" are not only the market and competition, but the family, privacy, autonomy, choice, consent, and so on. These are still occasionally treated today in the discourse of jurists, legal scholars, and politicians as if transactions within these domains are somehow not legal—as if they exist outside the political-legal register and are somehow exempt from the ambit of law.

This is a flat-out error (as demonstrated in the lineage of works by Wesley Newcomb Hohfeld, Robert Lee Hale, Warren Samuels, Duncan Kennedy, Joseph Singer, and more).[73] Here the point is not to demonstrate the error. (That has been done.) Instead, the point is to understand how and why the error has worked—and remarkably continues to do work.

Begin with the recognition that the liberal democratic state casts some legal subjects (e.g., the market, family life) as "outside of law." The principal liberal strategy for realizing (i.e., making real) this commitment lies in defining and delineating "domains," "spheres," "realms," "zones," "sectors," and "areas," that are then described as outside the law. There (i.e., in those domains, spheres, realms) the liberal individual subject can do as he, and later she, pleases. We have here, *as a matter of form*, a spatialization and territorialization I have previously described as "the grid aesthetic."[74] In this grid aesthetic, law is apprehended and represented as a two-dimensional area divided into contiguous, well-bounded territorialized legal spaces. These spaces are further subdivided into the usual legal artifactual forms: doctrines, rules, concepts, and the like. Those doctrines, rules, concepts, and the like are then further subdivided into elements, and so on, and so on. Each *formal division is* frozen in place as it is endowed with the character of spatiality and territorialization: boundedness, fixity, and location. The divisions and subdivisions have insides and outsides that are separated by well-marked boundaries. As for the territorialized divisions and subdivisions, their fixed boundaries gives them the appearance of substantiality, strength, solidity.[75] Thus, the grid—form and content—appears strong, steady, solid, built for endurance.[76]

The spatialization and territorializion of the grid aesthetic was perhaps most acute in late nineteenth century law, the aesthetic remains powerful and enduring. Even today, the law of liberal democracy remains marked with references to such spatialized determinations: "private *sectors*," "*zones* of privacy," "*realms* of personal choice," "*areas* of liberty," "*regions* of activity," "*spheres* of public discourse," and "*spaces* of private life." These, in turn, are defined and demarcated by "borders," "boundaries," "lines," or "distinctions" so that their scope, limits, and bounds can be defined, delineated, demarcated, and mapped.

For a law that aims to remain appropriately detached from socioeconomic details (lest civil society become juridified), the "grid aesthetic" with its spatialization, territorialization, borders, and boundaries was almost tailor-made. Admittedly, law would still intrude somewhat on the freedom of the liberal individual subject (no way around that) but only minimally—*at the edges*—by defining the boundaries and the borders. The actual substance of the protected activity, *the interior*, would remain the domain of the rights or power holder. Only minimal legal cognizance would have to be taken of social or economic particulars—only at the boundary lines when a question arose as to which side of the line a case might fall. The lines and boundaries, of course, would have to be rigorously policed and maintained.

There was thus an intimate association between the liberal democratic state and the grid aesthetic. If classical legal thought or nineteenth-century Langdellian legal formalism looks so bizarre from contemporary perspectives,[77] it is in part because it displayed a sustained effort to avoid taking notice of the social and economic substance of the transactions regulated by law. Instead, that "substance" was to be supplied by transactional encounters (e.g., contracts) between free-willed liberal individual subjects. To a contemporary legal thinker, this aversion to recognizing social or economic actualities seems almost inexplicable and possibly perverse. And, indeed, it was this persistent avoidance of the social and the economic that led Lawrence Friedman to famously ridicule Langdellian formalism as an "astronomy without stars" and a "geology without rocks."[78] Friedman's quip is funny, apt, and memorable, but what is easily missed amid his witticism is that the Langdellian avoidance of "the stars" and "the rocks" was, in one sense, ideologically attuned: *this was precisely the kind of legalism called for by the liberal democratic state!*

Indeed, there was method to the Langdellian madness: avoiding the stars and rocks was functional in terms of protecting the freedom of the individual liberal subject. If, by contrast, excessive notice were to be taken of stars and rocks, then the law might become unduly involved in running the affairs and traffic of civil society. That, in turn, would involve the whittling down of the freedom of the individual liberal subject whose choices and actions would become increasingly juridified—that is to say, specified by the state rather than remaining up to the individual liberal subject. The grid aesthetic, by relegating law to the establishment and enforcement of borders, boundaries, and dividing lines, appeared to enable the law to avoid such predicaments. And yet this was self-delusion. Even as the Langdellian formalists steadfastly declined to engage in any hardheaded examination of the social or economic spheres, they nonetheless allowed the social and the economic to intrude into legal analysis *sub rosa*. The social and the economic intruded—as Wesley Newcomb Hohfeld and his followers would show—in the form of underrecognized images and metaphors. Hence, for instance, the major implicit inspiration for the construction of all kinds of rights and privileges was the agrarian fee simple owner who holds dominion over his plot of land and does with it, within limits of his acreage, whatever he wills. As Jennifer Nedeslsky showed not long ago, property as metaphor and image came to play a huge formative role in the construction of many other very different rights—privacy, freedom of speech, and so on.[79] So, contrary to its self-image, it's not really true that classical legal thought, or Langdellian formalism, developed without relying upon the social and economic aspects of civil society. This law appropriated and deployed images, schemas, and metaphors having their roots in the affairs of civil society. It's just that these formalist images, schemas, and metaphors found their way into law *sub rosa*, uncritically and often inappropriately—a point that many legal realists delighted in exposing.[80]

Many problems and vexations quickly arose with this form of legalism—some having to do with the character of the liberal democratic state and others having to do with the jural forms through which the legalism was shaped and expressed (i.e., the "grid aesthetic").[81] Here, we consider one of the major problems.

At the beginning of the twentieth century, there was an increasing realization that the "law-free zones" were, in fact, not law-free. Instead, where an individual appears to have been granted discretion to act as he wishes with regard to an activity (in other words, where it looks like there is no law), he is actually protected by a legal relation—one that Hohfeld called a privilege—no-right relation.[82] That is to say, where it might appear that there is no law, but simply "free competition" or "free choice" or something of the sort, what we have is the state *permitting* individuals to interfere with each other as they pursue their own ends. There is a great deal of social, economic, and interpersonal interference that is permitted by law. This was a point initially articulated by Hohfeld and amplified during the 1930s by noted legal realists such as Arthur Corbin, Karl Llewellyn, Walter Wheeler Cook, and Robert Hale. The point was that, in any classic cooperative-adverse relation, as Duncan Kennedy notes, the permission given to one party to pursue his own ends to the detriment of the other alters the bargaining position of the parties. Take away or increase some of the privileges of one of the parties and they are now permitted to do (or not do) something that they couldn't before . . . and to do it (or not do it) in some circumstances, to the detriment of the other party.[83] Meanwhile, in these cases where Party A (e.g., creditor) has permission to do (or not do) X to Party B (e.g., debtor), Party B has no legal claim to prevent Party A from doing (or not doing) X. It follows that in structuring these cooperative/ adverse relations, the state is every bit as involved when it *permits* Party A to do (not do) something as when the state is engaged in *prohibitions* or *commands*. Permission was just as real a legal relation as prohibition or command. And, indeed, viewed from the perspective of the state, permission becomes one of the tools available for structuring the relations of private individuals in civil society.

The intellectual proliferation of this move was performed by the "legal realists" of the nineteen twenties and nineteen thirties. Among the major movers in Hohfeld's wake were Corbin, Llewellyn, Cook, and Hale. Cook and Hale, in particular, were also important in recognizing that the various privilege and rights arguments of the courts (then based on a moralistic discourse of transactions between free-willed subjects) had important distributional and allocational effects. In economics, John Commons (also a follower of Hohfeld) had similar thoughts.[84]

The upshot is that the liberal democratic state's attempt to establish, conceptually and materially, a sphere of civil society where law would not intrude or would not intrude too much became, for many legal and economic thinkers, untenable. And as it became untenable, it also became harder to refrain from investigating the social and economic effects of law in those spheres previously believed to be law-free. Legal realism counts as perhaps the first major American broadscale effort in this direction.[85]

Once it became clear that there was no way for law to avoid acting upon social and economic relations in civil society, it became an easy step to recognize that such legal action should be done knowingly and intelligently (rather than not). This did not mean that the realm of social and economic interference should be juridified in terms of prohibitions and commands. That did not follow. It did mean, however, that permissions (what were previously conceptualized as domains *outside* of law) were already subject to law. It became obvious that the rights of individuals in civil society vis-à-vis each other were delineated by the state. Put differently, the "*horizontal*" dimension (entitlements and disablements among individuals) had an inescapable "*vertical*" aspect (the securing of those entitlements and disablements by the state).[86] The clear implication was that the liberal-democratic imperative of "hands-off civil society" was no longer plausible—except as a utopian aspiration that would go unrealized.

This vexing condition did not make the "hands-off civil society" imperative go away completely. But it did render the "hands-off" imperative intellectually incoherent. As in many other precincts of law, there was a "crisis case"— that is to say, a case that presented the dilemma in stark and inescapable terms. This case, one well known to American jurists and legal scholars, was *Shelley v. Kraemer*. The case involved a racially restrictive covenant between private parties.[87] The issue before the court was whether the enforcement of such a common law-based racially restrictive covenant was "state action"—a predicate for the application of the Equal Protection Clause of the Fourteenth Amendment. Insofar as *the court* was being asked to *enforce* a racially restrictive covenant, the court's action would seem to satisfy the state action requirement. But to follow this line of argument to its logical conclusion would have sweeping implications: if the mere presence of court action enforcing common law were sufficient to find state action, then very little would be left of private law per se. Private agreements would all become subject to constitutional rights claims as soon as an otherwise viable claim reached a court. On the other hand, it seemed wholly unacceptable that a court enforcing a racially restrictive covenant could escape state action merely because the state actor was a court enforcing the common law. Courts, after all, are instrumentalities of the state, and surely they were subject to constitutional norms. Thus, it was, in *Shelley v. Kraemer*, that a finding of "state action" as well as a finding of "no state action" vividly demonstrated that the separation of public law from private law, vertical relations from horizontal relations, state from civil society was intellectually suspect (if not bereft). Worse, perhaps, *Shelley v. Kraemer* showed that the only "principled" solutions, given the state action requirement, were politically and legally untenable: the "principled" choices were to find state action (which would immediately constitutionalize private law) or to find no state action (and exempt common law courts from observing the Constitution).

Not surprisingly, state action doctrine was and remains a complete mess. If horizontal legal relations between private parties in civil society are simultaneously vertical legal relations with the state, then asking in any given case whether the relations are horizontal or vertical is complete nonsense. In fact, it is precisely the kind of nonsense humorously described by the legal realist Thomas Reed Powell, who purportedly said, "If you can think about something which is attached to something else without thinking about what it is attached to, then you have what is called a legal mind."[88] And so it is that the crisis case of *Shelley v. Kraemer* remains on the books today—a somnolent but devastating indictment of the state/civil society distinction.

How does this analytical collapse of the liberal democratic distinction between state and civil society escape notice among legal professionals? Actually, it doesn't fully escape notice. If we move from these abstractions down to the actual practice of the private lawyer, the concrete social reality of lawyering both exemplifies and denies the collapse of the state and civil society distinction. As Richard Abel argued long ago, the private lawyer is a mediation of the contradictions of the liberal democratic state.[89] That is to say that the private lawyer is the one who internalizes these contradictions and who strives to offer, at least within the formal precincts of law (the courtroom, the legislative hearing, and so on), coherent resolutions.[90]

Among the several contradictions the lawyer internalizes is the one between state and civil society. We tend to recall that a civil law lawyer represents a private client. What we often forget is that the private lawyer is an agent of the state and a carrier and executor of state law. Putting these dueling allegiances together, we have the state/civil society contradiction internalized in the lawyer's professional persona.[91]

To give an example, as a "Washington lawyer" dealing with federal agencies, my experience conformed readily with this internalization. When I started, I saw myself as representing private clients vis-à-vis federal agencies. Soon, however, I came to feel that I was also playing a nontrivial part in the execution of federal law and federal regulations vis-à-vis the client. I wasn't just a pure representative of client desiderata; I was also an extension of the legal enforcement process. I am pretty sure that I did not conceive of myself at the time as a personification of the state/civil society tension, but I came to understand that de facto I worked for both client and state. All private lawyers do this whether they acknowledge it or not. To be a private lawyer is in one ineluctable sense to work for the state and its law.

At a concrete level, we can recognize *the blending* of state and civil society in the actions and experiences of the private lawyer. One can wonder whether the state/civil society distinction holds up—whether we can tell which is which:

lawyer advises business client of new legislation
business client requests advice as to meaning of legislation
lawyer furnishes business client memorandum of law
business client requests lawyer to outline changes required in business
practices
lawyer advises several changes and modes of implementation
business client institutes changes

five years later business client gets sued anyway
lawyer conducts interviews of business client's employees
lawyers helps prepare testimony of private expert witnesses
business client complains of lawyer fees and requests faster and
less legal research
trial yields verdict against business client
lawyer advises business client of legal meaning of verdict
business client requests counsel to review business client's operations to
minimize liability exposure
applicable statutes amended by legislature
lawyer advises business client of new legislation

(And so on—more or less in the same way).
So—does the state/civil society duality hold up?
Well, no.

It does not hold up in the sense that it is difficult to discern at what point the state (the law) leaves off and civil society (the client's interest) begins. It all looks and feels like a sequence of steps that, when placed in context, are blends. It is true that in many of these situations consulting the rules of professional responsibility may be helpful or even necessary. But for the alert lawyer, the recognition soon dawns that this consultation of the rules itself reproduces the dilemma.

Switching the perspective now from lawyer to client we encounter the same hybridity. Arthur Leff, a noted legal thinker, provides a telling example—in terms of the actions of the client. Leff offers a couple of imaginary dialogues between two businessmen:

1. BUYER: Hello, Morris? Those widgets you sent us. They're breaking
every minute. You want me to pay for such junk?
SELLER: Look, if your men don't know how to use widgets right, what do
you want from me? They're just what you ordered, Grade A-2 stainless
steel widgets.
BUYER: Stainless steel they're not. Swiss cheese maybe, orange-crate
wood, but not steel.
SELLER: Look, Kevin, maybe we've been having a little quality control
problem— just temporary. Do the best you can, and we'll make it up
next time.
BUYER: OK, but don't forget. The noise of popping widgets my partner
doesn't have to hear.

2. SELLER: Hello, Kevin? So, what's with our last bill?
   BUYER: My bookkeeper's been sick.
   SELLER: Uh huh. Your hand cramps when you pick up a pen?
   BUYER: Soon, Morris.
   SELLER: How soon? Tomorrow?
   BUYER: Come on, Morris; did I make such a stink when you were
       shipping out those cardboard widgets?
   SELLER: OK, OK. Maybe I'll give you a couple of weeks more. You're not
       really in trouble, are you?
   BUYER: Absolutely not. I got plenty of orders. Go check with some of the
       other guys.
   SELLER: Don't worry. I already did. OK, take a couple of weeks. Give my
       get-wells to your bookkeeper.
   BUYER: Hah![92]

Leff's point was that it would be folly to deny that the conversations are both coercive and competitive. Mine is that it would be folly to deny that the conversations above are both business and law.

The tendency among some of us (and particularly jurists) is to ask: "Well, are the conversations predominantly or principally or primarily or mostly business or legal?" While in some factual situations one may have a gut sense, the question is typically nonsense (and sometimes a bit disingenuous)—akin to asking whether singing is more language than it is music. (Good luck with that.)

Parting Thoughts

The state/civil society distinction of the liberal democratic state is *analytically* collapsed. This immediately prompts a question: What does it mean that this collapse is *analytical*? On the one hand, it means that, apart from extreme cases, the distinction does not and cannot do much serious intellectual work in determining what versions of the state are or are not consonant with liberal democracy. On the other hand, the collapse seems, at this point in the book, confined to the analytical. The distinction endures in the breach: its analytical collapse does not mean it has vanished from the ideational commitments and repertoire of jurists and legal scholars, nor of the lay public. Moreover, it remains entrenched in the political-legal institutions and practices of the American state. And to the extent that these material institutions and practices serve as an ideational source domain (they certainly do) for the thinking of jurists and legal scholars, the distinction remains. Its collapse will, however, prepare the grounds for later more material erosions of liberal democracy. (But later on that.)

As for the contradictions of liberalism and democracy, these remain potentially live but mostly somnolent among U.S. jurists and legal scholars. In part, this is because the unreflective blending of the particulars of the U.S. Constitution with the political philosophy of liberal democracy have effectively eclipsed the conundra of constitutive power and constituted form. Those conundra have been effectively defanged by a domestic and domesticated conversation about judicial review, the counter-majoritarian difficulty, the intertemporal difficulty, and interpretive methodology. As a result, this contradiction survives—but out of view.

So we have an interesting state of affairs here. The state/civil society distinction is intellectually unmoored, but honored in the breach and materially entrenched. The liberalism/democracy contradiction is intellectually live, but the available political-legal repertoire of American jurists and legal scholars have so far prevented any serious encounter.

Even though the contradictions remain potentially live analytically they are as a political-legal matter defanged. It is plausible to attribute the success of this stasis to the intense *juridification* of the Constitution combined with the adherence of the populace to constitutional *mythology* and the strong identification of constitutional law scholars with the *institutional* apparatus of the courts, particularly the U.S. Supreme Court.

Into the breach arrives a new iteration of the American state with its own discourse, institutions, governance mechanisms, and legitimation schemes: the administered state (which we move to next). One of the things to bear in mind throughout the rest of this book is whether and if so to what degree the compromised character of the liberal democratic state sows the seeds for later more destructive iterations of the American state.

III   The Administered State

Today no nation lacking in a big bureaucracy and a powerful government has the means of insuring either its liberty or its welfare. This proposition is so plain that it should not be labored.

—J. A. VIEG[1]

In the early twentieth century, the "hands-off civil society" imperative of liberal democracy left the American state without the means to respond to the social and economic crisis brought by the depression. Nothing short of major changes in the organizing logic, institutions, and structure of the state would serve to address the challenges and problems. Other countries responding to economic and social crises wrought in the wake of World War I instituted major changes: Germany turned to Nazism, Italy to fascism, Russia to communism, and Spain to Falangism. Some countries, like France, became an unstable mess.

The United States meanwhile developed an administrative state. Comparatively, it was a tame response—though that was not unequivocally the view at the time.[2] Relative to the liberal democratic state, the transformations in the U.S. during the 1930s were nonetheless significant. Indeed, there is little doubt among historians and legal scholars that a major change took place. Nor is there much doubt that when "things settled out," they were discernibly different from before.

Among legal scholars, there are various ways to describe the precise identity and character of the changes wrought in the political-legal register. Duncan Kennedy, speaking of the global scene, famously describes the transformation as prompted by a failure to "respond coherently to the *social* needs of modern conditions of *interdependence*." Describing the champions leading the charge, he writes:

> Their basic idea was that the conditions of late nineteenth century life represented a social transformation, consisting of urbanization, industrialization,

organizational society, globalization of markets, all summarized in the idea of interdependence. Because the will theory was individualist, it ignored interdependence, and endorsed particular legal rules that permitted anti-social behavior of many kinds. The crises of the modern factory (industrial accidents, pauperization) and the urban slum, and later the crisis of the financial markets and the Great Depression, all derived from the failure of coherently individualist law to respond to the coherently social needs of modern conditions of interdependence.[3]

Bruce Ackerman provides a roughly similar description of what he calls the rise of the "activist state" in the United States:

> By saying that we live in an activist state, I mean to mark a special feature of our self-consciousness: an awareness that our society's existence depends upon a continuing flow of decisions made by politically accountable state officials. . . . [T]here is the widespread acknowledgment that the distribution of wealth and status is a central issue for political debate determination. . . . It is within this context of social perception—a context that gained its historical reality during the administration of Franklin Roosevelt—that I mean to situate the evolving legal culture.[4]

Other such accounts of a "transformation" could be identified. The accounts all describe roughly the same break even if they do so from different vantages.

But all this is prefatory. Right off it is must be noted that the administered state is much more sweeping and pervasive than the administrative state. Similarly, it must be recognized tha the administered state does not fully supplant the liberal democratic state. The latter survives. The relations between the two iterations of the state are complicated. The terms that come to mind include symbiotic, complementary, compensatory, constraining, mutable, and oppositional. Of these, it is the oppositional and its variants (e.g., conflicts, contradictions, tensions) that will have pride of place here since opposition poses the greatest challenge to coherence and viability of the state. As we move to a discussion of the administered state, the main questions to bear in mind are the following: How well does this iteration of the state perform in responding to the conflicts and contradictions of the liberal democratic state and what new difficulties does this new iteration introduce into the body politic?

Administered and Administrative

In the United States, jurists and legal scholars almost never speak of "the administered state." Instead, they speak of "the administrative state." It is the latter that draws the attention of jurists and legal scholars and which provokes their sharpest criticisms and most impassioned defenses.

The administrative state is primarily an *institutional category*: it refers typically to the alphabet agencies of the federal government (e.g., FTC, FCC, FAA). By contrast, the administered state, as the term is used here, refers to *modes of governance and legitimation*. The administrative state is institutionally and legally bounded—the administered state is not. The administered state extends to all official state institutions and eventually migrates into the organization and institutions of civil society. What is crucial about the administered state is its transformation of law into administration. In one sense, it signals governance by experts and expertise. In a different sense, it is a juridical foreshadowing of Theodor Adorno's "administered world" and Marcuse's "total administration."[5]

The rise of the administered state is among the first great institutional blows to the liberal democratic insistence of the separation of state and civil society. In sharp contrast to the "hands-off civil society" approach characteristic of liberal democracy, the administered state embraces a "hands-on" approach. The very ethos of law as administration lies in *regulating, monitoring, adjusting, and ultimately administering* the affairs of civil society. The political-legal character of the administered state finds expression in a panoply of familiar programs: social welfare, risk control, product specification, professional licensing, hygiene requirements, and so on.

Among the reasons to examine the administered state more closely is the still widespread description of the United States as a "liberal democracy." This misnomer invites serious misunderstandings. There are clearly major aspects of the American state that are appurtenant to liberal democracy, but it is deeply misleading to suppose that liberal democracy describes the fundamental character of the American state. That sort of description is archaic: it neglects and obscures radical transformations that have already taken place, among them the rise of the administered state.

For the sake of clarity, consider a very brief description of the administrative state and the arguments, pro and con, that have attended its rise. Among other things, this is a way of showcasing the originality as well as the sweeping reach of the administered state.

The Administrative State

Typically, the genesis of the administrative state is traced back to the early twentieth century, particularly to Franklin Roosevelt's New Deal, which greatly increased the presence and power of administrative agencies. Legal scholars have documented earlier manifestations of the administrative state in the U.S.,[6] but these earlier manifestations are not generally included when jurists, legal scholars, or politicians refer to "the administrative state."

The conception of the administrative state as a shorthand reference for the collection of federal administrative agencies and their panoply of processes is not going away any time soon, at least not so long as the administrative state remains the target of intense controversy among its champions and critics. Controversy over the constitutional legitimacy and general functionality of the administrative state started early and has been enduring. In the late 1930s, Roscoe Pound used the moniker "administrative absolutism" to attack administrative agencies, claiming that their subjects were inherently political and not subject to resolution by expertise. He claimed that the agencies would violate individual rights as well as the rule of law and would ultimately lead to totalitarianism.[7] These sorts of claims, along with the idea that administrative agencies constitute an illegitimate or spurious branch of government not permitted by the Constitution, have been classic arguments for conservatives and libertarians. Progressives, meanwhile, have generally defended the administrative agencies, viewing them as a necessary progressive corrective to the excesses of markets, unrestrained profit-taking, and the like. This highly patterned political fight has played a huge role in keeping attention focused on the administrative state as either problematic or desirable.

As in so many legal disputes that fixate on some formal conception of a legal institution,[8] this focus on the administrative state and its agencies have distracted jurists and legal scholars from recognizing the emergence of an arguably much more significant phenomenon: the rise of the *administered state*. This state is not confined to the agencies, but traverses all branches of government. Indeed, ultimately it becomes inscribed outside official circles in the internal structures and organization of firms, businesses, and corporations as these come to internalize and mimic government administration within their own intrafirm organization. As firms adapt to regulation, they respond, consciously or not, by tailoring their own internal infrastructures to the regulatory protocols, incentives, and deterrents of the administered state. In a very real sense, firms introject the administered state into their own internal practices and organization—both as a matter of self-defense and in order to take advantage of opportunities. Hence it is that health law and insurance law yield health maintenance organizations (HMOs) and preferred provider organizations (PPOs). Hence it is that various federal laws (e.g., antitrust) influence the creation and character of departmental subdivisions in large corporations. The important point here is that the institutional formalism that may once have confined administration to the administrative state has spilled over not only to all aspects of the state, but to civil society as well. Law as administration is not confined to federal agencies, but spills over to all branches of government (courts, legislatures, the executive), all kinds of official law (common, statutory, constitutional, and regulatory), informal law (internal corporate protocols, professional practice, institutional norms) and even the institutions of civil society.

The Administered State

The idea of the administered state offered here is unorthodox, but it is not particularly radical. It is unorthodox in the sense that most American legal jurists and legal scholars have not focused on the ways in which liberal democratic law has been morphed or displaced by *law as administration*.

To be sure, jurists and legal scholars are very much aware of the ways in which various kinds of instrumentalism and consequentialism (e.g., policy analysis, economic analysis) have emerged as important forms of legal reasoning and exegesis. (Virtually no one in the law world has missed this). What has been largely missed, however, is a recognition that instrumentalist and consequentialist forms of legal reasoning are carriers. Specifically, they are carriers of law as administration. Policies, goals and objectives are realized through administrative mechanisms that break organizations down into *functionalized* decision trees.

In terms of contemporary legal thought, the administered state corresponds most closely to Duncan Kennedy's "Second globalization" of legal consciousness (the social) and to my own description of "the instrumentalist aesthetic" (rights) and to "the energy aesthetic" (law generally).[9] All three descriptions—the social, the instrumentalist aesthetic, and the energy aesthetic—overlap significantly, even as they exhibit noticeable differences. The differences are not particularly surprising given that the descriptions were worked out with and against different backgrounds: respectively, a globalized form of legal consciousness (the social), rights (the instrumentalist aesthetic), and American law generally (the energy aesthetic).[10]

The conflict between the administered state and the liberal democratic state is perhaps most obvious in the sense that liberal democracy strives mightily to avoid "interfering" in civil society, whereas, the administered state, on the contrary, embraces the vigorous oversight, monitoring, adjustment, and regulation of civil society. Where liberal democracy is "hands-off civil society" to the degree possible, the administered state displays no such forbearance. It is most definitely "hands-on civil society."

Part of this hands-on approach may be ascribed to explicit political-legal considerations—a desire to rectify market failures, to compensate for wealth and power inequality, or to address other social problems. Part of this hands-on approach may also be linked to the increasing friction (e.g., negative externalities) and the compounding complexity (e.g., reciprocal interference) that pose challenges to political-legal coordination. Here it is helpful to think of the advancing logic of administration in terms of positive feedback loops: increasing friction and compounding complexity motivate more intricate political-legal responses that, as these become internalized in various public and private institutions, create yet more friction and greater complexity, which in turn . . . and so on.

The administered state institutes governance mechanisms and legitimation schemes very different from the liberal democratic state. Below is a quick listing of the semantics of the administered state. Familiar and seemingly anodyne to us now, they were once transformative:

Social Engineering/Functionalism/Instrumentalism/Consequentialism
Public Interest/Public Policies
Goals/Objectives/Ends
Means/Methods/Tools
Risk/Probability/Discounting
Monitoring/Supervision/Oversight/Management
Control/Deter/Incentivize/Facilitate
Disclosure/Reporting/Warning
Standardization/Systemization/Specification

Notice that the dissonance with the semantics of the liberal democratic state is stark. It is not just substance that has changed, but the political-legal aesthetics of the state. This new aesthetic is in sharp conflict with the grid aesthetics of the liberal democratic state described earlier. Instead of the *stasis* of the grid, the administered state is very much steeped in the *dynamics* of the "energy aesthetic." This is an aesthetic of law where "conflicting forces of principle, policy, values, and politics collide and combine in sundry ways. Precedents expand or contract in accordance with the push and pull of policy and principle . . . Movement and flux are the orders of the day."[11] As stated in a prior article, in the energy aesthetic

> [p]recedents have direction; they pass from one juridical constellation to another. Like planets or meteors, precedents have "gravitational pull" or "gravitational force." Policies and principles "conflict." They are cast as vectors (on the blackboard and elsewhere) that push and pull the law in various directions. . . .
>
> With the energy aesthetic, the judicial opinion is no longer merely a set of legal propositions (subdivided into holding, *obiter dicta*), but a legal force in the social world. Particularly in the legal realist cosmology, precedents and laws are reconfigured as causes, effects, antecedents, and consequences. . . .
>
> Law becomes . . . a drive for "efficiency"—a force that imposes its inexorable transaction-cost-reducing, Kaldor-Hicks-market-replicating logic on one legal subject after another. Law is on a mission—propelled by its own moving principles, policies, and values. . . .
>
> Not surprisingly, the energy aesthetic with its invocation of physics imagery—mass, weight, push, pull, force, etc.—are conducive to "social engineering" and its more scholarly incarnation, "functionalism." The decisions of individual judges are seen as occasions to prescribe directives for the organization of "society."

Hence it is that in the administered state, law is apprehended and represented in terms of active forces. While *the grid* jurisprudence of the liberal democratic state required the establishment and maintenance of secure classification schemes (border police jurisprudence), now the law of the administered state is all about action and verbs: laws are said to

Predominate,
Override,
Require,
Extend,
Contract,
Constrain,
Direct,

Promote,

Achieve,

Deter,

Advance, and

Perform all sorts of other moving actions.[12]

With all this *verb jurisprudence*, it is no surprise that the administered state and its moving aesthetic should disregard and override any number of previously established boundaries and distinctions, including, most topically, the state/civil society divide of the liberal democratic state. Plunging institutions and individuals into a world of motion, the administered state drives a law that is actively involved in regulating and managing. This regulatory and managerial drive transforms the idioms of lawyers, judges, and legal scholars as well. Progress and efficiency become the new watchwords. Reform, regulation, change, maximization, optimization, and the like become the new marching orders of the reconstructed political-legal register. Expertise, social science positivism, empiricism, and technical proficiency become the ideal forms of knowledge.

This jurisprudential override is explicitly manifested in many of the forms of legal analysis that developed throughout the twentieth century—policy analysis, economic analysis, utilitarianism, welfare maximization, and legal pragmatism. The ubiquitous deployment of these well-recognized approaches in legal reasoning and legal exegesis makes it clear that law and its institutions are acutely involved in examining, responding to, and managing the affairs of civil society.

Slippage—from the Administrative State to the Administered State

One of the crucial points here is that while the *administered state* is different from and far more sweeping than the *administrative state*, the two are hardly unrelated. Indeed, the rise of the administered state can be ascribed in part to the migration of administration from the federal administrative agencies to all corners of law's empire ("slippage"). We now turn to a description of this slippage.

Gradually, but inexorably, the administrative state extends its bureaucratic logic—to wit, administration—throughout the various precincts of law (constitutional, statutory, common law). Beyond that the so-called private sector (especially the institutionalized corporate sector) comes to internalize the bureaucratic logic imposed or rendered available. For instance, the internal structure of the modern corporation—its departments, its subdivisions, its lines of communication and authority—is in part organized as an internalization of and response to law as administration.[13] What is at stake is the construction of

> a private legal order in its own right. In a very real sense, we suggest, today's organizations hold court, incorporating but also subsuming many of the public legal system's central functions. As private legislatures, courthouses, law offices, and police departments, organizations construct within and around themselves a semiautonomous legal regime that simultaneously mimics and absorbs even the most "official" institutions of governmental law.[14]

After a while, all manner of institutions—hospitals, schools, fire departments, daycare centers, recreational parks—absorb in their very practices and architecture, the character of bureaucratic forms of law. In turn, bureaucratic forms shape standardized human relations: the traffic patterns of everyday life become those of administration. Indeed, the facts and channels of our social and economic world are increasingly the constructions of the administered state. HMOs, PPOs, employment contracts, automobile financing agreements, and so on—these are all constructs of the administered state. Having internalized law as administration, individuals become administrators of their own lives: they compartmentalize, consolidate and outsource their activities, tasks, and roles. The expansion of administration as a mode of organization for social life does not stop here, however.

As administration becomes embedded in the facts of everyday life, an interesting feedback loop takes hold: the social and economic face of administration begins to appear as "the facts" in common, statutory, and even constitutional cases. Hence, it is only a slight exaggeration to say that the constitutional law of the twenty-first century has become the constitutional law of bureaucracy. Indeed, no one would mistake the punchy narrative style of an early twentieth-century Supreme Court opinion with the protracted bureaucratic style of Supreme Court opinions issued by the Rehnquist and Roberts Courts. The former seem almost off the cuff—the latter a bureaucratic journey through mazes without end.[15]

The positive feedback effect here is clear and one would think undeniable: over time, under the influence of reform, regulation, supervision, and correction, the juridification begat by law as administration drives itself. That is to say, that administration begets more administration. Complexity begets more complexity. The levers of social and economic control beget even more levers.[16] And friction begets more friction. This is the compelling logic of law as administration—one which feels as if no additional specification is beyond consideration, no elaboration is ever too much.

The crucial thing is to recognize is that once the positive feedback loops take hold, the logic of the administered state produces and reproduces itself as *facts on the ground* that it then re-uploads into law. Thus it is that the "polar night of icy darkness" cometh.[17] And it cometh seemingly everywhere. Indeed, just to put a fine point on it, consider that the practice of law as administration even penetrates into fictional accounts of the underworld:

> Part of what makes The Wire so brilliant is its revelation that the bureaucratic forms of modern institutions are so pervasive that they have come to organize not only official institutions but underworld activity as well. The business of drugs turns out to produce the same kinds of pecking orders, promotions and demotions, incentives for good work, quality assessments, and business mergers as the routines of official institutions.[18]

Much as the aesthetics—both ideational and material—of the administrative state may be off-putting, the substantive political-legal stakes are not trivial. The ends invoked are nothing less than the protection of workers, safety, health, foodstuffs, competitive markets—indeed, any number of goods that the liberal democratic state demonstrably and dramatically fails to deliver. Law as administration steps into the breach: it becomes the vehicle for the delivery of these substantive goods.

Design—from the Legal Academy to the Administered State

Besides the administrative state, a second juridical source for the advent of the *administered state* must be recognized: the American legal academy. It is generally understood among jurists and legal scholars that the legal realism of the 1920s and 1930s was a major driver of the dramatic rise of federal agencies in the early twentieth century. But more than that, the transformations inspired by legal realism rippled throughout law and legal thought to help create the administered state.[19] In this regard, it is difficult to overestimate the impact of legal realism, which, though unsuccessful in many of its more ambitious projects,[20] nonetheless provided the basic grounds and the intellectual motivation for a whole slew of important schools of legal thought in the twentieth century, including:

Policy-driven doctrinal analysis—still the dominant school of legal
   thought today. It is committed to the evaluation and development
   of law in terms of instrumental goals, ends, and objectives. Policy
   analysis is supremely important in American law schools because it
   plays a key role in the elaboration of law as doctrine in the classroom
   and serves as the mainstay of legal scholarship as well.
Law and society—committed to studying the formation and effects of law
   in terms of social science (positivist, empirical, and otherwise).
Law and economics—committed to the analysis of law and legal regimes
   in descriptive and normative economic terms (in particular, Kaldor-
   Hicks efficiency).
Critical legal studies—committed to the critical interpretation and
   analysis of law in terms of wealth and power distribution with a view
   to adopting more egalitarian norms in law, particularly as it pertains
   to class, race, and gender.
Feminist jurisprudence and critical race theory—committed to the critical
   investigation of law in terms of its disparate, subordinating, and
   discriminatory impact on race and gender.
Empirical legal studies—committed to the study of law in empirical terms,
   particularly quantitative empirical studies based on available data
   sets, surveys, and data-gathering.
Legal pluralism—committed to the internalization of social
   contextualism within law itself, thus recognizing informal law, folk
   law, law without sovereignty, and the like.

The extraordinary impact of legal realism can also be appreciated by taking note of the comparatively few (and relatively insular) schools of legal thought today that have remained largely immune to the impact of legal realism:

Analytic jurisprudence—for decades committed to the conceptual
   analysis of law and still today deploying the strategies of Anglo-
   American analytic philosophy.
Grand normative theory—committed to the normative and, in some
   cases, natural-law-like evaluation and prescription of norms and
   normative values to improve the fairness, justice, equality, or
   libertarian qualities of law.

Law and literature—committed to the literary analysis of legal texts or the improvement of law by the familiarization of literature to legal actors.

The Corrosive Consequences of the "Constructive" Approaches

In the chapter on the liberal democratic state, we canvassed the widespread destruction that the legal realists visited upon classical legal thought and Langdellian formalism. Here we focus on the importance of the corrosive effects wrought by the positive program of the realists. In their "constructive" moments—and here one thinks mostly of Karl Llewellyn and Felix Cohen— the realists elaborated a legal functionalism and a law–social science connection that, like the administrative state, would prove to be highly corrosive to the state/civil society distinction and its hands-off civil society imperative. Many of the descendant schools that have followed in the wake of this constructive legal realist work have propagated approaches that are truly antithetical to the law and civil society distinction and separation. Among them:

Policy analysis
Functionalism
Utilitarianism
Efficiency analysis
Legal pragmatism

All of these approaches not only enable but also counsel, as an analytical matter, setting aside the state/civil society distinction where necessary to produce salutary social or economic consequences.

All of the approaches above share a common consequentialist grammar. They posit some desired goals or objectives (the "ends") that are to be achieved through law, which serves as the tool (the "means").[21] Cast in this summary fashion, this consequentialist formula greatly understates the sophistication of and differences among the various approaches.[22] To give a sense of the sophistication, consider Michael Dorf and Charles Sabel's account of the pragmatism of Charles Sanders Peirce, John Dewey, and George Herbert Mead:

Thus, a central theme of the pragmatism of Peirce, Dewey, and Mead is the reciprocal determination of means and ends. Pragmatists argue that in science, no less than in industry and the collective choices of politics, the objectives presumed in the guiding understandings of theories, strategies, or ideals of justice are transformed in the light of the experience of their pursuit, and these transformations in turn redefine what counts as a means to a guiding end.[23]

We will stick, however, with the more simplistic formula, not only for ease of exposition, but because it is more descriptive of the typical implementations by jurists and legal scholars. Most of the actual analytical work involved in the various consequentialist approaches lies in selecting ends that are at once desirable and attainable while fashioning efficacious legal means to achieve them, all the while minimizing collateral damage elsewhere. The problem for the state/civil society distinction, of course, is that these approaches require that *law as means* (the state) be tailored to achieve *ends in social and economic life* (civil society). That in itself is already a breach of the state/civil society distinction. And to the degree the consequentialist approaches become ubiquitous (as they have) it becomes less possible, and less credible, to characterize such breaches as minimalist, exceptional, or inconsequential. On the contrary, each breach is prompted by expansionary forces and rationales poised to override and overrun limits, restraints, borders, and boundaries (i.e., the aesthetic of the grid). The integrity of limits, restraints, borders, and boundaries (in short, the aesthetic of the grid) is now only as strong as the consequentialist calculus that supports them. To give some concrete examples:

> *Policy analysis* threatens to overrun field-specific distinctions separating contracts from torts from property law.
> *Utilitarianism* treats every aspect of law as something to be evaluated in terms of utilities—with a constant risk that rule-utilitarianism will collapse into act-utilitarianism.
> *Efficiency analysis* likewise poses a risk of dissolving any legal distinctions and concepts (e.g. rights, powers, identities) into a roving Kaldor-Hicks/cost-benefit analysis that shows little respect for side constraints.
> *Pragmatism* has no leg to stand on in affirming what stays fixed (and could thus ground analysis) and distinguishing what is variable (and can thus be taken as eligible for modification). Put differently, pragmatism has no solid grounds for distinguishing the invariant from the variant.

The dissonance between the two iterations of the state, both in form and substance, runs deep and wide as shown in Chart I below.[24] Chart I maps out this dissonance along many different roughly homologous parameters (laid out on the vertical). While the chart may not mean very much to those not already well versed in American legal thought, it is relatively easy to sum up the major significance of the detailed chart.

Here goes: the reticence of the liberal democratic state to examine, study, and manage civil society is rejected in the administered state. Whereas liberal democracy is committed to leaving civil society alone as much as possible, the latter is committed to social engineering. Whereas liberal democracy contemplates a law that is fixed, stable, and enduring, the administered state embraces instrumentalism and consequentialism in seeking to have law attain goals and objectives. Whereas liberal democracy contemplates law as boundary setting and border policing, the administered state sees law as a question of evaluation, calculation, and measurement. Whereas liberal democracy aspires to a degree of abstraction and universality, the administered state hews to localized contexts and particularities. Whereas the ethos of liberal democratic law is restraint and abstention, the ethos of the administered state is activism and intervention.

There are, in short, sustained and pervasive differences and conflicts in ethos, aesthetics, politics, and methods between the two iterations of the state. There is very little, if anything, that can be considered liberal democratic about the administered state—except that the latter has emerged through liberal democratic processes.

The chart below bears similarity to the one developed by Duncan Kennedy about the "Three Globalizations,"[25] though the categories are different. These entries and their relations are loosely associated and generally fuzzy. Moreover, it is important to recognize that all sorts of hybridities do occur frequently.

All of this poses an interesting question: Between the liberal democratic and the administered state, which is dominant? One could argue that the liberal democratic state remains as the background structure of the state as well as its dominant legitimating myth—at the constitutional level and beyond. (Americans and others around the world are far more likely to describe the United States as a liberal democracy than as an administered state.) On the other hand, administration as a mode of political-legal thought and organization is pervasive and relentless—installing itself in every nook and cranny it uncovers. In this regard, law as administration has a huge aesthetic advantage: law as administration is dynamic. It has places to go, things to do, worlds to explore (and colonize). The law of the liberal democratic state, by contrast, is deliberately self-inhibiting and static.

Chart I. Liberal Democratic/Administered States

	Liberal Democratic State	Administered State
Jurisprudence	Legal Formalism Law as Propositions	Legal Realism Law as Tool
Legal Consciousness	"Classical legal thought"	"The Social"
Aesthetics	Law as "grid": spatialization, grid, territorialization, field, objectification	Law as "energy": force, quantification, measurement, calibration
Moral Emphasis	"The right" (deontological ethics)	"The good" (consequentialist ethics)
Overarching Objectives	Maintain order (preserve structure)	Increase welfare (achieve purpose)
Philosophy	Conceptualist, Formal	Pragmatic, Functional
Essence of Law	The letter of . . .	The spirit of . . .
Key Artifactual Dyad	Directives and Principles	Directives and Policies
Knowledge Base	Law	Social science
Knowledge Form	Juristic Science	Domain Expertise
View of Social Field	Homogeneous	Heterogeneous
Statutory Interpretation	Textualist	Purposive
Governance Techniques	Formalization, Integration	Deformalization, Goal Achievement
Rationalization Techniques	Law as systematicity: coherent self-relation	Law as adequation to both its object-field and its goal
Key Jural Operations	Classification, analysis, subsumption, boundary policing	Consideration, evaluation, determination
Key Common Law Source Domain	Property (Entitlements)	Torts (Correction/Regulation)
Chief Objective Serving as Legitimation	Maintenance of order/Rule of law	Welfare maximization/Progress
Conflict Avoidance Strategy	Isolation of conflicting activities and interests/Boundary setting and maintenance	Deterrence/incentives/oversight
Privileged Situs of Law	Trial/Adjudication	Regulation/Hearing
Preferred Temporal Intervention	Ex ante regimes/Get the right answers, enforce them, and stick with them	Process regimes (Ex ante and Ex post) Monitor continuously and correct process
Favored Directive Form	Rule	Standard/Totality of Circumstances, Multifactor Tests
Ethical Categories	Right/Wrong Vices/Virtues	Costs/Benefits Advantages/Disadvantage

Chart I—*Continued*

Conceptual Sources for Law	Property images and metaphors (borders, dominion, control)	Tort images and metaphors rule (risk, duty, scope, standard of care)
Externalities/Friction	As the exception	As the general case
Preferred Techniques of Reconciliation	Line drawing, Hierarchy	Balancing Proportionality, Holism

Overall, it would be difficult to make a meaningful assessment as to which dominates. And there are so many different ways of framing the issues, the contexts, and their relations that it seems like a quixotic venture to try. What matters is to recognize the striking dissonance.[26]

A case law example of the virulence of the clash may help here: consider this conflict between liberalism and administration over the right of a woman to choose "whether or not to terminate her pregnancy."[27] The key precedent undergirding this right, *Griswold v. Connecticut*,[28] is a classically liberal effort to protect an individual's right of privacy. That right in turn is extended as "a right to choose" whether to get an abortion in *Roe v. Wade*.[29] That opinion ultimately rests the legitimacy and rationalization of its holding on the deployment of medical knowledge, procedures, and technology. Decades later, as the right is processed through many legislative actions and judicial opinions, the right to choose ends up as the focal point of incredibly intense technical, medical, and administrative scrutiny.[30] Indeed, the right is calculated and litigated right down to the number of feet that protesters must accord a woman seeking entry into an abortion facility.[31] This is a painful and cruel irony: a right that was created to *protect privacy* ends up being subjected to an *intensely public administrative specification of the form and content in which that right may be exercised*.[32] And then the right is abrogated altogether.

Whereas liberalism and administration are clearly at loggerheads, the relation between administration and democracy is more complicated. Indeed, this is perhaps the great problem at the heart of the administered state: administration, whether in the agencies or elsewhere, was at inception supposed to vindicate something called "the public interest."

Here, because it is such a great example, we will slide back partially into the discourse of the *administrative state*. James Landis, a champion of the administrative state, held out great hope that the public interest could be ascertained and defined through experts wielding knowledge. Similarly,

Felix Cohen, the famous legal realist, held out hope that law's problems and challenges in adjudication could be resolved through a publicly minded functionalism.

Neither Landis's nor Cohen's hopes came to full fruition. Expertise could and would certainly contribute to the fashioning of the political-legal register, but the public interest itself would remain a site of political contestation between expertise and democracy. Thus, the people's will was to have some strong relation to the public interest—but not so much as to disregard sound technical expertise. Expertise, in turn, was to have some strong relation to the public interest—but not so much as to disregard the people's will. And there, of course, is the dilemma.

Accommodations between the two are possible and have been variously implemented. At the same time, however, the conflict is ongoing—not capable of full resolution. During the twentieth century there was a gradual collapse of any robust notion (whether politically or expertise-driven) of "the public interest" in favor of policy adoption and regime setting in accordance with the aggregation of group or private interests.

Morton Horwitz captured the ethos of decline in the notion of "public interest":

> [O]nce the idea of a substantive public interest began to confront ridicule after World War II, the function of the state came to be redefined as simply a reflection of the sum of the vectors of private conflict. Private self-interest, which under the progressive program was to be kept suspiciously in check, once again became the only legitimate political reality, and the idea of an autonomous public realm began correspondingly to sink into oblivion.[33]

This devolution can be described in various stages:

Stage 1
Legal administration qua "the rule of expertise" (Landis, Frank
     Goodnow) to . . .
          Stage 2
          Legal administration qua "the rule of accounting" (Gary Becker,
               Richard Posner, Frank Easterbrook) to . . .[34]
                    Stage 3
                    Legal administration qua "the rule of cognitive
                         managerialism" (Richard Thaler, Cass Sunstein).

In long form, the stages are as follows:

Stage 1: Legal administration as the rule of expertise. This first stage is the "policy science" moment: discrete goals are stated in ostensibly politically neutral welfare-enhancing ways (e.g., reduce accidents, improve health, prevent fraud, and so on). At some point it became clear to most legal professionals that law as administration—law as an effort to manage the affairs of civil society—could not be accomplished without making value judgments as well as distributional choices about who should get what. The work of agencies and the administrative state generally could no longer be viewed only as the seamless outgrowth of expertise. Something more was going on. Distinguishing and shielding the administrative state from politics so as to allow the flourishing of expertise was thus thwarted.[35] Meanwhile, the disturbing insights of Ronald Coase and Guido Calabresi about the ubiquitous reciprocal interference of social and economic activities began to percolate throughout law and legal thought. Speaking of conflicting resource uses in the context of cattle ranching vs. farming, Coase famously argued:

> The traditional approach has tended to obscure the nature of the choice that has to be made. The question is commonly thought of as one in which A inflicts harm on B and what has to be decided is: how should we restrain A? But this is wrong. We are dealing with a problem of a reciprocal nature. To avoid the harm to B would inflict harm on A. The real question that has to be decided is: should A be allowed to harm B or should B be allowed to harm A? The problem is to avoid the more serious harm.[36]

This "causal agnosticism," also reflected in Calabresi's approach, had impacts on legal thought well beyond law and economics. Indeed, prior to this powerful insight, legal thinkers would cast conflicting resource use issues in a conventional "perpetrator-victim" frame, steeped in concerns about "fairness," "correcting wrongs," or in some cases the economic language of "internalizing externalities." Jurists and scholars would go about proclaiming, often with a great deal of armchair certainty and so-called good judgment, that it was "fair" or "economically sound" to hold this party liable to that one. Each case seemed to rest on its own bottom. When Ronald Coase's brazen causal agnosticism arrived on the scene it destroyed this unfounded doctrinal confidence. Equally disruptive was Coase's demonstration in his famous railway-sparks hypothetical that a rule aimed at the "internalization of externalities" would not necessarily achieve the desired results. It was not possible to formulate a legal rule that would affect *only* the putative externality cost and *not* the costs of other related activities. The upshot was that a legal rule's reduction of a given cost was likely to have effects on lots of other costs—not just the those targeted by the rule.

A host of approaches were offered to take up the slack resulting from the causal agnosticism: pragmatism and its contextual pluralism, critical theory's intuitionism, law and economics' efficiency analysis. Of all the approaches, law and economics was most popular in that it offered the semblance of a formal method that could be applied across multiple contexts to repair law's crumbled architecture. The efficiency approach was problematic (relying as it did on the categories of law's crumbled architecture)[37] but nevertheless law and economics thrived. Thus it is that over the last quarter of the twentieth century, the jurists and scholars of the administered state turned to the rule of accounting.

Stage 2: Legal administration as the rule of accounting. "The Rule of Accounting" does not refer to "accounting costs," but rather to the ubiquitous reliance on cost-benefit analysis (CBA) and Kaldor-Hicks efficiency and thus the necessary *counting or conjectural approximation of costs*. In this second stage, the challenge of reciprocal interference among activities and goals transformed public values and concerns into CBA. This, in turn, produced the rule of accounting where the value of policies and legal regimes is assessed by aggregating private valuations according to some metric: "willingness to pay" (Chicago law and economics), "utils" (utilitarianism), rough ungrounded approximations of costs and benefits (the courts).[38] Whatever the metric, CBA quickly became one of the dominant forms of analysis for proposed political-legal regime changes. Sometimes so-called side constraints were invoked to confine CBA to various moral, dignitary, or process concerns. But all in all, and despite serious criticism, CBA became ubiquitous. Public value collapsed into a discourse of aggregating private value because that is all that was left. But even this backstop was vulnerable since the aggregation of private value entailed large doses of conjecture and rests upon conventional legal frames that remain intellectually unvalidated from an economic standpoint.[39]

Stage 3: Legal administration as the rule of cognitive managerialism. This stage brings us to the borderlands of neoliberalism: it involves the use of psychological techniques to influence individual behavior. Classic examples include Thaler and Sunstein's "nudges"[40] and Sunstein and Adrian Vermeule's "cognitive infiltration."[41] Consider "nudge" as an example (it is much more well known). Often, a nudge is just a "permissive default" from which the parties are allowed to deviate. Such permissive defaults can be legal, technological, architectural, geographic, and more. The great appeal of nudge is threefold. First, nudges are happening anyway—so they might as well be designed rationally rather than allowed to occur randomly. Second, nudges can be designed to achieve social as opposed to, say, antisocial ends. Third, nudges are arguably less intrusive than "command and control" mechanisms.[42]

Whatever the welfare benefits of cognitive managerialism as practiced by the state, it is clearly at war with the psychological precepts of the liberal democratic state.[43] To put it simply: if the presuppositions of cognitive managerialism are right, then it can only be because the presuppositions about the free-willed individual liberal subject of the liberal democratic state are in need of radical revision, if not outright abandonment. The entire idea that human beings are free-willed individual subjects who nonetheless suffer from sundry cognitive errors and biases requires a bit of work on what exactly is meant by the "free-willed individual subject."

Stepping back to look at the whole, there has been a tendency over the course of the twentieth century to move from a conception of the public interest as independent of and distinct from private interests to a conception of public interest as a mere aggregation of various private interests. This transformation might easily be seen as a hollowing out of more robust notions of the "public interest" and the "generality of norms."

At a basic level, we are left without a serious account of the economic impact of the legal actions of the administered state—common, statutory, constitutional, and regulatory law. To be sure, with the availability of state of the art software and "available data sets," academics now produce many localized quantitative empirical legal studies. Many of these are extremely sophisticated—and display clear aesthetic allure. The best studies would be very hard, if not impossible, to contest. But whatever intellectual pleasures or rewards methodological perfection may bring, generalized insight is rarely among them. In the main, what we get are discrete studies that do not scale up easily. And sometimes the results are shaped by the interests of the institutions that produce the "available data sets" in the first place. We are thus frequently left without any serious accounting.

Economic analysis of law is no exception here. On the contrary, it is Exhibit A for the substitution of conjecture for knowledge: "If we can assume this, this, and this, then that follows, whereas if . . ." This formula and its manifold deployments are frequently right given their predicate assumptions. They do, however, suffer from a serious shortcoming: indeed, it almost always turns out that the predicate assumptions—"this, this, and this"—rarely hold in any world we have ever encountered, leaving the actual attainment of the resulting "that" rationally unreachable.[44] Moreover, law and economics is partial equilibrium analysis—one legal regime analyzed after another—but with no guarantee of exhaustiveness, and virtually no accounting at all for the overlap and interference among various legal regimes.[45] It is certainly very hard to figure out, for instance, whether a given property rule is efficient or not unless one also considers the tort and contract rules that overlap, supplement, or countermand that property rule.

Certain things we do know, however. We do know that the administered state's regulation of distinct activities in context is an endeavor that facilitates (subsidizes) or deters (penalizes) persons and activities in civil society. Note that this was also true (if one takes a Hohfeldian perspective) in the liberal democratic state as well: it too engages in the imposition of subsidies and penalties. But what is distinctive about the administered state, and its fine-tuned managerialism, is that it becomes possible for private parties to obtain *special, targeted, highly localized, even granular dispensations*—the sorts of subsidies that are now known generally by such unsavory names as "loopholes," "rent-seeking," "regulatory arbitrage," "capture," and "pay for play." Here we come within reach of the neoliberal state.

Now, make no mistake, it may well be that, in some or even many senses, law has always been for sale. Certainly, the critics of the liberal democratic state, on both the far right and far left, have offered significant arguments to that effect—again both Marx and Schmitt come to mind here. What makes the administered state different from their classic indictments of the liberal democratic state is that the logic of administration—to wit, managerialism, contextualism, localism, and so forth—enables much *greater granularity*, and therefore much more possibility for thoroughgoing rent-seeking, regulatory arbitrage, capture, and pay-for-play. To put it differently, the granularity of the administered state means that there is something to be had, if not for everyone who can pay, at least for a great many.[46] Note that once legalism catches on to the idea of granularity, it becomes a wonderful vehicle for the creation and exploitation of further granularities. Once analytical atomization takes hold intellectually, it's pretty hard to stop. The political-legal measures that would need to be taken in order to stop atomization become themselves new additions to the atomization . . . soon to yield further . . .

For jurists and legal scholars who are intimately involved in the practice or teaching of law, the administered state is so familiar that it is difficult to find it odd or strange. We are like the fish as described in David Foster Wallace's commencement speech at Kenyon College. In his story, two young fish are asked how's the water? "[O]ne of them looks over at the other and goes 'What the hell is water?'"[47] Well, regarding the administered state, we legal professionals are the fish and it is the water.

The irony is that for fish, little is more intimately related to their lives than water. For jurists and legal scholars, the same might be said regarding the administered state. Jurists and legal scholars have no need for deep understandings of the administered state in order to participate in its practice, growth, or rewards. But if jurists and legal scholars did want to understand the administered state, they would have to estrange their professional selves (even if momentarily) from this state so that they could experience its strangeness relative to the ethos of the liberal democratic state.

That doesn't happen much. With the exception of some libertarians and conservatives on the right and some radicals on the left, most contemporary jurists and legal scholars do not seem terribly bothered (or indeed, bothered at all) by any of this dissonance. Many seem neither to notice nor to care. It's simply law, and it is what it is. Correspondingly, legal professionals are who they are and do what they do. Again, they are the fish and it is the water.

For now, notice the big picture: the liberal democratic state demands a law and legal thought that stays aloof from the affairs of civil society, while the administered state demands a law and legal thought responsive to the disparate needs and wants of groups and interests in civil society. The first approach tells legal professionals to stay above it all and try to remain neutral, objective, and detached, while the second tells them to dig in, pay attention to particularities, and adjust the rules contextually. The first approach points to Herbert Wechsler's neutral principles[48] while the second points to Felix Cohen's functionalism.[49]

Against all this, it might be argued that the administered and the liberal democratic state stand in a symbiotic or complementary relationship. One might imagine a situation in which liberal democratic "self-inhibition" and administered "interventionism" might be dedicated to *different domains, issues, and problems* depending on suitability. Or one might imagine a scenario in which each iteration tempers the other. To some degree, this must surely happen. But it does not make conflict and contradiction go away.

The conflicts and contradictions run deep. In this regard, consider that the logics of the two iterations does not occur merely at the level of law. The two iterations will describe and frame transactions, domains, and issues differently. There is no field of application that preexists description through the law of liberal democracy or the law of administration. Every political-legal transaction, domain, or issue is thus susceptible to the descriptive logics of the administered and the liberal democratic state. (Whether any resulting description is convincing or not poses a different question.)

Going further, these two different logics also shape the identity and character of our very selves. The liberal democratic state asks that we imagine ourselves as autonomous individuals able to choose their life paths freely, protected by the rule of law and individual rights in a democratic state. The administered state asks that we recognize, in a very pragmatic way, that we are material beings, afflicted with cognitive biases and errors, subjected to social engineering by an administered state that deploys mechanisms designed to deter, incentivize, facilitate, and nudge us along in hopefully welfare maximizing ways (the administered state). OK. So just who are we here?

A different question now: Is the mere existence of the conflicts and contradictions identified problematic? Conceivably. What is certainly problematic, however, is the denial of the conflicts and contradictions. In time, actors and forces in both state and civil society learn, adapt, and reorganize to take advantage of these conflicts and contradictions.

How might this happen? Well, to some degree it has already happened: here we begin a transition to the neoliberal state. The dissonance between the liberal democratic and the administered state yields an *arrested dialectic*. This dialectic is one that doesn't go anywhere but simply repeats itself. It becomes entrenched: the resulting stasis prepares the grounds for the emergence of the neoliberal state.

If one peruses the oppositions in Chart I above, it becomes obvious that neither side triumphs. Each side is subject to nontrivial critiques from the other. Indeed, the story of U.S. legal theory in the twentieth century is a litany of ingenious but nonetheless failed efforts to synthesize the two approaches in a coherent whole.[50] Many solutions have been offered—meta-approaches,[51] pragmatism,[52] theoretical minimalism,[53] oxymoronic jurisprudence,[54] and more. All have been tried. None has succeeded.

Synthesis eludes, as the dialectic travels throughout law's empire to shape and form different content. While the dialectic is ubiquitous, there has been a generalized failure to appreciate that *this* dialectic is arrested—that at *the level of form*, it doesn't lead anywhere other than to this or that version of itself. All of this I have elaborated at great length elsewhere and need not be repeated here.

Why does the arrested dialectic endure? One easy answer is that once an arrested dialectic becomes entrenched as part of the political-legal register, no side can afford to leave the site of struggle. Leaving the site of struggle would be akin to unilateral disarmament—simply allowing the other side to prevail. Thus everyone remains engaged in playing out the same roles, making the same arguments, advancing the same positions.

The disputes ironically are not purely oppositional. There is a bizarre sense in which the antagonists also stand in a symbiotic relation. With sufficient exposure to the various instantiations of the arrested dialectic, one can experience the uncanny sense that, structurally and functionally, the antagonists are in some sense allies as well. The deep political-legal significance of this highly stylized opposition may well be that, in enacting the opposition and its panoply of arguments, *all other versions of the political-legal are perforce excluded.* The two antagonists have rented out all the rooms in the jurisprudential hotel.[55]

Political-legal stasis ensues because, amid the visible disagreement and antagonism of the two groups, there is a shared understanding that their discourse exhausts the realm of the "reasonable," the "sensible," and the "realistic." Everything else is extreme or radical. Amid the animation of the disputes, the sameness that undergirds their putative opposition goes unremarked: heads nod yes or no while law and legal thought repeat themselves as largely the same.

Now, translate the intellectual stasis of this oppositional discourse (discussed elsewhere) into its correspondent political-legal implications. The result is a decay and atrophy of vital political-legal thought and action. As will be argued in the next chapter, neoliberalism is the virulent political-legal exploitation of this decay—both its accelerant and beneficiary.

IV The Neoliberal State

We had a hierarchy in my office in Congress. . . . If you're a lobbyist who never gave us money, I didn't talk to you. If you're a lobbyist who gave us money, I might talk to you.

—U.S. CONGRESSMAN MICK MULVANEY FROM SOUTH CAROLINA[1]

There are many neoliberalisms.[2] The expression is polysemic and, absent further specification, a bit nonreferential.[3] Moreover, the expression is prone to tendentious uses—functioning as an all-too-convenient conceptual repository for whatever seems objectionable in the current political-legal climate. Complicating matters is that virtually no one these days wants to own up to the designation "neoliberal," nor defend it for that matter. Taking these things into account, some thinkers believe it would be better to do without the concept altogether.[4]

I am not one of them.

Still, the points above are not trivial: if ever there were a political-legal condition so self-evidently lacking a stable and discernible identity, neoliberalism would certainly rank. To be sure, analyzing any contested social political or legal "it" (e.g., the U.S Constitution) is often problematic because the identity of the "it" in question is necessarily presupposed by the analysis that follows.[5] Accordingly, much intellectual analysis consists of little more than unpacking from the conceptualization at issue that which has already been packed into it.

No one is immune.

One reason to call the iteration of the state soon to follow "neoliberal" as opposed to something else is that the account here joins up with much of the literature on neoliberalism. And this is so in two senses.

In one sense, the account here offers up something complementary and largely missing from the literature on neoliberalism—namely, the specific contributions of law, legalism, and lawyers.[6] Many accounts by legal scholars miss this possibility altogether by viewing neoliberalism as merely new neoliberal economics absorbed within the same old liberal legal forms. That take is decidedly unhelpful. (More on this later.)

In another sense, calling this iteration of the state "neoliberal" seems appropriate because the account joins up with whatever consensus there is among commentators on the traits that constitute neoliberalism as a political-economic phenomenon. While the identity and character of neoliberalism are contested, there is nonetheless a kind of rough common denominator or a family resemblance among the various conceptions of neoliberalism: Hence neoliberalism characteristically references some or most of the following:

An origin in the thought of European and American mid-twentieth-century canonical figures (e.g., Friedrich Hayek), many of them associated with the Colloque Walter Lippman and the Mont Pèlerin Society.

A motivation in the pre– and post–World War II period to reinvigorate liberalism by new means and new ideas—the then-shared sentiment being that with the rise of mass movements and the various totalitarianisms, liberalism had failed to protect itself and had to be rethought.

A rejection of laissez-faire as naïve and self-destructive.

The view that while government planning is generally bad and markets generally good, nonetheless the state has to intervene affirmatively to both support and monitor competition, to prevent encroaching social programs, and to defend against monopolization and other market failures.

A plan to expand market forms of organization as the means and ends of governance combined with a commensurate effort to contain the scope of democratic decision-making and to submit cultural and intellectual activity to market discipline.

A deliberate effort to control government through the concerted action of quasi-public-private institutions such as think tanks, expert networks, conferences and the like.

An erasure of the state/civil society distinction largely at the instigation and in the service of powerful market actors and interests generally designated as belonging to civil society.

This is hardly an exhaustive list. Many commentators would add to or subtract from the list. Many would adopt different takes on these substantive traits: neoliberalism as ideology, as epistemic program, as disciplinary project, as global politics, and so on. Nonetheless, this list seems to include many of the characteristics that a great many commentators find relevant to the description of neoliberalism.

One reason for this partial agreement among the commentators is that many of the characteristics listed above are traceable to the canonical figures and institutions generally recognized as giving shape and substance to neoliberalism in the first instance. In other words, while commentators may differ as to the precise identity or character of neoliberalism, nonetheless a great many of them affirm and elaborate (albeit with varying intensity) *a shared origin story*. And lucky for them, the master referents of this origin story (e.g., the Colloque Walter Lippman and the Mont Pelèrin Society) were composed of a rather articulate and voluble cast of characters: intellectuals.

The now well-elaborated origin story has been important in establishing the identity and character of neoliberalism. Indeed, it would be difficult to explore neoliberalism without acknowledging (or covertly relying upon) the screening and enabling effects of this intellectual history.

So this is not the place to criticize this origin story. Among other things this origin story has enabled some rich and textured genealogies of the deliberately orchestrated and synergistic relations of neoliberal thinkers and institutions across time. Philip Mirowski's description of the neoliberal thought collective is particularly edifying.[7] At the same time, two limitations of this origin story are particularly relevant to an exploration of the neoliberal state— particularly in its late stages.

One limitation is that excessive fealty to the conventionalized origin story misses other genealogical sources of what some (myself included) would want to call "actually existing neoliberalism" or "neoliberalism on the ground." This is one of the classic conceptual problems with origin stories and the flows of the ideas they occasion: as flows converge and separate, the connection to the putative origin becomes increasingly strained and less revealing. Two options are then open to the commentators. One option is to preserve the origin story and attach new revisionist chapters—hence the emergence of insightful books that emphasize the evolving character of neoliberalism: *Nine Lives of Neoliberalism* and *Mutant Neoliberalism*.[8] A different option comes to mind (as it has here) and that is to background the origin story and consider the possibility of a different genealogy—in short, to address, as others have called it, "actually existing neoliberalism" or "neoliberalism on the ground," or something of the sort.[9]

A second limitation of the origin story is that as the story unfolds and its manifest contributions become more definite, so too do its shortcomings.

Put succinctly, it becomes increasingly apparent what has been left out. And what has been left out is particularly salient here: the role played by law, legalism, and lawyers in the establishment, invention, and maintenance of neoliberalism.[10] Perhaps the most significant exception is Honor Brabazon's pathbreaking book *Neoliberal Legality*. Significantly she writes that "the role of law and its interrelations with the politics and economics of neoliberalism has remained almost entirely ignored as a subject of research and debate."[11]

Yes.

A More Materialist Account of Neoliberalism

With its focus on "actually existing neoliberalism," the account here accordingly *declines to elaborate neoliberalism as derived from articulate intellectual or political projects.* Instead, the account takes its cues from Jamie Peck's insights: "If there is an enduring logic to neoliberalization, it does not follow the pristine path of rolling market liberalization and competitive convergence. . . . It cannot be reduced to the high-church pronouncements of Hayek and his followers. . . . In fact, there was never a pristine moment of mountain top clarity or blackboard proof."[12]

Nor was neoliberalism simply an upgrade of liberalism. The strongest relation between the two remains at the ideological level. But even there the ideological aspects of neoliberalism is more patchwork opportunism than the conscious elaboration of an articulate intellectual political-legal project.

This poses a question: if neoliberalism on the ground has no clear or coherent ideology, then how can it possibly *transmit and institute* its preferred governance regimes? The short answer is it doesn't and it doesn't have to. Neoliberalism—and this is an aspect of its insidious character—institutionalizes itself through the self-reinforcing compulsions of its own governance mechanisms. Neoliberalism requires no articulate moment to expand, colonize, or prevail. Neoliberalism emerges when powerful market actors adapt to competition, consciously or not, by trying to have less of it . . . for themselves. Competitors have internalized the notion that often there are greater returns to be gained from the exploitation of

> rent-seeking,
> arbitrage,
> barriers to entry,
> selective socialization of costs,

selective externalization of costs,
selective creation and use of public options,
selective government subsidies,
work-arounds/bypasses,
carve-outs,[13]
dispensations,[14]
and the like.

The crucial imperative for the successful market actor in the neoliberal moment is *subsidization of costs for me—competition for everybody else*. Or as summarized by Peter Thiel, "competition is for losers."[15]

The high point of lucidity for a competitor in the neoliberal moment is thus to recognize that their firm is not simply in the widget business, but in the law business, in the cultural mining business, the cognitive errors and biases business, the arbitrage business, the transaction cost reduction business, and more. In short, "widgets are for losers."

This understanding of markets and competition is the moment *par excellence* of neoliberal lucidity. This lucidity likely helps the competitor, but it is no way necessary. Neoliberalism is operational. It is not in need of an articulate moment—still less a theory. All that is required is a self-interested adaptation to search for and extract profits anywhere and in any way they can be created and realized. The possibilities are wide open. Side constraints emerging from cultural thematics, intellectual resources, and moral or social norms no longer serve as inhibitions. Instead, these side constraints now serve as reliable indicators that there are untapped remunerative opportunities still left for the taking. Thus it is that cultural thematics, intellectual resources, morality, social norms, and so on are just another set of commons to be milked, mined, and selectively juridified so as to secure comparative advantage. The end is cost-cutting and the means are whatever works. All of this can function perfectly well for powerful market actors, though of course at some point the social coordination mechanisms that sustain their activities will be sucked dry. (Later on that.)

This process might be considered a "race to the bottom," but the neoliberal variant is distinct—it is insidious (as in insidious onset), virulent (as in powerful), and viral (as in self-replicating). It is in short, dynamically poised for success—at the individual level.

Indeed, it is striking how profoundly and pervasively the imperatives of the sophisticated neoliberal market actor are in stark opposition to the neoclassical model of the market. The imperatives:

Smash decentralized competition—aim for monopoly.

Make sure that contract and property rules are (so far as you are concerned) neither well known nor enforced.

Enlist legal officialdom in reducing your transaction and information costs.

Never incur costs when these can be externalized.

Capitalize on first-mover advantages by securing legal protection, barriers to entry, and monopoly positions.

Capitalize on second-mover advantages by letting competitors incur costs for design and R&D, then mass produce slightly less expensive versions.

Always leverage asymmetries (in information, power, timing, transportation, and so forth) to your own advantage.

Free ride whenever possible.

Be the last holdout.

The neoliberal market actor imperatives above share a common formula: try to violate or circumvent the assumptions described in the neoclassical model of the market whenever it is to your benefit. There is no floor.

It is important, therefore, to appreciate fully the profound depth to which neoliberalism has turned liberalism on its head. The differences are stark and unmistakable:

Liberal Democracy	Neoliberal State
From protection of *competition*. . . .	to protection of *competitors*
From *universal rules* for markets . . .	to targeted *legal subsidies* for select firms
From a *state/civil society separation* . . .	to the *colonization of the state by civil society*
From *egalitarian* political-legal regimes . . .	to *preferential treatment of groups*
From *regulatory oversight* . . .	to *market protection* and *barriers to entry*
From *private firms* . . .	to *industrial complexes*
From *passive monetary policy* . . .	to *aggressive monetary policy*
From *labor as employment* . . .	to *labor as gig work*
From *union/management negotiation* . . .	to *individual/management nonnegotiation*
From *national sovereignty* . . .	to *global market imperatives*

Notice that if we take the traits in the right-hand column as characteristic of neoliberalism, it is evident that there is not much of an intellectual *there* there. That is to say, that while the traits in the left-hand column are capable of elaboration and justification in some cogent, even if contestable, ideological program, it would be hard to say as much for most of the traits in the right-hand column.

Accordingly, in its contemporary self-representations and justifications, neoliberalism is less a robust political or economic theory or project than a mobile army of fetishized expressions designed to elicit both allegiance and somnolence. In the kingdom of *neoliberal ends*, we have terms like "free markets," "globalization," "innovation," "disruptive innovation," "entrepreneurialism," "growth," "development," "maximization," and "consumer choice." If now we move from the kingdom of ends to the panoply of *neoliberal means*, we have the canonization of "strategic planning," "accountability," "target goals," "benchmarks," "metrics," "outcome testing," and the like.

Most interesting is that with neoliberalism, the means have a tendency to become the ends. However we take it—means or ends or the means that are ends—the *crucial terms* marking out neoliberal practice and mindset appear on the scene undertheorized and underthought. And understandably so: when pressed, these neoliberal tag-terms generally reveal themselves to be the shallow, unschooled enthusiasms for the things and celebrities of business. The relative vacancy of the terms helps explain how it is that neoliberalism can end up meaning so many things to so many people. Neoliberalism doesn't have a lot to say about or for itself, because its own ideational (as opposed to material) character is relatively vacant. This in turn explains why so many theorists of neoliberalism turn back to the origin story: *that* story at least has some *there* there. That story has a text. This also explains why so many commentators (particularly in law) default into treating neoliberalism as a kind of upgraded liberalism.

At this point, having turned away from neoliberalism as an articulate intellectual project originating long ago to a material condition, a caution becomes necessary. Here goes: just because the conceptual markers of neoliberalism might be elusive, contrived, or counterfeit does not mean that neoliberalism is without power and effect. Nor does it mean that simply because neoliberalism resists its own theorization, it can't be theorized. It can.[16]

What Neoliberalism Is Not

Neoliberalism is not the resurrection of liberalism by other means. It is not the revival of *laissez-faire*. It is not the revival of classical economic liberalism.[17] In fact, neoliberalism is a misnomer. It is neo, but whatever it's neo about, it's not liberalism. Of course, everyone is free to conceptualize neoliberalism (or in fact anything) however they want. But the conceptual move that casts neoliberalism as the continuation of liberalism by other means is not helpful. By appropriating the term neoliberalism for what is fundamentally an amped-up liberalism (liberalism 2.0), this move effectively backgrounds a more important political-legal tendency—"actually existing neoliberalism."[18] It's true that neoliberal tendencies often present themselves in the ideology of free market, competition, and the like. But that is ideology.[19]

Still, why and how is it that so many thinkers in law describe neoliberalism as a kind of upgraded liberalism? One answer is suggested by Honor Brabazon:

> Neoliberalism generally has been understood as an economic phenomenon: it celebrates the supremacy of the market, it is justified using economic rationales, and it is measured through economic or socio-economic indicators. . . . Even critiques of neoliberalism have centered either on the economics of its goals or on its socio-economic outcomes *without due attention to how these goals are devised or these outcomes reached*, beyond the mere insertion of "neoliberal" content into policymaking.[20]

By and large, the legal scholars who have addressed neoliberalism in the past few decades have apprehended neoliberalism as *a kind of economic or political project ensconced within the same old liberal legalist structures.* And, as Honor Brabazon notes, even "critical political and economic writing tends to characterize law as an institutional vehicle through which neoliberal reforms can be effected (when law is mentioned at all)."[21] This downplaying of the role of law in the construction of neoliberalism is odd: if neoliberalism is successful at the economic or political level (and it is), there is no reason to suppose that it has not also been successful in changing the identity, character, and relations of law, legalism, legal practice, and lawyers.[22] (Ironically, Hayek understood the importance of law to his project).[23]

A second explanation for the tendency of legal scholars to describe neoliberalism as liberalism 2.0 has to do with the conserving character of legal thought generally. For many legal scholars, there seems to be nothing quite as good as following the well-hewn paths—especially if the paths can be severed from their antecedent history and presented as new and novel. This observation is admittedly not terribly nice. It is, however, terribly true. And it matters: to conflate and reduce neoliberalism to liberalism 2.0 is to effectively, even if unintentionally, eclipse that which most urgently demands political attention and intellectual analysis.

What would that be? Well, a different neoliberalism. How about this one:

> [W]e should not be under any illusion that today's neoliberalism is, as is too
> often said, the resurgence or recurrence of old forms of liberal economics
> which were formulated in the eighteenth and nineteenth centuries and are
> now being reactivated by capitalism for a variety of reasons to do with its im-
> potence and crises as well as with some more or less local and determinate
> political objectives. *In actual fact, something much more important is at stake
> in modern neoliberalism. . . . What is at issue is whether a market economy can
> in fact serve as the principle, form and model for a state. . . .* It is not just a ques-
> tion of freeing the economy. It is a question of knowing how far the market
> economy's owners of political and social information extend. . . . The relation
> between an economy of competition and a state can no longer be one of the
> reciprocal delimitation of different domains. . . . There will thus be a sort of
> complete superimposition of market mechanisms, indexed to competition
> and governmental policy. Government must accompany the market economy
> from start to finish.[24]

That was Michel Foucault some forty years ago. As yet another way to recognize the marked difference between liberalism and neoliberalism, consider S.
M. Amadae's elegant summary of liberalism juxtaposed with her summary of
neoliberalism. Again the differences are both stark and telling:

> Classical liberalism . . . is premised on individual freedom typically concep-
> tualized in terms of sanctity of personhood and private property sustained by
> the negative virtue commitment to avoid harming others. Self-determination
> and individual initiative sustain voluntary exchange, efficient production, the
> gradual accumulation of wealth and mutual prosperity.[25]

Now, neoliberalism:

> [I]n neoliberal political economy, individuals are identified by their prefer-
> ences and opportunities. Freedom becomes the prerogative to make any avail-
> able choice and thus conveys more of a tautological rather than normative im-
> perative. Agents profit throughout effective risk management of the creation
> of "externalities," that is, self-gain at a cost to another party. . . . The role of
> government is to improve social equilibria through monitoring behavior and
> threatening sanctions.[26]

So, if neoliberalism is a novel and problematic form enacting new aspects, just what are those?

One key aspect of neoliberalism is the intense pursuit of commodification and marketization where profit or its analogues (e.g., power? status? leverage?) are to be had. For some commentators, this translates into the recognition of "strong property rights." But this is not quite right: neither marketization nor commodification depend upon *strong* property rights. Marketization and commodification do depend on property rights or crypto property rights (e.g., the interests protected by tort law). But in neoliberal regimes, whether property rights are strong or not depends crucially on who gets them. The modus operandi of neoliberalism is *the selective and asymmetrical allocation* of various legal regimes (property, contract, legality, alegality) depending on the who and the what. To give an example, while Uber has "strong" intellectual property rights in its business m.o. relative to potential competitors,[27] it does not have strong property rights over its gig labor. On the contrary, the gig labor relation (the Uber-driver relation) consists in the main of (extensive) contractual provisions with drivers (Uber calls the drivers "customers") to distance Uber from any obligations to the driver and the rider.[28] Uber does not principally insist on rights. It insists mostly in establishing immunities. Neoliberalism doesn't just intensify processes of commodification and marketization (although it does do that); it intensifies these processes by enabling the sophisticated and variable use of different legal regimes. This enablement will both exploit and produce asymmetries of information, wealth, and power. And, of course, in these regards, lawyers will play a crucial role.

A second crucial aspect of neoliberalism is the exercise of a *granular selectivity in the application of different legal regimes* to capital and labor, rich and poor. If momentarily, a la Hohfeld and Hale, we can view the classic neoliberal contract as an instantiation of state power, the granularity makes for an unseen but virulent and thus pervasive abrogation of the rule of law virtues. Neoliberal practice implements elaborate forms, byzantine processes, time stalls, time accelerations, automatic waivers, palliative remedies, extensive bureaucratic deferment, cyber harassment, rigorous channeling, deferral phone menus, and techno-legal mechanisms that, in the aggregate, gradually but effectively induce despair, inaction, and ultimately resignation among its targets. Neoliberal law and legality are, for those on the receiving end, a Kafkaesque jurisprudence.

Everyone (some more than others) has experienced this granular asymmetry. But rarely do legal scholars write about it in general. In all these ways, the neoliberal state distinguishes itself from earlier iterations of the state by its tendency, as Wendy Brown shows, to invisibilize its own character, methods, and outcomes.[29] And in regard to Lon Fuller's famous articulation of the rule of law virtues—generality, publicity, prospectivity, intelligibility, consistency, practicability, stability, and congruence—neoliberal legalism routinely violates three (generality, publicity, and consistency) while frequently placing stress on three others (intelligibility, stability, and congruence).

A third aspect of neoliberalism is the necessity, akin to the famous prisoner's dilemma, that competitors exploit the greatest advantage from any available precinct of culture, norms, morality, law, and so forth, in order to prevail or simply survive.[30] The New Normal is thus a continuous disequilibrium (which generally translates into "precarity" among the deprivileged). Regarding mature neoliberal regimes, it is simply wrong to suggest that markets tend to equilibrium. On the contrary, in neoliberalism disequilibrium rules. This is one of the reasons that the expression "precarity" (the implicit risk of falling into poverty at any moment) has become so ubiquitous.

A fourth aspect is the relentless extension of neoliberal economic and legal norms to all aspects of culture, media, art, knowledge, and knowledge production. Philip Mirowski, among others, argues that neoliberalism is an *epistemic program* that seeks to replace expertise and knowledge by the one institution that supposedly knows best—to wit, the market.[31] But, according to Mirowski, it is not so much the market per se but rather market norms, market ideals, and market metrics displaced onto institutions, and governance itself that is crucial to neoliberalism.

A fifth aspect is the historic replacement of the political-legal functions of legitimation with the inducement of apathy and incapacitation, alternating with disruptive but ineffectual rebellious eruptions. This change is historic: while prior forms of the state required and enacted various forms of legitimation (e.g., freedom, self-rule, security), neoliberalism disciplines its populace largely through incapacitation. None of this occurs by design. It appears instead to be the by-product of the dispiriting processes of neoliberal advent.

A sixth aspect is a radical intensification of alienation, atomism, anomie, and nihilism across culture, which, somewhat counterintuitively, promotes compliance with neoliberal norms and the cultivation of neoliberal individual subjectivity (later on that).

Given the magnitude and pervasiveness of these new developments, we can ask again, with greater incredulity, how is it that actually existing neoliberalism has been so largely overlooked in the legal academy? To insist so forcefully on posing this particular question may seem odd. But the oddity vanishes once it is understood that this failure to recognize and understand neoliberalism is itself a crucial aspect and effect of neoliberalism itself—what Wendy Brown elaborates as invisibilization.[32]

The Legal Mechanics of Invisibilization

When one pauses to think about how it is that neoliberal legalism remains underinvestigated, it has to be recognized that legal scholars, still to this day, are most comfortable dealing with the *artifacts of official law*—judicial opinions, statutes, regulations. These are formal artifacts, public in nature and easily analyzed by legal scholars. Strip the scholarship of substantive content and what you get are a limited set of highly stereotyped forms of argument—deployed over and over again almost regardless of the substance.[33] The presumption underlying the ostensible value of this kind of scholarship is that the artifacts of official law in effect rule and can, with a little legal tinkering here or there, be made to rule better. Insofar as the courts, the legislatures, and the regulatory bodies declare the law, the presumption among jurists and legal scholars is that when the former do their job well, the subject parties, persons, and citizens will by and large conform and comply. Hence it is that if the legal scholar's arguments are well formed, they too can contribute to this enterprise of jurisgenesis—the creation of law. Or so the argument goes.

All right. But now imagine that the political-legal register has quietly morphed over the last several decades such that the primary legal actors are no longer official bodies—the courts, the legislatures, the agencies. Instead, consider that the prime movers are now powerful market actors in civil society represented by lawyers who draft up various legal documents that effectively create client- or industry-specific bypass mechanisms, work-arounds, carveouts, dispensations, exemptions, client- and industry-specific state subsidies, and so on.[34] If this were the case, then courts, the legislatures, and the agencies would no longer be the uncontested prime movers of law. For one thing, the effective law would be occurring largely (not entirely) *before and beyond* the jurisdictional reach of legal officialdom. Before—in the sense that it is the lawyers for the private client that draw up the relevant bypass mechanisms, dispensations, whathaveyou. Beyond—in the sense that once the bypass mechanisms, dispensations, whathaveyou are executed, legal officialdom has no more to do with it. Cipher law.

The effective law would be happening in localized transactional dealings rendered largely invisible in the shrouds of law firm practice and the confines of corporate boardrooms. Much of the effective law accordingly would never make it to courts, legislatures, or regulatory bodies. It would fly under the radar, so to speak. Hence, what was once considered to be the crucial interface of legal power conflicts—to wit, *private law firm vs. legal officialdom (with the client as subordinate)*—has been displaced by the increasing dominance of a different interface of legal power conflicts—to wit, *private law firm vs. client (with legal officialdom as subordinate)*. Thus, the key locus of crucial power contests, which was once between private law firms and legal officialdom, is now between private law firms and clients. In terms of jurisgenesis, legal officialdom has been demoted from the status of key player to that of subordinate and derivative.

Not only is this demotion happening, but it has already largely happened. This striking change, along with its effects, is none other than *neoliberal legalism*. This evolution inaugurates new intellectual challenges. These challenges are particularly daunting for most legal scholars, whose training, inclination, and aptitude are still even now to view legal thought as the dissection and analysis of the public artifacts known as judicial opinions, statutes, and regulations—in short artifacts focused on the private law firm vs. legal officialdom relation.

We would be confronting a striking dissonance. Indeed, in order to describe and theorize neoliberal legalism, it would be necessary to study what legal scholars are neither prepared nor disposed to study—namely, *the arcane legal documents and transactional practices* that form, in all their dispersion and complexity, the infrastructure of the neoliberal state. To undertake such a project, legal scholars would have to turn away (at least momentarily) from their favorite legal artifacts (e.g., constitutional provisions, statutes, and judicial opinions) to examine less formalized, far less accessible, and much more intricate artifacts (e.g., lawyer's transactional documents). By way of example, consider a UK contract between Uber and its customers (i.e., drivers)—conveniently available on the net.[35] This, by the way, is a commendably succinct contract. But while commendably succinct, the contract is nonetheless aesthetically forbidding. Imagine now reading contracts like this going on for hundreds of pages. I once had to read such a contract in law practice: it occurred to me at the time that one of the prime functions of this contract might well be to deter any of the parties from delving into it to settle any future disputes. A kind of contractual mutually assured destruction pact. A contractual Pandora's box.

For legal scholars to plunge headlong into the extensive and particularistic viscera of such a private-public bureaucratic morass is daunting. It is likely more than most legal scholars could stomach. Indeed, few of them are intellectually equipped (to say nothing of emotionally or aesthetically prepared) to undertake such a plunge. To the contrary, it is pretty much the wish to escape this jural morass that made these legal scholars leave the far more remunerative large law firm practice for the groves of academe.

Complicating matters is that those persons and firms whose practices would need to be studied are exceedingly unlikely to volunteer their work product for public discussion. In the bulk of cases, they cannot do so. Add to all this that if few legal scholars want to research or write about this stuff, even fewer will want to read it. Indeed, to seek out this world of byzantine transactional documents and other arcane legalisms (many of which would be difficult to access and evaluate because they are not fully "public") would take a fortitude of spirit and a tolerance for mind-numbing detail that few mortals, even those trained in the law, would be capable of sustaining. There are some for sure, but they are few.

Notice, ironically, that these observations about the aesthetically off-putting aspects of neoliberal legalism already give some hint of how the neoliberal state operates: the production of transactional complexity constructed off-scene, through law, legalism, and legal practice, is neoliberalism's automatic go-to technique. This hidden complexity (hard to learn/harder to master) immediately restricts neoliberal law practice to the acutely well-versed, highly specialized, and thus the very well-compensated legal experts who attend to the workings of various neoliberal transactional schemes. The attendant invisibilization, as Wendy Brown elaborates the term, not only outmaneuvers its victims and its marks but also discourages scholarly investigation of neoliberal legalism. That, too, is part of the m.o.: law is to be formed by and issued from law firms representing business clients to keep their businesses (particularly the most questionable and unsavory parts) far away from what remains of what was once called the "public" sphere.

So when thinkers like Wendy Brown rightly note that neoliberalism operates through its own invisibilization, it has to be added that law, legalism, and law practice play a huge role in this operation. We lawyers are absolutely terrific at invisibilization. As but a small sample, consider the more well-known instances: attorney-client, work-product, NDAs, confidentiality agreements. We can produce these at a moment's notice straight from the cloud to render transactions invisible. We are really good at it. We are known for it. At our best, we can even make our clients—indeed ourselves—invisible. Add to all this that we are simply terrific at amplifying the arcane linguistic complexity of the law we create as we go along. We are synergistic and self-compounding. (You are very welcome.)

Legal invisibilization is thus pervasive, as are its mechanics. The modes of invisibilization are reflexive: they are themselves invisibilized. But the mechanics of neoliberalism are not total and they are susceptible to inquiry.

The Legal Mechanics of Neoliberalism

Despite all of the above, some courageous legal scholars have plumbed the legal mechanics of neoliberalism. To be sure, these thinkers have not always called it neoliberalism. And their work has often focused on specific legal practices. But if we assemble their work together, we can piece together more or less discrete legal "mechanisms"—what the French call "dispositifs"—that warrant designation as neoliberalism in action.[36] With their work, we can begin to answer more concretely the question of how law, legalism, and lawyers contribute to the advent of neoliberalism. A mechanism here means a kind of discrete, standardized, and portable device that can be deployed in a variety of contexts to bring about certain characteristic effects or results. A mechanism can be characterized as military, medical, cultural, commercial, and most saliently here: legal. (Few if any mechanisms are pure—nearly all are combinations—but let that pass.) From now on, for the sake of brevity, the expression "legal mechanisms" will be abridged to simply "mechanisms."

To illustrate the idea of a mechanism, begin here with a simple mechanism, one that greatly antedates neoliberalism—to wit, the civil complaint. On one level, a complaint *informs* the party sued of such things as the claims made against that party, the factual bases for those claims, the redress sought (and more). What is often missed (even in law school), but is crucial to the understanding of the complaint, is *its character as a mechanism*. A complaint is not merely a standardized document conveying information: it is also effectively (John L. Austin would say "performatively") the initiation of a lawsuit.[37] A complaint doesn't *say* (it need not say explicitly) that it initiates a lawsuit. It simply *does*. To receive a properly executed and duly filed complaint that names you as a "defendant" (John L. Austin would have called the proper fulfillment of these requirements "felicity") is not merely *to know* that you have just been sued, *but to have in fact been sued*. Your legal relations and status have just been altered. You are now saddled with new legal obligations that did not exist prior to the proper execution of the complaint. Perhaps the most obvious one: if you do not answer the complaint, a default judgment can be entered against you.

Law is, of course, full of these performative mechanisms: the deed, the power of attorney, the surety bond, the . . . (we have a virtually endless list of mechanisms that effectively create new legal relations upon their proper execution, delivery, acceptance, whathaveyou). These mechanisms have been around since time immemorial—certainly way before the advent of the neoliberal state. What neoliberal legalism does add here is its own twist on power relations.

How so? Recall that one of the crucial hallmarks of neoliberal legality is an alteration of the power relations among three different actors: legal officialdom, the private law firm, and the client. Whereas once the dominant situs of law was considered to be the interface between the private law firm vs. legal officialdom (with the client as subordinate), now the dominant situs of law is increasingly the interface between the private law firm vs. the client (with legal officialdom as subordinate). We have moved from a law whose crucial situs was conceived as adjudication to a different situs conceived as transactional. Increasingly, adjudication is viewed as a derivative of the transactional.

What does such a shift imply? Well, it is now the private law firm and the client that are the main drivers of the character of the mechanisms. Concomitantly, legal officialdom is either relegated to a derivative position or, through invisibilization, ignored altogether. This is all rather strong and sweeping language even if it's not absolute (which it isn't). Accordingly, it might be reasonable to ask, how are such radical colonizations, displacements, and demotions of legal officialdom possible?

The answer is that private law firms and clients have over time successfully devised and exploited a series of transactional possibilities that sideline legal officialdom. Indeed, the very names of the mechanisms used—"bypasses," "work-arounds," and the like—tell us so: it is after all legal officialdom and its legal processes that are effectively being bypassed and worked around. Especially with clients who are powerful market actors, private law firms are able to craft mechanisms that combine some or all of the following features:

transactional invisibilization,
power/informational/transactional asymmetries among the parties,
technological execution through software or software-driven
     agreements,
channeling,
standardization and modularity,
minimization and deflection of legal redress

Here a quick but familiar example illustrates the combination of these characteristics. Consider, for instance, the typical "accept" or "decline" contract executable on the web. This contract is one where the seller determines the nonnegotiable terms. This is accomplished through the familiar "accept" or "decline" (*technological execution and channeling*). The many terms added (*standardization and modularity*) permit the seller to benefit from comparative advantages (*economies of scale*) in lawyering. The articulation of these additional terms in lengthy fine print is virtually never read by purchasers or subscribers (*transactional invisibilization*). Typical consumers do not know the terms. They are submitted to a succession of steps they will have to follow in order to obtain redress (*channeling*). Over time they become habituated to not knowing. What the consumers are often missing is an understanding of what rights and remedies they have waived away and what other *redress minimization and deflection* they have accepted. This then is a nearly perfect example of *a neoliberal mechanism*. It both relies upon and reinforces power asymmetries, transactional invisibilization, technological execution, channeling, standardization and modularity, redress-minimization, and deflection.

Now, one could find examples of these techniques (the fine print, the take-it-or-leave it language, and the like) in standard transactional deals far older than the advent of neoliberalism. It would thus be wrong to suppose that these techniques are entirely novel. But let us not be fooled: what neoliberalism does is *perfect* these legal mechanisms and render them *ubiquitous*. This is the difference in degree that yields a difference in kind. Indeed, there are even multiple templates of these mechanisms to be found on the web—ready for download. And many of these are positional templates—designed to favor, for instance, landlords, venture capitalists, and creditors in their respective bilateral relations. In one sense this technological achievement might be considered a positive attribute—this is technology effectively reducing transaction costs and making law "available" to all comers. In another sense, this is the reinforcement of asymmetrical neoliberal mechanisms as a form of life. It is as if, to put it strongly, human life had become the occasion or the vehicle for the deployment of neoliberal mechanisms and their remunerations.

This is the ideal[38] that market actors strive to achieve—indeed, that they are compelled to achieve in order to survive. And it is important to understand that these mechanisms and their effects do not remain confined to conventional contractual relations. These neoliberal mechanisms migrate into "informal law." Thus, for instance, in one breakthrough study, the authors show how business and commercial firms have internalized law's legalistic modes of dispute resolution (and the attendant inequalities and asymmetries) within the firm's own dispute resolution processes.[39] This is one of the striking aspects of the increasing dominance of transactional law: the forms of law can migrate almost effortlessly from "official law" to the kind of "informal law" just described. But of course, as this migration occurs and the formal law is internalized into informal law, the latter will have been lawyered to serve the client's interest.

The Erasure of the State/Civil Society Distinction

Implicit in the foregoing discussion is the reconfiguration of state–civil society relations. What has occurred, as will be seen below, is the radical intensification of the administered state's erosion of the state/civil society distinction inaugurated by the administered state. Ultimately, the aim of the discussion below is to describe the transformation of the political-legal register wrought by the neoliberal state. But insofar as the state/civil society distinction has been eroded overwhelmingly from the side of civil society, the analysis begins there and moves gradually to the neoliberal state.

What is key to this new iteration of the state is the reconfiguration of the political-legal register in the idioms, mechanisms, and images of the market. The political-legal register, its identity and character, has been colonized by mechanisms, metaphors, images, and idioms of the market. As Will Davies puts it, "Neoliberalism is the pursuit of the disenchantment of politics by economics."[40]

Note that this is not the old school narrative of "capture" or "control" of the state by actors in civil society (the classic tropes variously elaborated by various Marxist, Leninist, Schmittian, Hayekian, and Buchananite thinkers). Rather, the key tropes are *insinuation and colonization.*[41]

Just to be clear, it is true that the logics of capture/control on the one hand and insinuation/ colonization on the other partake in a common form— namely, structural and institutional corruption.[42] But the two logics—capture/control and insinuation/colonization—are different and yield different consequences. The logic of capture and control imagines two referents (e.g., the state and civil society), one of which renders the other *subservient.* Thus, for instance, when Marx speaks of the state as "the executive committee of the bourgeoisie," he is effectively deploying the logic of capture and control. Importantly, the logic of capture and control allows the two referents to retain whatever distinct or separate identities they might have had—it's just that now one "works for" or "at the direction" of the other. In the logic of insinuation and colonization, by contrast, the language, practices, and institutions of one referent (e.g., the political-legal) are infused with the other (e.g., market forms of knowing, thinking, speaking, hearing, and evaluating). The activity previously designated as the political-legal is thus gradually effaced. When everyone speaks the language of markets, of market actors, of business, there is nothing else left. The political-legal has been *denaturalized*, but not in a positive sense of a "denaturalization" that indicates a sloughing off of natural-istic metaphysical pretensions. Rather the political-legal has been denatural-ized in the negative sense that its discourse (the markers of its identity) has been morphed into and ultimately supplanted by the idioms and structures of markets, commerce, and finance. The logic and unfolding of neoliberal colo-nization is thus *qualitatively* different from the logic of capture and control.

How did this happen?

Here, for expository purposes, we will consider three stages in the evolu-tion of the neoliberal state: the market colonization of culture, the fashioning of the neoliberal self, and the neoliberal dissolution of the state/civil society distinction from the private side.[43]

Market Colonizing Culture

This first tendency is exemplified in embryonic form by Justice Lewis Pow-ell's famous 1971 memorandum to the Chamber of Commerce delivered right before he became a Supreme Court justice. In the memorandum, Justice Pow-ell bemoans the influence of the New Left in U.S. culture and recommends to the Chamber of Commerce an ambitious plan to remake and refashion pub-lic universities, scholarship, textbooks, television, book publishing—in short, what is generally known as the culture industry.[44] In his view, the Chamber of Commerce and the business community should combine to espouse ideas favorable to the "free enterprise system." In Justice Powell's own words:

The Chamber should consider establishing a staff of highly qualified scholars in the social sciences who do believe in the system. . . .

Perhaps the most fundamental problem is the imbalance of many facul-ties. Correcting this is indeed a long-range and difficult project. . . .

The staff of scholars (or preferably a panel of independent scholars) should evaluate social science textbooks, especially in economics, political science, and sociology. This should be a continuing program. . . .

The national television networks should be monitored in the same way that textbooks should be kept under constant surveillance. . . .

The newsstands—at airports, drugstores, and elsewhere—are filled with paperbacks and pamphlets advocating everything from revolution to erotic free love. One finds almost no attractive, well-written paperbacks or pamphlets on "our side."

There should be no hesitation to attack the Naders, the Marcuses and others who openly seek destruction of the system. There should not be the slightest hesitation to press vigorously in all political arenas for support of the enterprise system. Nor should there be reluctance to penalize politically those who oppose it....[45]

Here Justice Powell outlines an approach that goes well beyond Hayek's notion that the rule of law should be designed to enable the "spontaneous order" of markets to thrive.[46] Justice Powell wants to intervene in the culture industry—to win "hearts and minds" by deliberate intervention in public cultural and educational institutions.

Fashioning the Neoliberal Self

In a second tendency, neoliberalism matures into an ambitious fashioning or refashioning of the individual liberal subject as a particular *kind* of self—one disciplined as suitable for market governance and market functions.[47] In this regard, neoliberalism appropriates moral, cultural, and political discourse by refashioning its key terms in instrumentalized market terms:

community becomes *networking*
self-realization becomes *branding*
achievement becomes *impact*
knowledge becomes *expertise*
importance becomes *hits/likes/downloads*
quality becomes *rankings*
moral integrity becomes *reputation*
intellectuals become *thought-leaders*
commitment becomes *buy-in*
creativity becomes *innovation*
ideals become *goals*
values become *best practices*

Everything—all cultural moments—become increasingly subject to quantification, commodification, instrumentalization, and functionalization.

Everything is thus eligible for transformation into market-cognizable terms wherever profit is to be had. And, of course, profit is to be had wherever use values can be rendered in market cognizable terms.

Perhaps the most successful effect of neoliberalism is to fashion the self through numerous institutional venues—the school, the workplace, the home, the web—all become occasions to train, rehearse, and fine-tune market-oriented and market-ready selves. Individuals become start-ups of their own selves, entrepreneurs of their own personality, self-generating nodes of their own networks. And with the omnipresence of social media and the web, there is the opportunity (perhaps the obligation) to upgrade the self continually. For those who are anxious about being left behind, there is an endless array of self-help videos available on the web. All of this combines to construct the self as a compatible plug-in for market-ready organizations. The popular image of the cyborg and the academic concept of the posthuman are apt manifestations of a condition that is close at hand.

Of course, for some people or from a certain perspective, this can all seem really cool. This can feel like energy unbound. In another sense, and simultaneously, this is the panopticon on steroids—in which the self learns to observe, monitor, and re-present itself on an accelerated 24/7 timeline of post to post, tweet to tweet. The noxious effects on children and adolescents of working on their social media self have been widely noted. Children and adolescents are rendered more anxious and depressed—only as cool as the next post, the next tweet. Adults likely fare better. Still.

Consider that in the span of a few decades the only things that are transcendent in the neoliberal state are social media, the web, cyber reality, and their constitutive algorithms. These are the only logics that are transcendent because they are the only ones that effectively traverse all aspects of life while demanding, as if from nowhere, that the self do this or that. Everything else is subject to domain limitations or compartmentalization. The substance of social media, the web, and cyber reality may be particularistic and localized, even intensely so, but the form is monistic and universal. (Click, click.) And in the end, form triumphs: the particularistic and localized substance paradoxically becomes a vehicle for the universal form.

The sinister rhetorical beauty of all this—and this is the pseudo-liberal part of the term neoliberal—is that since neoliberalism is presented as a market ideology, it's all about the individual: what the individual chooses to do, has done, has earned. So even though the self has been socially constructed and disciplined (culturally/technologically/institutionally) by market norms and algorithms, it has been constructed in the image of the market to understand itself as *free*—free to choose, free to be responsible for itself. Those who are inured to the liberal discourse of law assimilate and resonate to the freedom/ choice/responsibility aspect, while simultaneously discounting the social construction and disciplinary aspect. This can make neoliberalism seem coextensive with liberalism—as if the two were largely synonymous or at least continuous. Once that particular misapprehension takes hold, there are no grounds for complaint. No matter the circumstance, *you* freely chose this: "Eat what you kill." "Take personal responsibility." Moreover, in constructing the individual as a choosing being, neoliberalism institutes a consumerist variant of choice. That is to say, neoliberalism smuggles in the addictive aspect where "choosing" between this and that consumer good becomes arguably (how can one tell?) a compulsion.[48] There is, absent dropping out, no choice about whether to choose or not.

Notice that, even as all this is happening, neoliberalism does not forego the language of community, caring, compassion, and the expression of moral concern. On the contrary, neoliberalism can and frequently does emote in good vibes that resound in empathy, caring, and the like. It is the substitution of marketing and P.R. for politics. "We feel for you." "Our thoughts and prayers are with you." This soft touch is not surprising: insofar as neoliberalism designs not simply markets, but the culture, the self, the community, and social relations, the soft touch is perfectly congenial.

In law, this transmutation of soft normative language to service the interests of power is certainly not new. The long-standing conceit among jurists and legal academics has been that normative values and morals are a restraint on power. But the critique of this conceit is also long-standing.[49] Indeed it was noted some time ago that normative prescription in legal thought was becoming increasingly anemic in its capacities to hold power accountable—that, indeed, normative language had become the go-to language for the advent of bureaucratic and corporate enterprises.[50] Put bluntly, normative language (particularly in law) has become the vehicle of choice for power moves. Given the success of neoliberal modes of thought, this critique—now a few decades old and perhaps ahead of its time—has become more salient, quite possibly incontestable except perhaps at the margin. Again, as seen above, we have a flip: the upbeat normative substance has become the carrier of the form—a form of performative power (which may or may not coincide with the normative substance).

One consequence is that, in the neoliberal state, value-talk turns out to be no guarantee against cynicism, coercion, or simple leveraging. On the contrary: value-talk has largely become the carrier and tool of cynicism, coercion, and leveraging. Accordingly, to approach value-talk stripped of its actual uses in social life (in the characteristic manner of academic moral philosophers) is to engage in a serious category mistake. In the neoliberal moment, there is even a negative denaturalization pattern visible for all to see. Thus, a particular value assertion arising first as

> a *moral precept* for a desired corrective,
>> becomes an *institutionalized entitlement*,
>>> becomes a *weaponized claim* to launch at enemies,
>>>> becomes a *flipped claim* advanced by those very same enemies,
>>>>> until it becomes *flippable* by any and all parties,
>>>>>> and is thus left *devalued*—without force.

In this regard, what distinguishes the neoliberal moment is the stunning alacrity with which these transformations follow one another. Such processes once seemed to take decades to morph. Now the changes transpire in a year or less. Neoliberalism has culturally imperialist tendencies and it is apparently very good at bringing them to fruition: this capacity for and metamorphosis of ideas, values, theories, and other such cultural-intellectual artifacts is neoliberalism's forte. Many sectors of cultural life (media, religion, politics, health care, universities, infrastructure) have already succumbed. Perhaps these institutions are not beyond hope. But they are certainly on a degenerative trajectory and it is not at all clear what or whom will alter their present course.

Decomposition, Recomposition, and Reconfiguration

The neoliberal state effectuates major changes in the political-legal register through processes of decomposition, recomposition, and reconfiguration. These processes are generally subsumed under the (somewhat infelicitous) heading of "privatization." Regardless of what this process is called, the m.o. is well-known: previously public infrastructure services are first defunded and then privatized. In principle, the entire state can be "unbundled" in this way—schools, universities, prisons, detention centers, police forces, military operations—everything can be subdivided, severed, spun off, and turned into for-profit private enterprises subject to and protected by state involvement and oversight.

The libertarian version of decomposition of the state would be *laissez-faire* (or the so-called nightwatchman state) in which only a very restricted set of functions would be served by the state (e.g., police, military defense). But the nightwatchman state *is not* the neoliberal state. Neoliberalism does not aspire to the reconstruction of a *laissez-faire* state. Neoliberalism is not out to reestablish the "law free zones" of the liberal democratic state. Foucault is especially lucid on this score:

> The problem of neo liberalism is rather how the overall exercise of political power can be modeled on the principles of a market economy. So it is not a question of freeing an empty space, *but of taking the formal principles of a market economy and referring and relating them to, of projecting them on to a general art of government.*[51]

The neoliberal state is thus not one that seeks the reduction of the state so much as its co-optation by market actors and market ways of knowing and governance. While some systems (feudalism, theocracy, fascism, communism) aim for total political control of civil society by the state, neoliberalism aims at market control of the state by certain idioms/knowledges/governance mechanisms emanating from civil society. How far the neoliberal state will or can proceed in that direction is yet to be seen. The distinction between state and civil society or public and private is erased not as a self-conscious project, nor all at once, but rather as the consequence of millions of localized self-interested incursions.

Neoliberalism thus turns Hayek on his head—neoliberalism is the spontaneous disordering of society. Schmitt and Hayek were not wrong to see the future of liberal democracy as threatened by the race for material advantage through various appropriations of the political-legal register. They were wrong, however, in fearing that this development would occur through unions and leftist institutionalization of social democracy. The danger came from an entirely different direction: the state was reconfigured by firms in the image and language of business and finance.

The Neoliberal Entanglement of State and Civil Society

In practice and in theory, liberal democracy repeatedly asserted and promised to assure a separation between state and civil society. This separation was in important senses illusory, but it nonetheless took hold in theory and practice. In sharp contrast to liberal democracy, neoliberalism has no respect in theory or practice for the strict separation of state and civil society. Neoliberalism is in no way inhibited from traversing or even erasing that distinction. Indeed, neoliberalism embraces cooperation and even partial or incremental fusion between state and civil society, the public and the private.

This neoliberal erosion of the state and civil society distinction is not an abstract matter. It is not, for instance, a right-wing mirror image of the Marxist ambition to bring civil society in toto under the aegis of the state. Instead, the neoliberal erosion proceeds interstitially. Emanating from the actions of powerful market actors in civil society, various specific tasks, functions, and roles previously conducted by the state are discretely and incrementally identified and spun off. In the U.S., this "spinning-off" has existed for decades, even centuries, in the form of government contracts, grants, franchises, licenses, and so on. (The late nineteenth-century railroads provide a particularly rich example.) What distinguishes neoliberalism is the intensification, magnitude, and ubiquity of the public-private entanglement ensuing from this spinning off. The objective of market actors is not to substitute private activity for public provision of goods, but rather to create a remunerative and tenaciously intertwined public-private entanglement. Thus, the ideal neoliberal arrangement is for the state to remain intimately involved with the private parties as a partner, co-venturer, overseer, regulator, protector, and so on. The neoliberal m.o. entails continued cooperation, repeated consultation, and sustained collaboration between previously or nominally distinct public and private actors. One of the major effects is that the state is, piece by piece, part by part, reconfigured in the images, mechanisms, and idioms of the market and thus rendered more hospitable to business.

The immediate political-legal threat (and the one most likely to be noticed at the outset) is a semicorrupt win/win scenario of symbiotic deals between government administration and private businesses. But over the long term, the more serious neoliberal threat is the onset of a state run like a business— that is to say, a state that treats its citizens like consumers and its services as goods to be sold. By way of example, the day after I wrote that last sentence, the White House put out a government fact sheet entitled "Putting the Public First: Improving Customer Experience and Service Delivery for the American People."[52] This document is a helpful description of what the federal government does to ensure that its services are easily available to the American people. Now, in one sense, an appropriate reaction is "good for you—job well done." In a different sense, however, this fact sheet evidences the classic neoliberal slide where the government already conceives of itself as a business and its citizens as customers.

Things will surely not stop here. The ultimate in "cooperative" or "collaborative" governance would be a state that deals with its citizens on the business model of social media like Facebook—literally selling access to citizens as potential consumers to private contractors. In this capacity, the state would then serve as a kind of cyber-intermediary. We do not often think of private-public cooperation or collaboration in such terms. Our classic image is a triadic transaction where the state purchases private goods from market actors to deliver services to citizens. But that triadic relation can simultaneously be viewed another way with more sinister implications: an image of the state using its power to deliver citizens as consumers to market actors. Examples might be include the mandatory coverage provisions of the Affordable Care Act whose very design (it was no accident) was to coercively induce citizens to become consumers of private insurance. Most of the complaints about this came from the right, but there was clearly something for the left to be concerned about here. Another example might be the IRS 401(k)s, which effectively ties the individual worker's pension to the performance of stock and bond markets.

All this entanglement is a far cry from the formal rules that are often thought to undergird free competition. No one should be fooled. What may be desirable for *competition* is not the same as what is desirable for individual *competitors*. Indeed, competitors are at best ambivalent about competition. In the main, competitors are more interested in securing legal protection *from* competition for themselves. Formal rules are certainly not optimal in this regard. Formal rules imply, at least in theory, a level playing field. But competitors (and this is how we get to neoliberalism) do not seek a level playing field—they seek competitive advantages. And they care not a whit whether these advantages are derived through R&D, the creation of a better product, the establishment of reputation, the milking of culture, the extraction of nature, the plundering of the intellectual commons, the securing of governmental largesse, the regulatory arbitrage of law, the externalization of costs, the threat of lawsuits, or whatever. Competitive advantage is the end—its source is irrelevant.

As cynical as this account may seem to some readers (I view it as realistic), it still understates the wonderfully perverse economic logic of neoliberalism. It turns out that the quest for competitive advantage from indiscriminate sources is not optional, but mandatory. As S. M. Amadae shows, firms subject to competition must, precisely because of competitive pressures, view any resource of whatever kind as a possible vehicle for cost-cutting and price enhancement.[53] Hence, it is that law itself becomes a source of rent-seeking and regulatory arbitrage—in other words, a source of *competitive advantage*. And, as Amadae shows, the sterling, self-reproducing logic of neoliberalism is that competitors must treat the search for competitive advantage not merely to thrive, but to *survive*.[54] Why? Because in an exquisite variation on the prisoner's dilemma, the other competitors will be doing the same thing. If those competitors are to survive, they too must regard the law not merely as an *opportunity* to exploit, but as a production factor. Indeed, that is one of the grim and rarely noticed implications of Ronald Coase's pathbreaking work in *The Problem of Social Cost*.[55] If, as Coase says, in the concluding part of his article, factors of production should be considered as legal entitlements, then one can surmise that there is no reason, no reason whatsoever, why firms would not seek to cut the costs and increase the rents from that particular production factor—in other words, to try to tailor the law, legalism, and law practice governing productive activities to their own advantage. Indeed, once this becomes obvious, a competitor (who wishes to remain a competitor) would be crazy not to do so. Retirement in Boca Raton may beckon, but that course of action is what it sounds like: an exit from the market, the surrender of status as "a competitor."

All of this places extraordinary stress (to the point of surrender) on the efforts of legal officialdom and law itself to maintain so-called neutral norms and fixed baselines. And that is one of the implications of the rise of neoliberalism: in this competitive world, there are no fixed baselines. On the contrary, legal and moral baselines are in principle and practice negotiable and renegotiable. This does not mean that market actors necessarily act illegally or immorally. It does mean, however, that legality and morality increasingly have to be priced out. Neoliberalism exercises pressure on redefining baselines down. It is not entirely clear that there is any countervailing pressure nor where it might come from—particularly if the downward drift of baselines is invisibilized.[56]

Some baselines, by contrast, are extremely attractive to powerful market actors. And they would very much like these baselines to be fixed—if at all possible. Among the choice possibilities is to obtain a cooperative arrangement where the business (or the industry) in question is protected and subsidized by political-legal advantages of a symbiotic and deeply entangled nature. Entanglement here refers to anything from the revolving door, to profit-sharing, to informal contracts, to the "favor bank," to any number of political-legal arrangements that can serve as vehicles for protectionism, barriers to entry, subventions, special dispensations, special deals, and the like.

The ultimate objective, the *non plus ultra*, is the establishment and institutionalization of elaborate, byzantine, barely comprehensible, highly contex-

tualized political-legal entanglements that ultimately lead to what we have
come to know as the

> military-industrial complex,
> prison-industrial complex,
> health-industrial complex,
> education-industrial complex, and soon,
> the anything-whatsoever industrial complex.

It is important to appreciate that at this point we are very (*very*) far from the
Hayek's "spontaneous order" or Smith's "invisible hand."[57] Rather, neoliberalism yields a *plurality of decentralized state-civil society entanglements* where
competition in any robust sense has become the exception rather than the
rule.

   In economics, neoliberalism was de facto championed early in the work of
Gary Becker of the University of Chicago. Becker applied rational actor theory
to aspects of human existence (e.g., family relations) that *at the time* seemed
extremely far removed from the domains usually claimed by the dismal science.[58] In law, neoliberalism was advanced de facto by the highly successful
work of Judge Richard Posner. He pioneered and popularized the idea that law
should facilitate, promote, or replicate markets in sundry doctrinal fields.[59]
Judge Posner came to argue that legal rules regimes should be evaluated by
the market criterion of Kaldor-Hicks efficiency, as measured by the metric of
"willingness to pay." This means that the law would be used to effectuate what
he aptly called "forced exchanges." Thus, contrary to what many liberal and
left critics of law and economics believed during the early years (the 1970s
and 1980s), Chicago law and economics was *never* principally a libertarian or
laissez-faire project. Neither was it a classically conservative project. Instead,
efficiency analysis was a kind neoliberalism *avant la lettre*—a paternalistic
project aimed largely at replicating through government means (i.e., in this
case, through legal doctrine) what markets ostensibly would have produced
had markets been possible. The ideal proposed and celebrated was a state
of affairs where the only relevant indicium of human satisfaction was willingness to pay. The canonization of this specific metric was the paternalistic
moment: the determination by law and economics' analysts of who would be
willing to pay what for this or that entitlement and then the inscription of the
conclusion into law itself as either a hard or soft default.[60] The paternalism
also lay in the summary dismissal of other ways of expressing and register-

ing value. As for law and economics' designedly disruptive anticonservative streak, it lay in a forthright willingness to vitiate the security of traditional legal arrangements in favor of a sometimes roving cost-benefit formula formalized as Kaldor-Hicks efficiency.

Chicago's use of Kaldor-Hicks efficiency could hardly have been anticipated or foreseen from Nicholas Kaldor's original article and its rather anodyne example about the corn laws and the inefficiency of tariffs.[61] But in the hands of Chicago law and economics, Kaldor-Hicks efficiency became almost a free-range formula for imposing "forced exchanges" in cases where (1) some cost was thought to preclude exchange *and* (2) educated guesses, conjectures, guesstimations, or contingent valuation studies revealed that "willingness to pay" counseled the imposition of a forced exchange.

Kaldor-Hicks efficiency became an extremely important vehicle for the rise of the neoliberal state—namely, the formation of a political-legal register subject to construction in terms of the desiderata of private interests. Public interest became the aggregation of private interests *as measured by willingness to pay*. The formula appeared to many jurists and legal scholars to be clear, simple, and universally applicable across legal regimes. It was in many ways devastating to both the liberal democratic and the administered state.

Now, I have focused on the market universalism of neoliberalism in regard to the political-legal register, but it is important to appreciate that the political-legal ambit of neoliberalism is vastly more sweeping. Philip Mirowski points the way here when he talks about the "neoliberal thought collective" as pursuing "an epistemological project that aims to substitute market ways of knowing for expertise and knowledge generally."[62] Neoliberalism as law and state is thus an epistemic construction: law and state play an important role in the social control of what is and can be known. And in the case of neoliberalism, that turns out to be not much other than market universalism: the substitution of market forms and norms to evaluate everything—the self, politics, social life, wisdom, everything. As William Davies put it:

> [W]hile neoliberal states have extended and liberated markets in certain areas
> (for instance, via privatisation and anti-union legislation), the neoliberal era
> has been marked just as much by the reform of non-market institutions, so
> as to render them market-like or business-like. Consider how competition is
> deliberately injected into socialised healthcare systems or universities. Alter-
> natively, how protection of the environment is pursued by calculating a proxy
> price for natural public goods, in the expectation that businesses will then
> value them appropriately.[63]

This will turn out to be destructive—not only of the intrinsic values and aims of culture, art, morality, and intellectual life, but in a turn of poetic justice to neoliberalism itself. In its lack of restraint in the celebration of market epistemics as the governance mechanism *primus inter pares*, and in its intense social construction of the self as an instrumentalized strategic market actor, neoliberalism leads to the strip-mining of the other social control and coordination mechanisms that are ironically necessary for business and markets to run (morality, law, social bonds, solidarity, community, and so forth).[64]

Morality becomes a form of self-promotion and branding (virtue-signaling)
Law becomes a market-mimicking device (Kaldor-Hicks efficiency)
Social bonds become instrumentalized relations (means-ends)
Community becomes a network ("connected atomization")

The culture morphs into a dispersion of relations, into ephemeral communities where everything and everyone is a means to everything else. This goes well beyond Marx's ghoulish description of "commodity fetishism."[65] Neoliberalism is a perfected regime in which all aspects of life come to be monitored, surveilled, and manipulated by metrics, rankings, and data gathering. No one should underestimate the extent to which this evolution of capitalist rationality (i.e., neoliberalism) has amped these processes to a degree that establishes a very different form of life. Indeed, this is one of the key strategies of the neoliberal advent—the gradual transformation of distinctions of kind into matters of degree: quantification, measurement, calculation, calibration.

The resulting form of life does not have much to do with liberalism. To be sure, the liberal ideology of markets, competition, freedom, and choice remain and continue to be deployed. But this is completely consonant with the colonizing logic of neoliberalism: liberalism too can be mined. Why should liberalism enjoy an exemption?

The world of moral, political, and aesthetic value is, as previously stated, not a deep concern of the neoliberal state. This is why it is possible to have conservative neoliberals who happen to value traditional marriage, family values, a strong military, and law and order alongside progressive neoliberals who happen to value gay marriage, freedom to choose, cosmopolitanism, and identity politics. For the neoliberal state, these political inclinations are simply conservative or progressive social issue "add-ons." They are the epiphenomenal plug-ins to neoliberalism (which is indifferent to culture except as a means—a way to cut costs, enhance profits, make the sale, win the election, discipline workers, and distract voters). For the perfected *neoliberal* politician, conservative cultural issues and progressive identity politics are each political auras to be exploited as a way to glean support, attract donors, finance elections, cultivate a virtuous self-image, and, in some cases, inspire antagonism. Indeed, for neoliberals, the culture wars have served for several decades to distinguish putative antagonists (Democrats from Republicans) and thereby eclipse their shared allegiance to donors keen on promoting their own interests. Again, this is the symbiosis of putative antagonists.[66] The symbiosis is invisibilized in flashes of antagonism that remain irrelevant to the rule of neoliberalism. Indeed, neoliberalism solidifies its grasp on the political-legal even as voters are distracted by the culture wars and the aura of spiraling polarization.

The Contradictions of the Neoliberal State

One would think that a political-legal register constructed out of such opportunistic appropriations and the facile deployment of ideas as superficial mantras would be rife with contradictions. Oddly, however, the neoliberal state is such a syncretic product of decentralized entrepreneurial bricolage that it never establishes strong claims or sets down solid markers through which it might be intellectually embarrassed or nudged into reforming itself.

That is not to say, however, that neoliberalism is entirely free of contradictions.

Of Means and Ends

One contradiction of the neoliberal state is the radical dissonance between its governance mechanisms (as described above) and its legitimation schemes (largely borrowed from liberal democracy). Usually, such a contradiction between governance mechanisms and legitimation schemes produces the sort of dissonance between the actual and the ideal that prompts charges of failure, fraudulence, and hypocrisy. And those are the sorts of charges that, once experienced viscerally on a sufficiently large scale, often motivate change.

In the neoliberal state, however, this contradiction does not appear to be doing that work. The reason is one that is consonant with and, indeed, an extension of what has been said above. The opportunistic character of neoliberalism means that the deviation of its governance mechanisms from its legitimation schemes, the dissonance of actuality from ideal, is resolved (or rather never arises) because the legitimation schemes are "redefined down" to the "actually existing" governance mechanisms. In other words, *what should be* is redefined in terms of *what it is possible to achieve.* Thus, the gap between the actual and the ideal never fully materializes.

In law and legal thought, this collapse of values and ideals into actualities was identified as the structure of normative legal thought in the 1990s.[67] The ends become defined in terms of the means available. Or as former secretary of defense Donald Rumsfeld said in a different context, "You go to war with the army you have, not the army you might want or wish to have at a later time."[68] There is a kernel of truth to Rumsfeld's realpolitik statement. At the same time, one wonders what happens when ends are redefined down in terms of the means. If the ideal-actual gap is understood to be the driving force for taking moral or political stock of our conditions and guiding the direction of change and reform, just what happens when the ideal has been folded into the actual?

In the neoliberal state, it does not matter. Nor does it matter that the intelligentsia, the commentariat, or the people might notice. As previously discussed, neoliberalism has no deep need for legitimation. It pacifies the populace through the inculcation of apathy, resignation, and despair: "It is what it is." "Why ask why?" "There is no other way." And so on.

Self-Cannibalization

Not surprisingly, neoliberalism is self-cannibalizing. Neoliberalism, in eroding communal ties and human solidarity, is not sustainable. Why not? Well, because whatever meaning and bonds people create for themselves—in terms of traditions or projects—must be constructed with the cultural resources at hand. If the culture consists of endless instrumentalized relations—not just in work, but in cultural forms and artifacts, in social relations, in personal life, and in law and legalism themselves—then human beings will not have a whole lot to work with. Nor, to put it more vexingly, are there a whole lot of individuals left to work with either.

In a biting irony, the gradual erosion of social coordination mechanisms—law, morality, social bonds, community, selves—undermines the preconditions for the existence of businesses and markets. Markets, contracts, agreements, and expectations depend upon these social coordination mechanisms. If all that is left are rational utility maximizers who do not have each other's welfare registering on their indifference curves (this is arguably the economic expression of psychopathy), then we will have a population of individuals that simply cannot be trusted. And if we cannot trust agreements executed, documents signed, or representations made, then how can we have well-functioning markets?

Law, Oliver Wendell Holmes said, is constructed for "the bad man," the man who views a criminal penalty as a tax.[69] But what happens when all we have are Holmesian "bad men"—when the legislators, judges, and lawyers are also "bad men?" Now, the rational actor is not strictly the equivalent of the Holmesian bad man. In one sense, the bad man is worse: beyond the reach of socialization through moral norms. On the other hand, the rational actor has no limits on his preferences (they are taken as given) and he is a champion of means-end rationality.

The point here can be articulated in more conventional law and economics terms: simply put, moral norms, communal ties, and a civic-minded educated populace—all these things cut down on transaction costs. Concomitantly, their erosion increases transaction costs.

And, once again, here too there is a positive feedback loop. If individuals cannot trust their business partners, co-venturers, lawyers, accountants, and consultants, what kind of legal or financial leverage can be used to ensure loyalty and efficiency? And in deploying instrumentalized means of leverage, will this not entail training the very same contractual partners to do likewise? How can one teach people to manipulate others without the very same people turning the manipulation back on you? Pause. Now imagine this picture on a society-wide scale.

There is yet one more sense in which neoliberalism is unsustainable. Once the state becomes in effect one huge opportunity for private gain at a regulatory auction or a constellation of opportunities for joint ventures, deals, and the like with the state, the result will be rising inequality: those best positioned economically to secure advantageous entanglements with the state will do so. The outcomes will be to their benefit at the expense of those more poorly positioned. This is true at the static level. At the dynamic level, the effects are compounding.

In ways akin to "industrial policy," "dirigisme," "new governance," and "fascism" (these are hardly equivalent) neoliberalism de facto moves the liberal democratic and the administered state in the general direction of a corporatist mode of political-legal representation. De facto, the U.S. has already moved some distance down this path. One revealing indication is the contemporary use of the term "stakeholder" as a habitual term for representation in hearings in private and public decision-making. The mantra is that "all stakeholders must be represented." In one sense, there is something positive (and even admirable) about this: the term "stakeholder" signals a need to consult *all* those who might have an actual "stake" in the matter at hand. But there is also a more disturbing exclusionary and corporatist aspect. The exclusionary aspect lies in the possibility that the term "stakeholder" effectively limits participation to *those deemed* to have a sufficiently important "stake"—thereby excluding all others. The question is who gets to do the *deeming* and on what criteria? The disturbing corporatist aspect is that it is interest groups that are represented—very often without regard to the size of the groups or how the policies or legal decisions will affect them.

At the level of national politics, and putting aside the Political Science 101 and the basic first-year Constitutional Law conceit of viewing the U.S. Congress as a "democratic institution," it is evident that, de facto, congressional legislation is very much the product of corporatist representation rather than popular representation. As a formal legal matter, Wall Street, the Fortune 500, the hedge fund managers, the insurance companies, the elite professional groups, and the military contractors do not have a single representative in Congress. Realistically, however, they each already have close to a supermajority on many (most) of the issues that matter to them. If we look past the facade of congressional "democracy," what we have de facto is something that looks very much like corporatism—representation of corporate entities, industries, professional groups, and religious organizations.

The development of corporatist modes of organization under what is increasingly a veneer of democracy is advanced in various ways. Perhaps the most obvious are campaign financing and lobbying. At this point, such claims are in no need of demonstration. But there is also the political-legal character of the linguistic—and its effect on democracy. Thus, consider, for instance, a sequence of equations routinely used in news media: When Americans are supposedly doing well economically, it is because . . . the economy is doing well . . . which in turn is doing well because . . . the Dow is doing well. The implication in this series of false equations is that what really matters is the Dow. The result is that "the Dow," which is almost personified, now has an important role to play in economic policy. It becomes a political-legal matter to ask and answer what effects a policy will have on "the Dow."

Most Americans (indeed, most legal professionals) probably do not generally think of "linguistic representation" as an aspect of "political-legal representation," nor vice versa. But the two are intimately related as in the manner of a Möbius strip. *Political-legal representation* happens in the executive, legislative, or judicial branches in part because *linguistic representation* has already fashioned the conceptual architecture and apparatus that will enable the political-legal work to be done, which in turn . . . and then we continue to go around the Möbius strip. The taxonomies of everyday life—of social and political identity (of employee, corporation, income)—have already done a lot of political-legal work. In turn, the creation of our everyday taxonomies, their staying power, their transformation, the intensity and speed of their currency and demise are in part a function of political-legal construction.

The traditional liberal democratic take on all this is a bit different. The traditional take is that individuals forming groups of voluntary associations play a large role in constructing political-legal reality. But this is an archaic and arguably pernicious romanticism. With the onset of neoliberalism, the entire panoply of liberal legalist concepts ("the individual," "choice," "consent," "intent," "privacy," "autonomy," and so on) has been hollowed out by neoliberal practices. This conceptual architecture, which was already strained in liberal democracy as largely illusory for the precariat and the poor, becomes in the neoliberal state flat out incredible. One may well bemoan the increasingly fragile condition of the liberal conceptual order. It certainly isn't clear what would replace this conceptual order should it collapse entirely. But what is difficult to excuse is to pretend the intellectual and political hollowing out of this discourse has not happened. The continued invocation in the first year of law school ("the individual," "choice," "consent," "intent," "privacy," "autonomy," and so on) contributes mightily to the systemic misinterpretation of contemporary social and economic life. What needs to be recognized accordingly is that the liberal democratic conceptual architecture, even as it does (occasionally? sometimes? often?) serve liberal democratic ends, also simultaneously facilitates the neoliberal reconfiguration of state and civil society in ways that ironically undermine those very same liberal democratic ends.

Neoliberal Futures

Where does neoliberalism lead? In one sense, the neoliberal state helps prepare the grounds and instill the motivations for an evolution toward authoritarianism. How so? In several ways. Four can be mentioned here.

First, the neoliberal entanglement of state and civil society makes it much easier for authoritarians to assert control over civil society. Much of the structure enabling state control has already been laid down and institutionalized. The networks of entanglement are already in place. To analogize, Franz Neumann of the Frankfurt School pointed out long ago that the ability of the National Socialists to control the economy in interwar Germany was greatly facilitated by the fact that much of German production was already highly cartelized and monopolized.[70] State control was just an easy add-on. While the neoliberal entanglement of state and civil society seems to issue mostly from the private side, when the entanglement is politically and legally institutionalized, it becomes easy to flip it.

Second, once neoliberalism has paralyzed politics by degrading it into market opportunities and market imperatives, the possibility of correcting market excesses diminishes. This was evident with the Great Recession of 2008 and the subsequent failure to prosecute Wall Street wrongdoers. Indeed, not only was Wall Street too big to fail, but apparently it was also too big to prosecute. In fact, given the thundering silence of the Obama administration, it was apparently even too big to blame. The interconnections between the governing financial class and the governing political class were simply too intricate and too symbiotic for the prosecutions to proceed or blame to be affixed.

Third, once neoliberalism instrumentalizes and degrades morality, law, and community, there are not a whole lot of political or social mechanisms left to control the body politic or to reconstruct community. As Wolfgang Streeck puts it, the elites can hardly call on "shared values" in a society where everything is commodified and "up for sale."[71] He adds that if the elites ever had to legitimate their rule, they would find themselves "morally defenceless" and would have to become highly "creative." Indeed: the resources of solidarity and community have already largely dissipated. With this dissipation of solidarity and community, the neoliberal state increasingly promotes the politics of disdain, hatred, and revanchism—hence the gradual but ever increasing intensity of the "culture wars."

Fourth, having degraded democracy and the rule of law (the hallmarks of the liberal democratic state) and having demoted the public interest goals of the administered state to aggregations of private interests, neoliberalism then fails to deliver on its own economic promises. It effectively leaves the populace ready to sign up for any form of governance that promises, fraudulently or not, to give them integrity, security, and a means of livelihood.

All these considerations reinforce the opposition between liberal democracy and the administered state on the one hand and the neoliberal state on the other. Below, then, we have another chart—one which draws attention to the stark detailed differences among the liberal democratic, the administered, and the neoliberal state. The main point of this chart is to highlight the dissonance across the horizontal dimension. Less important but also interesting are the manifest similarities or homologies across the vertical dimension.

Chart II. Liberal Democratic/Administered/Neoliberal States

	Liberal Democratic State	Administered State	Neoliberal State
Jurisprudence	Legal Formalism Law as Propositions	Legal Realism Law as Tool	New Governance Law as Managerial
Legal Consciousness	"Classical legal thought"	"The Social"	"Third Globalization"
Aesthetics	Law as "grid" spatialization, grid, territorialization, field, objectification	Law as "energy" force, quantification, measurement, calibration	Law as "Perspectivism" Contextualization, Particularism
Moral Emphasis	"The right" (deontological ethics)	"The good" (consequentialist ethics)	"The efficacious" (operationalism)
Overarching Objectives	Maintain order (preserve structure)	Increase welfare (achieve purpose)	Growth, efficiency, development (maximize wealth)
Philosophy	Conceptualist, Formal	Pragmatic, Functional	Managerial, Empiricist
Essence of Law	The letter of . . .	The spirit of . . .	Context-specific
Key Artifactual Dyad	Directives and Principles	Directives and Policies	Directives and Defaults
Knowledge Base	Law	Social science	Business, empirical data, surveys
Knowledge Form	Juristic Science	Domain Expertise	Industry Know-how
View of Social Field	Homogeneous	Heterogeneous	Particularist
Statutory Interpretation	Textualist	Purposive	Mixed
Governance Techniques	Formalization, Integration	Deformalization, Goal Achievement	Buy-in, Consensus, Strategic Planning, Nudge
Rationalization Techniques	Law as systematicity: coherent self-relation	Law as adequation to both its object-field and its goals	Law as engine of wealth, growth
Key Jural Operations	Classification, analysis, subsumption, boundary policing	Consideration, evaluation, determination	Data gathering, Computation, Data processing
Key Common Law Source Domain	Property (Entitlements)	Torts (Correction/ Regulation)	Contracts (private ordering)
Chief Objective Serving as Legitimation	Maintenance of order/ Rule of Law	Welfare maximization/ Progress	Promoting Growth, innovation, progress
Conflict Avoidance Strategy	Isolation of conflicting activities and interests/ Boundary setting and maintenance	Deterrence/incentives/ oversight	Consultation/Strategic Planning/Stakeholder Buy-in Extrajudicial Process

Chart II—*Continued*

Privileged Situs of Law	Trial/Adjudication	Regulation/Hearing	Informal Meeting
Preferred Temporal Intervention	Ex ante regimes/Get the right answers, enforce them, and stick with them	Process regimes (Ex ante and Ex post) Monitor continuously and correct process	Continuous self-monitoring and engagement
Favored Directive Form	Rule	Standard/Totality of Circumstances, Multifactor Tests	Mixed
Ethical Categories	Right/Wrong Vices/Virtues	Costs/Benefits Advantages/Disadvantage	Costs/Benefits Consultation, Buy-in
Conceptual Sources for Law	Property images and metaphors (borders, dominion, control)	Tort images and metaphors rule (risk, duty, scope, standard of care)	"Accounting" images and metaphors (measurement, calculation).
Externalities/Friction	As the exception	As the general case	Mixed
Preferred Techniques of Reconciliation	Line drawing, Hierarchy	Balancing Proportionality, Holism	Particularism, Contextualism

As before, this is a loose and fuzzy chart meant to indicate tendencies, *not* absolutes.

Notice from this chart that neoliberalism cannot easily be conceived as a reconciliation of the opposed tendencies of liberal democracy and the administered state. It is instead a third contender arising amid the arrested dialectic of the liberal democratic and the administered state. It is amid the inconclusive oscillations wrought by this arrested dialectic that neoliberalism gains its foothold and flourishes.

Neoliberal Domination?

If we credit neoliberal ideology and its repertoire of semantic niceness (consensus, collaboration, growth, stakeholders, and buy-in), neoliberalism can easily seem anodyne. For those powerful market actors and the elite professionals who serve them (managers, lawyers, bankers, accountants, consultants) the genial phrases will likely seem fitting. The cheery and accommodating character of such neoliberal expressions allows many people to view neoliberalism as committed to "soft power."[72] While not entirely wrong, such a view is incomplete. This is neoliberalism as seen from the inside—from the perspective of the privileged. Soft power is what they see, what they experience. But there is also an outside. And neoliberalism de facto accords different treatment to those on "the inside" as opposed to those "on the outside." Neoliberalism is soft power for those who are inside and hard power for those outside. For those who are on the outside—that is to say, the precariat, the terminated, the jobless, the detained, the incarcerated, the feared and despised—"hard power" rules. Think here of the town of Ferguson, Missouri and the use of the criminal justice system against Blacks to raise municipal revenues as an example of neoliberal hard power.[73]

Then, too, once one moves from the abstract character of doctrinal legal categories—contract, offer and acceptance, private ordering—to their realization among the precariat and the poor, entirely different images emerge: repo agreements, lease eviction terms, pawnshop loans, and the like. At that point, for the precariat and the poor, neoliberal uses of soft-power doctrinal legal categories (e.g., contract—private ordering) quickly turn into instances of hard power. And for those on the economic edge or beyond, the failure to conform to contractual obligations can quickly turn into a cascade of successive negative legal consequences. For the precariat and the poor, the law sometimes functions as serial trip-wires to misery.

We have entire groups of people that become walking financial risks to themselves and their families by virtue of obligations on their credit card loans, their student loans, their mortgages. Many of these people are leading leveraged lives. They are de facto indentured. And, in a very real sense, they become the occasions for economic processes of the neoliberal state—processes already in place.

The concept of domination comes to mind here. Except that if this is domination, it is a peculiar kind of domination. This is *polycentric domination* dispersed in sundry legal relations in ways that typically remain out of public view—hard to trace, and accordingly difficult to dismantle or neutralize. Occasionally, we get partial glimpses of this polycentric domination when the news media publishes a story on the student loan crisis, or on arbitration clauses preventing class actions, or on serial false charges by a bank. What is rarely seen, however, is *the total result* stemming from the aggregation of these discrete instances. But once aggregation is considered, it is not hard to imagine its concrete manifestations. Thus, it is not hard to imagine that in cities and towns, there are individuals subjected not just to one of these mechanisms, but to several—at once and successively. Human fodder for the neoliberal economy.

With this kind of polycentric domination comes habituation. Even people in the middle class become accustomed to signing away their rights, powers, and privileges and conforming to the protocols and the unnoticed algorithms of legalistic market stratagems. ("Accept" or "Decline.") Over time, the habituation of individuals to such institutionalized impairments constructs a population that is paradoxically docile and despairing while also angry and hostile. That is to say, a nearly perfect constituency for authoritarianism.

V The Dissociative State

The crisis consists precisely in the fact that the old is dying and the new cannot be born.
—ANTONIO GRAMSCI, *PRISON NOTEBOOKS*

In the contemporary moment, the various iterations of the state are still with us. The iterations are—moment by moment, context by context—symbiotic yet antagonistic. They fuse and separate, penetrate and envelop; indeed, they engage in any number of interactions. Hierarchy, equalization, subordination, alliance, and enmity are but a few of the possible relations. The prospect of identifying and tracing all the actual permutations is, if only for reasons of time and space, impossible.

But that was never the point. Instead, the effort was to bring into sharp relief the dissonant forms of governance of the American state and to show that they cannot, in any satisfying way, be reduced to or subsumed by any *single unitary overarching whole*. And yet oddly many jurists, legal scholars, the media, and the public presume as much: typically, they describe the American state as a liberal democracy (with other aspects and strains duly subsumed and subordinated). That view is an exaggeration: the American state is not only or even principally a liberal democracy. The mistake (and it is common not only in law, but in history and the social sciences) lies in presuming that a state can 1) be reduced and stabilized to a specified identity which in turn 2) can be grasped as a single, unitary, overarching whole that encompasses and subordinates its various aspects. This is a widespread mistake wrought of many sources, but chief among them is the denial of time.

A particularly prevalent aspect of this denial of time is the failure to recognize that past epochs (e.g., feudalism) economies (e.g., laissez-faire) political organizations (e.g., fiefdoms) and social tendencies (e.g., tribalism) are not entirely overcome in history, but survive and reemerge over time. History has no ratchet. Teleology is but one temporal ordering among many. And the absence of the past often turns out to be mere dormancy—a condition from which awakening can be expected.

A second prevalent aspect of the denial of time lies in positing an origin (i.e., the Constitution) and presupposing that the origin not only severs itself from the past (just how would that happen?) but that it is the secret key to what comes after. There is no singular origin. All origins are posited. And though thinking might well *require* the affirmation of origins, intellectual requirements do not legislate into being their own conditions of possibility.

A third prevalent aspect of the mistake lies in a specific, though particularly widespread, denial of change. This is the denial of change that posits that all change can somehow be captured by periodizing successive stages in sharp (therefore rigorous?) conceptualizations. If change is taken seriously, there is no reason why it should observe boundaries. Heraclitus helps here.

All of these points could be turned against my description of the various iterations, except that there is no suggestion here that the iterations appear in actual life in a pure or unadulterated or distinct form. On the contrary.

All of this brings us to the fourth iteration of the state—the dissociative state. What we see in the dissociative state is that the various iterations variously confront, subsume, colonize, elevate, incorporate, repulse, and fuse into each other. Their relative fortunes rise and fall depending upon power, time, and context.

Ironically, in the American state, much of this grand drama is played out on a micro-scale—in the incremental contributions of discrete judicial decisions and the interstitial enactment of statutes, regulations, and executive orders. In one sense, there is nothing particularly surprising about the prevalence of this micro-scale. Indeed, any version of the state, in order to realize and safeguard itself, must imprint its own political-legal character on the micro-institutions of law, legality, and adjudication. In turn these micro-institutions will serve as the "micro-channeling" through which the "grand dramas" of macro-challenges are either neutralized or translated into forms that can allow processing by micro legal institutions, directives, and practices. But this channeling is neither fully successful nor fully determining. Nor is the direction all one way (i.e., macro to micro). On the contrary, at some times, in some contexts, conflicts and contradictions can erupt into frontal challenges to the micro legal institutions, directives, and practices. The conflicts and contradictions can *in theory* disrupt nearly any aspects of the political-legal register—federalism, climate change policy, civil rights, antitrust, whathaveyou. Legal institutions, law, and legal practices can only do so much to govern the relations between macro and micro and the traffic between them. In the dissociative state, legal institutions, law, and legal practices are particularly vulnerable in this regard.

The conflicts and contradictions of the various iterations yield a great deal of disordered ordering. Hence, the legitimation myths and governance mechanisms appurtenant to the liberal democratic state with its insistence on a sharp demarcation of a division between state and civil society conflicts with the insistence of the administered state on managing the affairs of civil society. Complicating matters, the neoliberal state creates all manner of new arrangements that effectively eat away at the liberal democratic state, the administered state, and ultimately the neoliberal state itself.

This unrationalized mix helps bring about the dissociative state. Importantly, given the absence of rationalization, there is no "meta state"—no overarching political-legal logic, agency, or agent that effectively delineates the appropriate arrangement of the various iterations of the state. Questions as to which iteration of the state should prevail, how much so, about what, when, and for how long receive no cogent answers—indeed, often no answer at all. The various bodies of thought, knowledge, institutional relations, legal techniques, legitimation schemes, and governance mechanisms appurtenant to each iteration of the state could in theory yield answers, but these will often be conflicting. The question then becomes: Amid the contestation of the various iterations, which one is the default? Which is meta?[1] According to whom?

On first impression, one might think that the U.S. Constitution and the Supreme Court would serve this function or role. That, all on its own, is a truly frightening thought. But pause a moment and ask: this is the document and those are the people who are de facto deciding how to allocate and organize the various iterations of the state? Well, in part: yes. But in terms of deliberate conscious design, almost certainly not.

Why not? Well, for one thing, the constitutional pronouncements of the U.S. Supreme Court are interstitial—not comprehensive. For another, the Constitution is not immune from, nor does it stand above, the conflicts and contradictions of the various iterations. On the contrary, as elaborated by legal officialdom (and the Supreme Court in particular) constitutional law is itself infused with the conflicts and contradictions of the various iterations.

Again, this is not much noticed or discussed in political-legal circles. This great failure to recognize these problems could easily be seen as odd, because the stakes are nothing less than the Enlightenment ethos and the aspirations of both the liberal democratic state (the rule of law as the rule of reason)[2] and the administered state (sound governance as the rule of expertise).

The stakes are not small.

Meanwhile, without any synthesis or coherence in sight, the perspective from each iteration of the state, renders the other iterations seemingly dysfunctional, possibly illegitimate, even perverse.

From the perspective of the liberal democratic state . . .

> the administered state looks
> like serial substantive inter-
> ferences with individual
> freedom and democracy

> > the neoliberal state looks
> > like a corruption of the
> > political-legal system.

From the perspective of the administered state . . .

> the liberal democratic state
> looks like an irrational
> forbearance from necessary
> social control and social
> sustenance functions

> > the neoliberal state looks
> > like a politically and morally
> > compromised hijacking of
> > the legal system by powerful
> > market actors.

From the perspective of the neoliberal state . . .

> the liberal democratic state
> looks like an archaic and
> unnecessary rejection of
> public/private cooperation—
> and thus an inefficient
> formation

> > the administered state
> > looks both like a captive of
> > procedural complexities and
> > unnecessary meddling by
> > cloistered and unknowing
> > experts arrogating power.

If to all this we add the realization that the various states' institutions, knowledges, and governance mechanisms often conflict, this implies a certain amount of friction—political-legal frustration at the level of both means and ends. We have seen this well enough in the arrested dialectic of the liberal democratic state and the administered state.[3] Neoliberalism, meanwhile, arrives on the scene declaring government to be dysfunctional and demanding that the state be decomposed and recomposed so that "cooperation" can enable private market actors and the market to "more efficiently" deliver the goods.

All of this leaves those who claim to follow and honor law, notably jurists and legal scholars, with only the thinnest, most fragmented shared account of what this "law" might be. It is accordingly unclear what "law" it is they are honoring, other than the poorly rationalized and often gratuitous dictates of legal officialdom (whatever these dictates may be). Indeed, that has become the default: the assertion of legal authority wrapped in syncretic and interstitial rationalizations rendered up as reason itself. This has become the "default law"—what legal officialdom says or is understood to be saying. But legal officialdom has no more clue than legal scholars (or indeed anyone else) about which of these iterations rule or how, where, or when.

So how did we get here?

A Lack of Awareness and Reconnaissance

The argument here has been long and elaborate and yet the main storyline has been simple: in order to craft and maintain itself as a viable state with all that entails (e.g., democracy, liberty, and more), the practices and institutions of law and politics had to maintain an awareness and reconnaissance of their own structures and their own actions, lest their law and politics drift off in some undesirable direction. How, we might ask, have the various states failed to maintain awareness and reconnaissance? Two basic narratives have been key:

Self-generated blinders. The first narrative is that each state has blinders that lead it to pursue political-legal agendas that are, from its own perspective, corrosive of its legitimation strategies as well as its governance mechanisms. The vexing aspect of this phenomenon is that the failure of awareness and reconnaissance is not always a severable or remediable aspect of the state. Instead, as in the liberal democratic and the administered state, the failure is the downside of deliberate and desired design choices. Hence, for instance, the liberal democratic state is, by its own lights, designed to leave civil society alone as much as possible, but as a result the liberal democratic state fails to address the pathologies (e.g., the immiseration of the populace, cultural warfare, cyber manipulation) that arise in civil society and pose a threat to the ostensible values and aims of the liberal democratic state. The administered state deploys expertise to secure multiple conflicting ends, but that devolves into such technical intricacy that the original public interest polestar is lost amid an intractable complexity. The neoliberal state authorizes marketization and market forms of knowing to colonize culture, law, and politics, thereby destroying "the social" through which the personal bonds, informal norms, and collective action necessary for markets are possible in the first place. As the various states become, given their state-specific disabilities, unable to fulfill their raison d'être, they yield alienation and anomie.

The ideé fixe. While each of the three iterations described is attended by a complex set of moves, it is important to appreciate that at a certain level of abstraction (a high one) each iteration is stuck on an *idee fixe*.

The liberal democratic state allows incremental movements or relocations of the line between state and civil society. The liberal democratic state can even tolerate a certain fuzziness in the line itself. But what it cannot abide, without surrendering its identity, is abandoning the idea of the line itself. Relocation is one thing, erasure is another. There are limits. In this instance, the range would be bounded by laissez-faire at one end and the welfare state on the other. As between the two (and everything in between), it's trench warfare.

The administered state authorizes experts and managers to administer in the public interest. The end is *progress*, the means are *administration* and the charge is *reform*. Over and over again. The task at hand is to improve an ever more complex social life by subjecting it to ever more complex regulation. As a result, things become more complex, thus requiring more complexity to regulate them. At some point in this synergistic production of complexity, the relevant participants lose track of their polestar and the public interest disintegrates into fragmented accounting statements of private costs and benefits.

The idee fixe in neoliberalism is that all aspects of culture, politics, law, and language become subject to colonization and reconfiguration in the image of markets, market metrics, and market idioms. Religion, universities, knowledge itself. Increasingly, everything is commodified, instrumentalized, measured, and calculated. Concomitantly, all matter of things on which markets depend—moral norms, social solidarity, language—are conscripted into neoliberal service. Humans, animals, the environment, the Earth itself—everything is rendered disposable, dispensable.

The contests of the three iterations along with their clashing **ideés fixes** yield the dissociative state. As this collage state, this nightmarish postmodern apparition comes into view, it introduces a fourth challenge to awareness and reconnaissance—what can be called "the absence of legal mind" and the rise of "uber-positivism." These are the juridical variants of a more widespread cultural nihilism. In the political-legal register, this nihilism manifests in a condition where jurists and legal scholars have largely given up on any robust account of law as a social steering mechanism. This is not to say that legal professionals have given up on "law." Obviously, we still have law firms, courts, and legislatures. Lawyers and judges still "apply" and "interpret" the law. And there is every reason to believe that in the future briefs will still be filed and opinions still written. But the sense that something has gone missing—that the expression "law" has no robust referent—seems close to recognition: on some dim, poorly articulated, not fully formed, tentative level, jurists and legal scholars understand that something once believed is no longer on the scene. And it is not clear that there is anything terribly appealing poised to take its place.

Among legal scholars, whatever shared sense of law there might be seems to be carried forward mostly by the *artifactual forms of law* itself: the stylizations known as the judicial opinion, the law review article, the faculty workshop, the conference panel, the job talk. These antiquated forms remain the shallow, but nonetheless well-entrenched common denominators. Indeed, the artifactual forms go unchallenged—as if everything worth saying about law from an intellectual standpoint could be said within these rigid stylizations. As if form were inconsequential and genre-neutral. Ironically, despite their archaic character, these jurisprudential forms are rigorously enforced through state of the art standardizing practices—formal mentorship programs, elite law school academic boot camps, the rule of citation rates, downloads, twitter feeds, and so forth.

The Absence of Legal Mind

What jurists and legal scholars have lost and are unable to conjure is a shared coherent sense of what law is or is supposed to do.[4] Most striking is that, with the well-publicized death of legal theory and the stagnation of analytical jurisprudence, virtually no one in the law schools is seriously looking to find an organizing logic anymore. Either they are not serious or they are not looking for it. Or it's not an organizing logic they're looking for.

To be sure, there are still interstitial and localized efforts at *rationalization*: law and economics, legal pragmatism, institutionalism, utilitarianism, and the like continue to be deployed at the micro level.[5] And occasional calls for *normative redemption* in the name of political or moral ideals such as justice, equality, self-determination, and democracy continue to be issued. But among jurists and legal scholars, the first endeavor (rationalization) does not get much past the micro. As regards the second endeavor (normative redemption) it remains exceedingly thin—deprived of the necessary oxygen and way too lofty to scale down. Either way (rationalization or normative redemption) the mediations and agencies that would be necessary to effectively connect the *ideals* to the localized *actions* of discrete actors—judges, legislators, and lawyers—remain elusive or missing altogether.[6] As if to confirm (albeit unwittingly) these desperate straits, some legal scholars have appealed unabashedly to faith. Faith in what? Legal positivism? Legal history? The Constitution? The Court? Faith? Really?

To be sure, among American legal scholars (less so jurists) there are here or there some high moments of perceptive insight that pierce through.[7] But they are few and far between. Legal scholars almost never pose a question they cannot answer or a problem they cannot solve. In a way that seems almost perverse, they reframe all issues, all questions, all problems so that these are capable of resolution. They disregard the rest.

How to sum up? The point could be stated perhaps most simply this way: The jurisprudence of the dissociative state is one that has *no theory of legal mind*.[8]

It is true, of course, that there remain sundry "professionally approved ways" of interpreting and reasoning through the authoritative official artifactual texts. These "professionally approved ways" are also called "law"—perhaps stand-ins for the most fundamental law (what the French call *le droit*). But in the U.S., these "professionally approved ways" are pluralized, conflicting, and unrationalized. They too lack any discernible organizing logic. They too rule, not because they are demonstrably rational (reason) or right (justice) or agreed upon (democratic) but because for the moment they appear to be in place, which is to say authoritative. And so they are . . . until they aren't. Corresponding to the absence of a theory of legal mind is the triumph of an arid uber-positivism.

Uber-Positivism

Uber-positivism is the triumph of legal positivism. Robin West has perceptively traced the institutionalization of this positivism in American law schools back to the shared commitments of those legendary (and otherwise antagonistic) schools of legal thought—the Langdellian formalists and the American legal realists.[9]

Over the long term, as this legal positivism proliferated throughout the twentieth century, it has become more moralistic, more value-laden in tone. But, ironically, it is not so much the moralism or the value-talk that have tempered this positivism. Rather it is more the other way around: the positivism has appropriated the moral lexicon and sucked the values dry. Or as stated some time back:

It now becomes evident that the value (if any) of normative legal thought depends on a decentered economy of bureaucratic institutions and practices—
such as those constituting and traversing the law school, the organized bar,
the courts—that define and represent their own operations, their own character, their own performances, in the normative currency. Indeed, at this point,
normative legal thought takes on a completely different character. It becomes
the mode of discourse by which bureaucratic institutions and practices represent themselves as subject to the rational ethical-moral control of autonomous individuals (when indeed they are not).[10]

That was some three decades ago. This positivization of moral and political
values has proceeded apace.[11] All of this is to say that even moralisms and values have been largely stripped of their moral or political content. They remain
as the "hooks," as the "operational levers" in legal arguments:

> Law has apparently transformed itself into a bizarre bureaucratic form of life
> that reproduces itself, not just without consulting us or our wishes, but by
> shaping us and our wishes. What is the role of normative legal thought rela-
> tive to bureaucratic practice? But that is already the wrong question. Norma-
> tive legal thought isn't somewhere else, where it could then be relative to this
> practice. Normative legal thought is that inseparable aspect of bureaucratic
> practice that persists in mistakenly thinking that it is separate and distinct and
> then compounds this error by thinking that it rules over bureaucratic practice.
> Normative legal thought is at once an abstraction of and indistinguishable
> from the operations and practices of bureaucracy.[12]

Once we get here, once values are recognized and deployed as indiscriminate strategic operational devices, the realization dawns that no one is being
fooled. Ironically, the most value-conscious individuals are those who have
come to recognize this devaluation and its implications, while the most cynical become those who in service of their professional or academic training
continue to deny the devaluation.

One of the few normative thinkers who have taken the challenges to
normative thought in law seriously is Robin West. Her aim is to re-create a
form of normative thought that effectively addresses the critiques and moves
beyond them. This is certainly a much needed endeavor. But it is only by recognizing, as West does, the depth of the problems that we will get anywhere.[13]

Complicating matters now (as they did not three decades ago) is that we
now have values and value-talk by algorithm and moral concern by menu. So
still and again: How did we get here?

For uber-positivism to prevail—for this deflationary greatest common denominator to triumph—it was necessary that all the other contenders fail (or at least appear to fail). For uber-positivism to triumph, it was necessary for legal institutions to rest on their laurels and "go along to get along." This is one of the great under-remarked and under-theorized aspects of law and legal thought—the extent to which it is a rhetoricized practice that pays *obeisance* to convention and power not because these are right, but because they are in force: law students are trained to practice law in accordance with this view though they are seldom given the intellectual equipment to help them recognize that this is what they are being trained to do.

Part of this is the famous Socratic method. There are things to admire in the Socratic classroom, but among those that are not admirable is that in the Socratic classroom, law is taught largely through *mimesis*—through the imitation of forms of thought, habits of elocution, and rehearsal of conventions as personified by the professor. The classic Socratic classroom teaches by training the law student to mimic the law professor—to ask her questions, to confront his issues, her counterarguments, his agon, and so on. This might be great were law students also given the intellectual equipment to reflect critically on all this. But that does not happen much. Again, if there were space, much more could be said about this.

How do we describe law then in the dissociative state? What then do law professors teach when they teach law? Like tradesmen who must sell a somewhat degraded product, they teach what seems most evidently to them to be law—namely, what the official legal actors themselves declare law to be. De facto, the ruling default jurisprudence in law schools is an *uber-positivism* that might be crudely summarized as follows:

(1) Law is what the official legal authorities say it is in their formal artifacts (e.g., opinions, statutes). Unless what they say is very (very) wrong, beyond their jurisdiction, or procedurally defective, what they say is law, counts as law, and, within its scope, is part of the corpus of law.

(2) Whatever difficulties are encountered in the deployment of the above formulation are to be resolved by the invocation of yet more law. In a pinch, reference may be made to terms such as "good judgment," "forms of life," "situation sense," "singing reason," and other such terms whose constative content remains vastly underspecified, but whose performative significance is to work as conversation enders. Invocation of authority also works.[14]

Few jurists or legal scholars, in fact close to none, would ever think that this is *their* jurisprudence. (For one thing, the account above is riddled with question-begging.) And if questioned specifically on the issue, the jurists and legal scholars will say, in all good faith, that *this is not* their jurisprudence—that their understandings are far more sophisticated, that their visions of law are far more urbane. And in that precise moment, they will be right. But at other times, when self-awareness is on holiday, when sophisticated interlocutors have left the scene, when law "speaks the subject" rather than the other way around, the default vision returns. One often finds this default vision in the shared working jurisprudence of the typical law school classroom, the conventional law review article, the typical faculty workshop, the standard law school conference panel, the core curriculum. It is the default jurisprudence in effect as the formal work product of legal officialdom that makes its way into all these artifactual forms. The law professoriat treats the formal work product of legal officialdom as law if, when, and because it is formally issued by the legislatures, the courts, and the agencies.

But therein lies part of the problem: legal officialdom most often has no shared overarching vision, no common commitment, beyond adherence to this tacit uber-positivism and to grand under-specified abstractions like "liberty" or "the rule of law." Operationally, their greatest commitments are to the small scale, the micro-problems, the localized, and the contextual. The point here is not offered as an insult: this is in some sense the fulfillment of their job descriptions as they see it. As for lawyers, who must answer to clients, they are largely compelled to conform to this vision.

But again, this one-sided and entrenched commitment to the small scale, the micro, and the localized has its effects: at the micro level, every rule may well be justified within its scope or place (notice the question-begging here). But at the macro level, who knows whether the aggregation of these micro rules are justified? Who could know? Who is keeping track? What means or criteria do we have to do *the cross-scope checking?* Who assures that the rules adopted in their various contexts within their scope do not interfere with each other? And what criteria for resolution are to be used when they do?

Enough on this. What then has this absence of legal mind and uber-positivism produced? A hint can be found in the work of Judith Shklar who described "legalism" as a dominant form of thought among jurists and legal scholars:

> Legalism is what gives legal thinking its distinctive flavor on a vast variety of
> social occasions, in all kinds of discourse, and among men who may differ in

every other ideological respect.... Legalism is, above all, the operative outlook of the legal profession, both bench and bar.... The dislike of vague generalities, the preference for case-by-case treatment of all social issues, the structuring of all possible human relations into the form of claims and counterclaims under established rules, and the belief that the rules are "there" —these combine to make up legalism as a social outlook.[15]

That was fifty years ago. Shklar was prescient.[16]

Fifty years on, it seems appropriate to ask: How has this legalism changed? Jurists and scholars have not abandoned their dislike of "generalities" (vague or not). They still prefer "case by case" treatment of social issues. Many still believe that the rules are "there." But now there is more to legalism than that. The attachment of jurists and scholars to legalism has produced over time a radical intensification in the variegation and intricacy and the untetheredness of law.[17] The first part (the variegation and intricacy) needs no demonstration. The second part (the increased untetheredness) does.

This untetheredness becomes most obvious upon thinking about law from the macro level. Nonetheless, we will start small, at the micro level, where, for most legal professionals, law can still seem to work well enough. At the micro level what lawyers and judges know seems sufficient at least for them (and also for many others). What is it then that jurists and legal scholars know? Here is a start on a list. They know:

A *juridical lexicon*—that is to say, *the compendium, in their field, of recognized legal doctrines, policies, principles, and concepts* (the bulk of the sort of material learned in three years of law school).

Certain formal relations—that is to say, how laws relate to other laws (assumption of risk is a defense to negligence, not battery; deterrence of accidents is a policy of strict product liability law, not contract law).

The juridically performative legal realm—the juridical consequences of the invocation of various legal statements (file a complaint and that starts a lawsuit, violate a court order and that will bring on sanctions).

The juridically performative social realm—the juridical consequence(s) of making various social statements in certain contexts (saying "deal!" in response to an offer for contract).

Beyond that, there are other important things that legal thinkers "sort of know." They sort of know how to navigate the system. They sort of know how legal institutions operate. They sort of know what their peers in the legal profession are likely to say or do about a legal matter. And they sort of know the social consequences of various legal regimes and doctrines.

"Sort of knowing" is the coin of the realm for lawyers and judges. They sort of know in the sense that they have no robust epistemic foundations to stand upon. They sort of know in the sense that what they know is sufficient to carry out their tasks, their job descriptions.

"Sort of knowing" is a shallow form of knowing—one that is incapable of tracing or discerning in any secure way the implications and consequences of regulation for the objects ostensibly regulated. Still, "sort of knowing" is not nothing. Sort of knowing seems to work for lawyers and judges in performing their daily tasks. In the issuance of rulings and opinions, in the writing of briefs and motions, in the delivery of arguments and testimony, in the drafting of affidavits and documents, sort of knowing works well enough. In part, it works well enough because the work of lawyers and judges is often routine and not in need of epistemic redemption. If this routine law can be analogized to carpentry, it might help here to recall that we seldom ask a carpenter for his epistemic warrants in choosing to use a hammer on a nail.

There is another reason (more interesting) about how and why law works well enough for lawyers and judges. And that is because the law is articulated and performed with and within the burdens of persuasion, burdens of production, default rules, and other tie-breakers that inevitably compel a decision this way or that. With such tie-breaking authority built into the frames and framing of law, there is never any chance (no matter how significant the knowledge or reason deficits may be) that law will fail to provide an answer. (Even the "hung jury" is an answer.) In this, there is something at once to admire (the law works automatically to produce results) as well as to horrify (same).

Step away now from this micro-perspective and think instead of law from the proverbial bird's-eye view. Think of the myriad legal regimes, doctrines, rules, exceptions, policies, principles—all providing for different penalties, subsidies, conditions, defeasances, transfers—all ruling within their micro scope and scale. If help is needed here, go take a look at a couple volumes of the Code of Federal Regulations or the Federal Register. Now, consider: What is the chance that the panoply of legal directives at the micro level we call law will not produce massive interference, a mutating disorder, at the macro level? And is there any—any reason at all—to suppose that the consequences and implications of any given legal regime, doctrine, rule, remains confined to its self-declared scope, its presumed scale, or even to its ostensible subject matter? No doubt there are many occasions in law and adjudication where an official declaration that "things are so" in fact makes them so. But no doubt there are many occasions where it doesn't.

Certainly when jurists and legal scholars operate at the micro level, they generally exhibit great confidence in the integrity of the micro-context that is the focus and limit of their attention. But what chance is there that the analytical or principle or policy work they undertake in the micro-context remains confined to that micro-context? What precisely ensures that the micro-context so carefully delineated and scoped out in the words of the judicial opinion or the law review article in fact translates from the words on the screen to the social architecture of the world—that one tracks the other? And what ensures that this demarcation of the micro-context has staying power? Is this any more than the perennial habit among legal professionals of dividing wholes into parts so that they can work on each of the parts in isolation from the others without having to think about the wholes?[18]

Realize that for a rule or a policy to produce its desired effect in a micro-context, this micro-context must be *relatively insular* from or *impermeable* to any destabilizing macro-forces. That is to say that either the operative rules governing the micro must be (roughly?) the same as those governing the macro *or* the micro must be insulated somehow from any operative macro that might disrupt, contradict, or frustrate the rules operative at the micro level. Those are the alternative necessary conditions. The problem is that, *ab initio*, there is no reason whatsoever to believe that these conditions hold. It's convenient to believe this, but that in no way ensures its truth or validity and thus it does nothing to validate any work issuing from such premises.

Now look at all this from another perspective: consider the effect that modifications of the part may visit on the whole. If working on a part without considering the whole is to work, then all the implications and consequences that we hope are effective in the part must somehow stop at the borders of frame, scope, and scale. If these consequences and implications register beyond the frames, scope, and scale, then other parts of the system might be disturbed or unsettled. This is a problem, of course, because apart from the words on the page or the screen, there is absolutely no reason, no reason at all, to believe that the implications and consequences are confined to the frame, scope, and scale of the part. In fact, absent a stubborn adherence to the grid aesthetic, it seems transparently odd to presume that such conditions would hold.

There are more daunting challenges yet to come. One of them is as intellectually interesting as it is socially dire:

The Dissolution of Identity

Identities ostensibly referring to institutions, legal methods, political persuasions, race, gender, sexual orientation, class, and so on are dying the death of a thousand cuts—a fine but relentless subdivision that effectively fractures essentialism (not a bad thing) but tends to drive identity out of effective intellectual, cultural, and political-legal existence (a decidedly more ambivalent thing). This fracturing is noticeable in all sorts of endeavors. Is this fracturing demobilizing? You bet. Is it happening? You bet. Can it become yet more refined, more intricate? Of course. Can anyone or anything stop it? Who knows?

Perhaps the most radical form of dissolution of identity is intellectual: one comes to recognize that previously cogent identities fracture into a series of disparate elements existing in different modes. Consider Felix Cohen's famous analysis of the question "What is a corporation?" Felix Cohen, a noted American legal realist in the 1930s, famously excoriated an opinion by Justice Benjamin Cardozo that sought to define the reach of personal jurisdiction over a foreign corporation. In his opinion, Cardozo hypostatized the corporation into a thing or person: indeed almost obsessionally so.[19] Said Cardozo:

> [T]he problem which now faces us is . . . one of jurisdiction, of private international law. We are to say, not whether the business is such that the corporation may be prevented *from being here*, but whether its business is such that *it is here*. If in fact *it is here*, if *it is here*, not occasionally or casually, but with a fair measure of *permanence* and *continuity*, then, whether its business is interstate or local, it is within the jurisdiction of our courts. . . . Unless a foreign corporation is engaged in business within the state, *it is not brought* within the state by *the presence* of its agents. But there is no precise test of the nature or extent of the business that must be done. All that is requisite is that enough be done to enable us to say that *the corporation is here*. . . . If *it is here* it may be served.[20]

The problem, as Cohen famously explained, is that a corporation is not a thing existing in space, capable of moving from place to place. Presuming metaphorically that it is such a thing, as Cardozo does, precludes a cogent answer to whether and in what circumstances a foreign corporation may be sued.

All right. Cohen has a point. But Cohen fared no better than Cardozo. Cohen also was forced to give the corporation physical and socioeconomic presence in order to answer his own questions.[21] Put differently, not using metaphors is not an option. If you think that a corporation is only a legal relation, then the only cogent answers are it cannot be sued anywhere (legal relations are not subject to suit in and of themselves) or it can be sued anywhere (since a corporation is a legal relation there can be no burden placed on it, and thus it really doesn't matter where it can be sued). Once one realizes all these points—that Cohen's analysis is subject to his own critique—it can dawn on the reader that a corporation isn't (excuse the expression) any one thing. Instead, for purposes of legal analysis, the corporation is a mutable aggregation: a nexus of *contracts*, a constellation of *legal relations*, a particular *form of social organization*, an *economic unit* known often as the firm, *a carrier of capitalism*, and on and on.[22] And, of course, one can take any of these aspects of the corporation, elevate it to superior status, and subsume all the other aspects. Hence, for instance, one can say that a corporation is fundamentally a form of social organization composed by a set of legal relations and a nexus of contracts, disciplined by the market and so on. Or one can say a corporation is fundamentally a set of legal relations that . . . Or one can say . . . And so it is that we end up with different conceptualizations of the corporation from which we can yield different implications.

The exercise can be repeated, en abyme, at a more granular level by taking one of the corporation's aspects, such as contract, and asking: What is a contract? Dissolution can strike again: a contract is an agreement by the parties, a set of legal relations, the written or oral expression of the agreement by the parties, that part of an agreement that is enforceable at law, and so on.[23] And we can keep striving for more even more granularity: What is an agreement by the parties? What is a party? And notice here that it won't do to say: "Terrific—we have just specified the various aspects of corporation, contract, and agreement so we can now isolate them and deal with them separately and rigorously." Nope. Isolation is not in the offing, because any particular aspect of contract relies, for its form and substance, explicitly or covertly upon an invocation of the other aspects. Please note that here we are well beyond what Lon Fuller, elaborating Karl Polanyi, described as "polycentricity." We have no centers here to be poly about. We know too much about how to pry centers apart and how to substitute different concepts of the concept (core/penumbra, radial category, family resemblance, aggregation, and so on), one for the other.

Similarly, it is important not to equate the above with the familiar perspectivism that approaches a legal identity or its corresponding legal concept in terms of the various contexts or perspectives in which it appears. In that familiar approach, the identity or the concept changes in meaning and implication as a function of the perspectives and contexts in which it appears. No, here we have something different—more interesting and also more disturbing. Here what we have is the falling apart of what were previously apprehended and thought to be whole legal concepts and legal phenomena. The disintegration is not produced from the "outside" (different perspectives/different contexts). Instead, the disintegration all happens from the inside of the legal identity. "Things fall apart" as Yeats said. "The center cannot hold." And why? Because there is no center but rather an aggregation of traits subject to sundry organizations and reorganizations. But what about H.L.A. Hart and core/penumbra? Well, what about Hart? Core/penumbra was also imagery—one image of the concept among many.

What does all of this have to do with the dissociative state?

Well, this is what legal identities and legal concepts look like, how they work (and not) when the political-legal has proliferated into the multiple iterations described. The conflicts and contradictions occur not simply on the outside, but within legal identities and legal concepts. The forces—political legal, cultural, linguistic, and so forth—that are deployed to keep the rationality of the various iterations intact (when they are not) yields tremendous stress on legal concepts and identities. Not only do legal concepts and identities fall apart, but it becomes possible to experience their undoing as well as the forces deployed to hold them together.

Law, in this regard, is especially interesting, precisely because it is so frequently crude and brutal in enforcing the integrity of legal concepts and identities. Law doesn't just adjudicate and prescribe the entitlements of persons vis-à-vis each other: along the way, law adjudicates and prescribes the meaning of legal concepts and identities—which when inscribed socially and economically enables the possibility of leading certain lives, while extinguishing the possibility of others.

The passage a few paragraphs ago about the dissolution of the concept of corporation or contract can be useful to the legal mind. On balance it would be a good (as opposed to a bad) thing for such an account to be read or heard in many judicial chambers.[24] But, at the same time, the passage in question would be utterly untenable in a standard judicial opinion or a piece of legislation. For one thing, its inclusion in a judicial opinion or a piece of legislation would reveal the general arbitrariness of law (think Kafka) and the unavoidable brutality necessary to affirm *this* version of the concept as opposed to *that* one.

Judges, legislators, and lawyers are not the unacknowledged poets of the world. Indeed, as a general matter, they tend to avoid complicating their tasks. They try, generally, to make things simple for themselves, and it is in that simplification that we can find the crudeness and the brutality. Think here: plain meaning of the text. Think here: legislative intent. Think here: the fixity of legal meaning. This is not subtle stuff. Neither in theory nor practice.

From the vantage of prosaic understandings of reason, knowledge, law, politics, and the like, all this dissolution feels like an unsettling encounter with Immanuel Kant's sublime. And not surprisingly so: what is at stake is the potential dissolution of cogent legal concepts and identities, and, along with them, intelligible structures in which we live and which live in us. The prospect of such dissolution is not comforting. But it is happening.

VI The Authoritarian Temptation

We have seen how the conflicts and contradictions within and among various states produces forms of denial that yield political-legal dysfunctions. These dysfunctions (real or perceived) prompt the rise of each succeeding state. We have also seen how the various states are not definitively synthesized or integrated, but rather preserved in a kind of fragmented-fusion state—namely, the dissociative state.

Where then does this all lead (assuming it leads anywhere at all)? What kind of governance comes next? Who or what inherits the problems and opportunities created by this chaotic state?

Authoritarian Opportunism

The weakness of the dissociative state and its manifest incapacity (if not paralysis) in the wake of challenges has two major effects. One effect is to discredit the American state and its self-declared associations including democracy, liberalism, and the rule of experts. Another effect is to render the authoritarian temptation increasingly plausible and appealing. Indeed, authoritarianism may look good not just to political opportunists and ruling economic elites, but to the masses, and to all those who are, as a matter of personality, already predisposed to authoritarianism.[1]

As numerous commentators have noted, the recent rise of authoritarianism around the world (the U.S, Turkey, Hungary, Poland, and so on) has proceeded gradually by steps.[2] This rise of authoritarian regimes does not emerge from nowhere: with every new onset of gridlock, paralysis, and dysfunction, the appeal of authoritarian command and control governance increases.

While this movement toward authoritarianism is incremental and insidious, the attendant political mythology is not. Indeed, the far-right populism (for lack of a better name) in the U.S. shows no strong adherence to democratic norms (of any kind) and shows clear signs of embracing a rather dark *political mythology* not seen in mass movements for a long time.

Consider, by way of example, Trump's campaign in 2016. There he managed to strike a number of themes and aesthetic displays that resonated with his audience. Among them were nationalism, authoritarianism, racism, anti-intellectualism, xenophobia, and revanchism. He punctuated many of those themes with arch-intimations and endorsements of violence. Perhaps most remarkable, Trump managed to evoke the fusion of revolutionary fervor and reactionary nostalgia. He also borrowed heavily from the scripts of the left (hence, the claim of politics as "a rigged system," and the endorsement of social programs for the benefit of workers). He celebrated working class physical culture.[3] His performances were attended with a stream of phantasmagoric stories—like the one about the roving gangs of criminals decimating U.S. cities or the "millions" of illegal immigrants stealthily stealing jobs.[4] His designated enemies were clearly identified: the immigrants, the elite experts, the swamp.

This is a *political mythology* we have encountered before.

Mythic Fascism

Fascism has many different registers: the political (totalitarianism), the economic (corporatism), the social (collectivist), the aesthetic (monumentalist) and the mythological (irrationalist). Here we focus on the mythological because this is perhaps the strongest aspect of fascism—the aspect most likely to entice and motivate the masses.

This "mythic fascism," as it will be called here, does not necessarily entail fascist governance mechanisms—such as those of interwar German National Socialism or Italian fascism. Indeed, any number of authoritarian governance mechanisms are compatible with "*mythic fascism.*" As will be seen, the portable largely indiscriminate character of mythic fascism renders it particularly dangerous: mythic fascism can be deployed by any number of movements or parties given to authoritarianism. Thus, mythic fascism can be invoked not only by neofascists but also by populists, garden-variety dictators, and political opportunists.

As will be seen, there is nothing rationally coherent about the fascist myth. At the same time, however, it is psychologically well attuned to eliciting, nurturing, and then satisfying a people's darkest needs and emotions—anger, fear, resentment, revenge. While the fascist myth is nihilistic to its core, it nonetheless presents through spectacle, elan, transport and the like as a grandiose project that overcomes nihilism. It presents as a grand mythic project of nation-building and recovery.

In 1995, Umberto Eco, the famous Italian intellectual, wrote a brief essay on the mythology of fascism."[5] In that essay, "Ur-fascism," Eco wondered how and why it is that fascism seems to recur across nations, epochs, and cultures both as a phenomenon and a diagnostic. This was no small challenge because, as Eco saw it, the classic fascist regime (Benito Mussolini's Italy served as his paradigm) was, at the level of both ideology and politics, a syncretic mess.[6]

But if fascism is a syncretic mess, then how then does it ever manage to replicate itself across nations, cultures, and epochs?

Eco's answer is important because it demonstrates how *particular instances* of fascism are anchored in *a generalized archetype that resonates at the affective and mythic level*. Moreover, Eco's answer helps explain how a mythic politics so fraught with contradictions can nonetheless appeal to wide swaths of the populace given certain circumstances. As Eco puts it, despite fascism's evident "political and ideological discombobulation . . . it was a *rigid* discombobulation, a *structured* confusion. Fascism was philosophically out of joint, but emotionally it was firmly fastened to *archetypal foundations*."[7]

Eco argued that, at the level of myth, there is some sort of primordial fascism recognizable to us—even if not all the features of the classic Italian or German examples are to be found in other concrete instances. To describe this primordial fascism, Eco invoked Ludwig Wittgenstein's notion of family resemblance—the idea that some concepts are organized in the manner of family resemblances. With family resemblance, each member shares a number of traits with some (but not all) of the others. Individuals can be recognized as part of the same family even if there is no single common trait shared. Using this notion of family resemblance, Eco thus proceeded to describe his archetype of "Ur-fascism" as a coalescence of traits.[8]

What follows here is a summary of Eco's "Ur-fascism," with very few deviations or additions. Eco's archetypal account is particularly useful because it shows how mythic fascism can travel so easily—not only across time and culture, but across different political tendencies. Moreover, Eco's linkage of traits is visible in the work of other well-known historians of fascism—such as Roger Griffin and Eugen Weber.[9] Similarly, the recent work of Jason Stanley on fascism likewise converges with Eco's account.[10]

Here the term "mythic fascism" is used rather than Eco's "Ur-fascism" to avoid any errors of ascription. But to be clear: what follows is a summary of Eco's views—views that are likewise shared in great part with many scholars of fascism. Much like Eco's effort, the aim here is to describe mythic fascism as an archetype that can emerge as an actualized version at moments of economic and social stress. As for the lasting significance of this mythic fascism, it can be ascribed in part a coherence that holds at the mythic and emotional (not the logical) level. Fascism is like superstition in this regard: at the level of propositions, it fails to parse rationally: leaps of faith, tendentious characterizations, and animistic invocations are repeatedly required. And yet, nonetheless, at the level of myth and emotion, it can feel coherent—again particularly for those experiencing economic and social stress.

The mythological coherence of mythic fascism finds its natural home in the reactionary mind that emerged forcefully in a response to the Enlightenment and its signal political moment—namely, the French Revolution of 1789.[11] This reactionary mind does not hold much appeal for those who live in intellectual and cosmopolitan milieus. Intellectuals and cosmopolitans are thus easily motivated to believe this reactionary mind has passed from the scene. But that belief is profoundly mistaken. It is a belief wrought of zip code bubbles and intellectual echo chambers. It is also prompted by an unfounded teleology: namely, the progressive notion that history works, by and large, as a ratchet—the triumphant advance of freedom or the gradual realization of rationality.

There is not much going for such a (mythic?) belief. The cultural achievement of "advanced" forms of consciousness over time does not in and of itself imply that this consciousness dominates nor that everyone has been brought along. Just because a voter owns a state of the art laptop or a 14th-generation mobile phone doesn't prevent the cable news channel he watches from delivering the most reactionary or primitive myths.

In times of economic stress and social anxiety, the reactionary mind may well find mythic fascism appealing because it offers a redemptive and consoling narrative. Mythic fascism is redemptive because it explains away individual failure (the designated enemies are to blame!) and it is consoling because it promises a way out (a bold new movement reviving the golden age will provide!) When constitutional democracies go awry, when the masses feel abandoned, the appeal of mythic fascism will be there waiting to be activated by an entire assortment of characters and movements seeking power.

How then does mythic fascism attract, motivate, and mobilize its adherents? Mythic fascism achieves its narrative appeal by invoking resonant, earthy, and thus highly abstract but nonetheless vivid referents ("volk," "blood," "struggle," "action," "sacrifice"). Mythic fascism idealizes (and even lyricizes) these referents. Beyond idealization and lyricization, fascism propagates its mythic order through sustained and repeated aesthetic spectacles of the myth itself. In the interwar years, particularly in Nazi Germany, this was done through the extensive and elaborately choreographed use of banners, uniforms, parades, monumentalist architecture, demonstrations, light shows, staging, cinema, and more. Today, of course, one can only imagine what a politics of spectacle could do with twenty-first-century technology.

Ultranationalism and the glory of the Nation, the People, or the State. Nazism revered the volk and celebrated it by reference to its supposed attributes—physical beauty, innate strength, racial superiority. Mussolini's fascism celebrated the state. The volk or the state, or both, thus became everything—the individual nothing. This ultranationalism serves as a kind of automatic tribal identity to create a sense of belonging in times that might otherwise be characterized by anomie, alienation, and despair. Moreover, ultranationalism is easily coupled to a sense of victimization at the hands of malign outsiders, strangers, and foreign powers. Ultranationalism thus leads to a friend/enemy or an us/them division of the world in which all problems are traced to the enemy—to those who are held responsible for the troubles of the nation and who must thus be vanquished.[12]

National palingenesis. This call for the rebirth of the nation is fascism's promised remedy for the wrong of national victimization.[13] The narrative holds that the nation is great, but that it has been unjustly wronged and betrayed by outsiders, strangers, and foreign powers that have taken advantage of it. Characteristically, the fascist myth cultivates a sense of collective injury. It will deepen the wounds and nurture the resentments to almost apocalyptic proportions and then offer itself as the only solution adequate to the daunting task—nothing less than a grand project of national rebirth. Fascists typically look to the past (even a distant ancient past) as a way of reconstructing a mythic community. This will be achieved through the political creation of some organic whole—the Aryan nation, the Italian state, or the like. The claim is that only fascism can lead the way because only the unitary organic character of fascism is able to avoid the schisms inevitably wrought by the other political tendencies—liberalism and Marxism. Only fascism taps into the true source of unity—blood, soil, nation, and so forth.

Tradition.[14] Fascists celebrate the pre-Enlightenment (and even the ancient) world when communities were shaped by folkways, folk heroes, and folk wisdom. Inverting the conventionalist modernist account, mythic fascism holds that the Enlightenment was the true dark age. Its great sin was to eclipse and destroy traditional modes of life and their hierarchical order. For the fascist, traditionalism holds considerable appeal. Tradition is both the legitimation and carrier of order. Moreover, tradition is timeless—its truth is timeless—and thus not susceptible to the wrenching progressive rationality of the Enlightenment. And, of course, tradition is what the common people know best. It is what is familiar and comfortable. Fascism will thus often tap into "ancient, and even arcane myths of racial, cultural, ethnic, and national origins to develop a plan for the 'new man.'"[15]

Anti-Enlightenment.[16] Fascism holds that the age of reason brought darkness to the world. There is thus a strong anti-intellectual and anti-academic ethos to fascism. Bolstered by the embrace of traditionalist myths, this becomes the classic fascist affirmation of irrationalism. Rational argument is both dismissed and disdained as if it were some sort of clever artifice meant to derail more fundamental, more important knowledges anchored, as the Nazi slogan had it, in "blood and soil." The chief political offshoots of the Enlightenment (liberalism and Marxism) are held in great disdain. Both liberalism and Marxism are viewed as the work of deracinated cosmopolitan intellectuals who know little about human nature or the nation or the common folk. Indeed, for fascists, the great harm of the Enlightenment was to undo the virtues of concrete tradition in favor of the universalist adventures of reason. Marxism, as an offshoot of the Enlightenment, is seen to bring class warfare and internal strife, thus destroying the true source of common bonds—namely, the nation, the volk. Meanwhile, liberalism, the other political offshoot of the Enlightenment, is viewed as weak, corrupt, indecisive, and destructive of the common identity of the volk or the nation. Liberalism is thus incapable of defending the volk or the nation against its enemies.[17]

Anti-deliberative democracy. Fascism locates sovereignty in an active unitary executive rather than a deliberative legislature. That is because fascism is opposed to political forms that are the outgrowth of Enlightenment norms of rationality (i.e., deliberation, public reasoning, criticism, and tolerance of dissent). These are seen to produce a kind of political weakness— making it impossible to reach resolutions. As Carl Schmitt wrote, "The essence of liberalism is negotiation, a cautious half measure, in the hope that the definitive dispute, the decisive bloody battle, can be transformed into a parliamentary debate and permit the decision to be suspended forever in an everlasting discussion."[18] In part, this indecision or incipient paralysis is ascribed to the universalist character of liberalism and Marxism.

Action for action's sake.[19] Practice is first, theory comes after. If at all. As the Belgian Rexist and Nazi sympathizer Leon Degrelle put it, "You must get going, you must let yourself be swept away by the torrent . . . you must act. The rest comes by itself."[20] As for theory, reason, and reflection—these are not to be trusted. Fascism is a kind of romantic politics dedicated to the idealization of heroism, courage, sacrifice, and duty.

The fascist negations. The famous "fascist negations" (some are mentioned above) are well known. Fascism is anti-liberal, anti-democratic, anti-parliamentary, anti-Enlightenment, anti-Marxist, anti-intellectual, and anti-cosmopolitan. Fascism's targets here can easily be associated with weakness, indecision, endless discussion and deliberation, and advantageously contrasted with fascism's hyper-masculinist, self-assertive, physically aggressive ethos.[21] Fascism's negative orientation is particularly persuasive in times of economic and social stress when the popular emotions are likely to run to the dark side: anger, fear, anxiety, and resentment.[22]

Designation of the enemy.[23] Fascism offers a bleak diagnosis of national conditions and immediately targets some named enemy as the responsible party. In contrast to liberal democracy, which, at least in theory, champions political community through reasoned and deliberative discourse, fascism establishes itself in opposition to a named and demonized enemy—the proverbial "other." It is in this way that *fear of difference* is inculcated to produce communal solidarity. Fascism is thus a clear instantiation of the classic diagnostics of scapegoat theory: communal bonds are achieved through the identification, demonization, and exclusion of the other—the stranger.[24]

Revolutionary aims. For fascism, the destruction of the political forms of the Enlightenment and the rebirth of the nation all require revolutionary action. Palingenesis can only be accomplished by dismantling the modern political and social institutions in favor of action and struggle. This means the glorification of violence and war itself are the crucible in which men and nations are tested. As Mussolini's *Doctrine of Fascism* states: "Life is struggle. War is a rite of passage. Sacrifice is a duty. Death is not to be feared."[25]

The warrior ethic. The rejection of the Enlightenment, together with the celebration of traditionalism, is also consonant with the celebration of the warrior ethic. The latter is much in evidence, for instance, in Leni Riefenstahl's famous film of a Nuremberg rally, *Triumph of the Will*. The warrior ethic represents the historical moment when warriors with their code of honor were the acknowledged leaders of the community (as opposed to the scholars or merchants).[26] From the warrior ethic, it is easy to slide into the celebration of the body and from there to the immediate, the primitive, and the sensual.

The celebration of physicalist culture.[27] Fascism valorizes purity, health, strength, and beauty, all of which are ascribed to "the volk" or "the people," while the absence (or negation) of these values are ascribed to the other, the enemy. This exaltation of physicalist culture not only entices those social classes most susceptible to this identification, but it also serves to reinforce the characteristic fascist "contempt for all that is reflective, critical, and pluralistic."[28] Physicalist culture is also closely linked to the idea that might makes

right—that there is virtue in strength alone. An important aspect of this celebration of physicalist culture is the somatic aspect of fascism—the masculin-
ist displays of hardship and endurance, physical strength, and the celebration
of the starkly sculptured and disciplined (militaristic) male body.[29]

The aestheticization of politics. Fascism champions not only the physical, but the sensuous, the immediate, the sensory, and the perceptual. All
of these are made to do a lot of the work otherwise done by morality, politics, argument, and reflection. Joseph Goebbels, Hitler's propaganda minister,
made this clear: "Arguments must therefore be crude, clear and forcible, and
appeal to emotions and instincts, not the intellect."[30]

Walter Benjamin famously drew attention to the Nazi aestheticization of
politics.[31] Later Susan Sontag elaborated Benjamin's insight with her dissection of Riefenstahl's Nazi art. In Sontag's famous essay, "Fascinating Fascism,"
she castigates Riefenstahl's disingenuous attempts to belittle her collaboration with the Nazi regime. Along the way, and this is what makes Sontag's
essay so memorable, she shows just how crucial art and aesthetics (including
Riefenstahl's work) were to the promotion as well to as the existential core
of Nazism. Consider by way of example Sontag's description of Riefenstahl's
Nazi propaganda films:

> All four of Riefenstahl's commissioned Nazi films—whether about Party con-
> gresses, the Wehrmacht, or athletes—celebrate the rebirth of the body and of
> community, mediated through the worship of an irresistible leader. . . . The
> fictional mountain films are tales of longing for high places, of the challenge
> and ordeal of the elemental, the primitive; the Nazi films are epics of achieved
> community, in which triumph over everyday reality is achieved by ecstatic
> self-control and submission.[32]

The fascist aesthetic itself has clear political implications: this aesthetic is mon-
umental, vertical, hierarchical, rigid, strong, pure, simple, brutal, violent, and
male. It has its idealist moments (the heights, mountains, clouds, flight, lights,
and fire). But it also has primal materiality (stone, iron, steel, machinery, and
human beings arranged in formidable columns). The fascist aesthetic is an aesthetic that seeks to overwhelm the individual, to awe him or her into submission with the grandeur of an order in which he or she is supposed to blend.

Can this really appeal to anyone? Well, recall the target constituency. It will
not be intellectuals or cosmopolitans. Mythic fascism is addressed to a population racked by economic precarity and social anxiety, a population that feels
betrayed and left behind by forces it cannot control. Mythic fascism promises

not only to hold those supposedly responsible to account—the intellectuals, the cosmopolitans, the Marxists, and other designated enemies—but it also offers a spectacle of renewal, redemption, and grandeur. It is not a politics of the frontal cortex, but one for the amygdala.

Violent drama plays an important role. This is accomplished in the first instance on a small scale (the drama is not epic and the violence is localized). But then, as in the logic of romantic transport, the intensity must be ramped up. More violence, grander struggles, rallies, military parades, war, genocide. It's all one way.

Thanatos unbound.

VII   The Contest of Diagnoses

The phrase "awareness and reconnaissance" has been invoked many times in this book. It is now appropriate to elaborate precisely what awareness and reconnaissance means, how it works, and what work it does. Soon it will become readily apparent why it is only now—in the last chapter—that this phrase can be unpacked and its various meanings elaborated.

Typically, awareness means cognizant, mindful, knowledgeable. While one can be aware in general, awareness is often an awareness of something. As for reconnaissance, it means a number of things. One of them is to reconnoiter, to take stock, to assess, as in, for instance, military reconnaissance. A second meaning, particularly if we rely on its original French meaning, is to know again. This implies that things were known before and now they are being known again.

In order to unpack the relations between awareness and reconnaissance, on the one hand, and law, on the other, we will proceed in stages—starting with the most simple and obvious and proceeding to the more obscure but possibly more important. There is nothing definitive about these stages: they are used here for expository purposes.

Begin then with the more conventional understandings.

Individual cognitive capacity. The most obvious forms of awareness and reconnaissance pertain to an individual's cognitive capacities: what an individual knows, can perceive, or discern. Clearly law school as well as law practice educate and train legal professionals to pay particular attention to certain things—whether a witness is lying, whether a will is likely to be contested, whether criminal law prohibits a course of action, and so on. Along the way, the lawyer, the judge, and the legal academic are trained as well not to pay attention to certain things. This is all obvious.

Conceptual architecture of law. There is a second stage of awareness and reconnaissance also pertaining to the work of the individual legal professional. The latter must be aware of the conceptual structure of law and, most importantly, what this structure means and does. Ideally, law students and legal professionals become aware that the conceptual structure of law is a template, a screen, a channeling, a process, a standardization (and more), and that law institutes a particular (legal) version of the things and aspects it claims to address and regulate. One may find the same sort of conceptual structures (e.g., template, screen) in other fields—business, psychology, and so on—but these structures will not have the same character nor purpose.

Then there is a further step, one that has frustrated, and even compromised, a great deal of interdisciplinary work. This step lies in recognizing that the various templates, screens, and so on in one field do not translate very well into each other. Very often, that is because the axiomatics or the root assumptions in one field are incompatible with or antithetical to those of another. One clear example is the neoclassical model in economics, which makes assumptions that are and have to be rejected in law.[1]

The social and institutional structure of law. Here we move from the possibilities of awareness and reconnaissance by the individual to those of the collective. This does not involve some controversial assumption of a "collective mind." Rather, it involves moving from the idea of law as conceptual structure to law as material inscription. Here an analogy to architecture or software might help. With architecture, there are first plans. At some point, with luck and construction, the plans beget buildings of "brick and mortar." With software, there is first an idea. At some point, with luck and coding, this idea becomes actual software. Now the interesting thing here is that in the translation from architectural plans to a building and the idea to software, what we get in both cases are structures (physical or coded, respectively) that organize and direct the activity of personnel. And not just what they think, but what they do. The law is such a structure.

Having arrived at this point, it now becomes possible to recognize that both as social process and conceptual architecture, law highlights or obscures, fastens upon or discards, exposes or reveals, organizes or undoes events, problems, challenges, and the like. In other words, awareness and reconnaissance are part of the political-legal structure and the social organization of the state.

In order to fulfill its roles and functions, the state needs to establish and maintain the channels of awareness and reconnaissance. Law, construed as litigation, adjudication, legislation, and regulation, establishes multiple tripwires, allowing or disabling all sorts of actors (subdivisions of the state, firms, the press, political parties, academia) to take cognizance of challenges and problems. Law enables and disables awareness and reconnaissance and it channels the possible responses.

To give a simple example: shortly following 9/11, the U.S. followed a set of policies and legal mechanisms that allowed "terrorist suspects" to be iso-lated from families, friends, and lawyers. The U.S. also engaged in a practice of "rendition"—whereby terrorist suspects were shipped off to allies overseas, where they could be questioned by professional interrogators free from any obligation to follow U.S. constitutional or statutory law.

All this happened in the dark. For some time, no one outside the intelli-gence agencies knew for sure what had happened to the suspects. There was thus nothing for the press to report. There were no indictments, no hearings, no court proceedings—in short, nothing in the way of formal legal events or records that served as trip wires to launch the press into reportorial action.

The upshot is that, for a while, no one outside the government knew. When the stories emerged later about these interrogation practices, it became evident that one of the great functions of *legal processes* pursued in public lies precisely in creating legal "events" that enable the press, elected officials, the legal profession, the people (and more) to take cognizance of what is happen-ing. Without such processes, these parties remain in the dark.

This story about the terrorist suspects is probably one of the most obvi-ous examples in which the political-legal register plays a major role in allying law and legal institutions with those of the press. This is one of law's ways of producing awareness and reconnaissance: the state establishes social and institutional mechanisms through which various important agents, the press, elected officials, the legal professionals, and the people can learn what is hap-pening and decide for themselves whether *this* or *that* warrants attention, study, and action (or not).

Now, this is a relatively simple example from criminal law, but the same sort of thing happens in civil law. Hence the availability of tort causes of action, the activation of antitrust civil suits, the holding of public municipal hearings, the publication of legal records, the agency-required "impact state-ments," the Freedom of Information Act requests—these are all ways in which awareness and reconnaissance are activated and thus enable further acts of awareness and reconnaissance (professional commentary, academic study, legislative hearings—in short, an institutional version of the "follow-up").

In law, these matters are very often treated under the heading of "trans-parency." Ironically, that very term itself hides a great deal about awareness and reconnaissance. The reason is simple: transparency is mostly about the wisdom (or lack thereof) of making various political-legal proceedings public. What transparency leaves out is the preliminary and much more basic ques-tion of whether there are any legal proceedings to make public in the first place. And that is crucial because, of course, if the political-legal register fails to actually hold the legal proceedings in the first place, there will be nothing to make transparent, nothing to make public, to study, or think about. This is a deeply ironic point, of course, because awareness and reconnaissance is precisely about enabling matters, issues, concerns, challenges, and problems to come to the light of day.

"*Sapere aude*," Kant said. Yes, certainly. But there's not going to be much sapere aude happening if the political-legal register is not organized and structured to enable important matters to rise to attention. If sapere aude is the aim, then the *material and intellectual resources* necessary for thought, reflection, analysis, and thought must themselves be provided. Kant himself worried about this: the transition from brutalized serf to self-actualized citizen would be difficult—it would not happen overnight.[2]

The same point can be made about the freedom of speech so cherished in liberal democracies. Freedom of speech typically concerns those methods, techniques, and processes that states use to regulate, suppress, or prohibit speech. What is often left unrecognized, even by the most passionate partisans of freedom of speech, is that before there can be speech to "regulate, suppress, or prohibit," there must first be a language, a conceptual architecture that allows this speech to occur and to be heard.

Here we now arrive at a central problematic. Awareness and reconnaissance are key to the vitality and existence of a political-legal order. (It must learn of challenges and problems.) At the same time, a political-legal order *is itself* already a duly institutionalized form of awareness and reconnaissance. Not surprisingly, to defend its identity and existence, to accomplish its goals and ends, the political-legal order must sometimes suppress the rise of any awareness and reconnaissance that threatens to displace it. Without going into any great detail, it's clear that all four iterations of the state establish (by design or not) serious impediments to awareness and reconnaissance. They must—any political-legal order must. Why? Because a political-legal order is, among other things, itself already constituted as a form of awareness and reconnaissance (which simultaneously entails a form of non-awareness and non-reconnaissance).

Hence, the liberal democratic state, in trying to honor its commitment to hands-off civil society, strives to be minimalist in supervising or monitoring the transactions and practices that occur in civil society. As explained earlier, the ideal liberal democratic strategy for civil society is to define and police legal entitlements and disablements in terms of the grid aesthetic. The idea is to leave the liberal individual subject free within a certain domain or dominion to choose what to think and what to do: the limits of the liberal individual subject's entitlements or prerogatives are defined by establishing lines, borders, boundaries. Within the realms, areas, domains, fields, and spaces demarcated by those lines, the aesthetically established "insides" are placed beyond regulation, perhaps even beyond examination. That is the vaunted upside of the liberal definition of rights. The downside, or rather one among several, is that this particular legalist strategy leaves the liberal democratic state without the legal mechanisms or feedback to learn what is or is not happening in and to civil society.

The administered state also establishes impediments to awareness and reconnaissance. Insofar as this is a "hands-on civil society approach," very much steeped in consequentialist reasoning, the administered state requires a great deal of expertise—and not just in law, but in the natural sciences, in engineering, manufacturing, finance, and so on. The intellectual and professional ability to trace chains of causation, feedback loops, interferences, externalities, and the like also require a great deal of expertise. Expertise is thus a sine qua non of governance in the administered state: consider, by way of obvious examples, environmental threats, toxic chemicals, product design, transportation, and communication.

This reliance on experts and expertise is in one sense commendable. In a different sense, dependency on expertise interjects into the political-legal register both the need for and the fact of highly rarefied expertise. Here the problems start. Governance requires the kind of expertise so refined that it will often be beyond the comprehension of the people, their representatives, the commentariat, and the press. In fact the expertise may well be beyond the comprehension of most judges, lawyers, and legal scholars not specialized in the particular issues under consideration. In an advanced society, this heightened degree of expertise may well be necessary. But the complexity recognized or produced by all this expertise in sundry domains poses a real challenge to democracy: the people do not know, cannot understand, and thus cannot evaluate the expertise or the domains monitored. The administered life is one they live every day, but without knowing necessarily the how, the why, or the wherefrom.

Often this problem is apprehended and described as one of transparency. But the description is inapt. Transparency is largely understood to be a problem of inception. Here, by contrast, we are talking mainly of a problem of reception. When reception is blocked, transparency ceases to work. And in the administered state it is easy for reception to be blocked. Transparency yields disclosures that are incomprehensible, far too specialized, far too numerous. Meanwhile those who "translate" the disclosures (suppliers, salespeople, brokers, and the like) are frequently not terribly reliable: "Sign here and here and here."

As for the neoliberal state, it operates according to a different grammar. It contributes greatly to the opacity of the political-legal register by invisibilizing the distribution of entitlements and disablements in public-private alliances. Recall the public-private deals, grants, subsidies, protections, licenses, and so on that are distributed in a highly localized and contextualized manner. The identity or substance of the deals largely escapes notice. Given their localized and contextualized character, they are not easy to access or decode. Neoliberalism operates largely behind closed doors (law firm conference rooms) or through unseen algorithms (click, click).

The dissociative state meanwhile introduces the chaotic into the political-legal register—not only cognitively and intellectually but also in terms of the levers that legal entitlements and disablements make available. The triumph of uber-positivism and the absence of legal mind leads to a proliferation of perspectives, viewpoints, agendas, plans, and solutions that can have no overarching coherence, unless by accident or fortuity. Increasingly, identities fragment into electronic dust while structures fuse into oblivion.

What to do about this?

Law in constitutional democracies is *organized reflexively* to enable a kind of self-observation and self-monitoring.[3] Moreover, the self-observation of law is directed not just at the rules, policies, principles, and values of the legal system, but at *the interaction* of these rules, policies, principles, and values, with their designated (or unintended) regulatory objects. This self-observation is also directed at how these rules, policies, principles, and values affect (or not) other precincts of the legal system. On these latter issues, there is certainly internal contestation among jurists and legal scholars: What kind of relations should there be—coherence or contextualization? Harmony or compensation? Reinforcement or competition? All of this would have to be observed and monitored in a sustained and revealing way to yield a copacetic reflexivity.

The political-legal register of the American state comes nowhere near achieving the sort of self-observation required for its sustenance. The main reason is relatively simple: while the political-legal register does permit, and even demands, a degree of self-observation, the pathways and methods of self-observation are themselves truncated. The pathways and methods of self-observation are themselves too narrow, too confined, too constrained: law does observe itself, but it uses the same techniques to observe itself that it uses on its regulatory objects. The latter form of observation is (unavoidably) truncated and thus the former is too. It does not help that the "self-observation" that might be performed by legal scholars is itself largely modeled on concepts, idioms, and practices of jurists.

The law school classroom furnishes a striking example. Law students must learn topics far removed from their own personal experience: corporations, securities regulation, and so on. They typically learn the law on these subjects through judicial opinions. The students also have to learn, of course, the facts and real world contexts of the transactions at issue. Almost always, they learn these facts and the real world contexts through the judicial opinions. The result is that the law is almost always a perfect fit with the transactions described. Amazing.

Another example: In the past several decades, interdisciplinary approaches have made significant headway in legal thought. Economics, philosophy, linguistics, and cognitive science have been frequently deployed in legal scholarship. One would think then that this interdisciplinary activity would provide vantage points from which to enhance the self-observation of law. And to some degree it has, but the contributions have been far narrower than might have been hoped for. No sooner is the foreign discipline introduced to law than it is conscripted into service to improve law's architecture and performance, generally on law's own terms. It's not hard to see that if the foreign discipline is subordinated to the dictates of legal officialdom, its capacity to enhance self-observation will be limited. Indeed, the foreign discipline can be expected to repeat law's official scripts (albeit in a foreign idiom).

Why so narrow?

In legal scholarship, there is a curious, albeit widespread, presumption that the legal scholar is supposed to provide solutions or prescriptions to fix whatever issues or problem are raised. This presumption is captured in the ubiquitous questions "What should the courts do?" or "What should we do?" As questions go, these are not invariably bad ones. But these questions are not all-purpose inquiries. Nor are they always helpful. They can truncate awareness and reconnaissance. And there are certain controversial predicate assumptions that have to hold for the questions to be sensible.

Consider this parable:

Suppose that you are walking on a road and you come to a fork. This calls for a decision, for a choice. So you ask your companions: "Which fork should we take? Where should we go?" You all begin to talk about it, to consider the possibilities, to weigh the considerations. Given these circumstances, given this sort of problem, the questions "Where should we go?" and "What should we do?" are perfectly sensible.

Now suppose that it gets dark and the terrain becomes less familiar. You are no longer sure which road you are on or even if you are on a road at all. So you ask, "Where are we?" One of your companions says, "I don't know—I think we should just keep going forward." Another one says, "I think we should just go back." Yet another says, "No, I think we should go left." Given the right context, each of these suggestions can be perfectly sensible. But not in this context. Not anymore. On the contrary, you know very well that going forward, backward, left, or in any other direction makes no sense unless you happen to know where you are. So, of course, you try to figure out where you are. You look around for telltale signs. You scan the horizon. You try to reconstruct mentally how you got here in the first place. You explore. You even start thinking about how to figure out where you are.[4]

This would be awareness and reconnaissance. This is what we have been doing here. This is what it looks like.

The principal focus has been on law—albeit a very sweeping conception of law (the political-legal) and an extended time frame (centuries). Still, even such a sweep can be considered somewhat limited. What reason do we have, after all, to suppose that what has happened to law is somehow unique or special? Why not think about the evolution in broader terms—as culture-wide, for instance?

Taking a broad view turns out to be difficult. Yet it seems worth trying if only because the limits of disciplinary perspectives (law, economics, whatever) have no a priori claim over domains and functions. The mere fact that most universities have an economics department, for instance, in no way signifies that there is a corresponding discrete domain called "the economy."

In this chapter then, we have a last chance to take a more encompassing perspective. Let's think of law, legal architecture, and legalism more broadly as social and intellectual constructs not immune from the wider cultural, economic, and political milieus. With this shift in perspective, different diagnostic narratives become possible. These diagnoses are neither mutually exclusive nor exhaustive and they are all consonant with the through line (awareness and reconnaissance) in this book.

Culture-Wide Decadence

The concept of decadence has not done much work in this book—not as an analytical tool and not as a mode of analysis. What then of decadence as a diagnosis?

The political concept of decadence implies some kind of fall from a prior more vital or more admirable condition. Not surprisingly, the diagnosis of decadence appeals most to conservative or reactionary thinkers: decadence is consonant with the idea of having deviated from a sound tradition or the wisdom of the ages. There is thus an implicit or explicit claim that a better past was abandoned for a disappointing present and a bleak future. (Not surprisingly, fascists are fond of the concept.).

On the left, decadence rarely appeals as a diagnosis because it negates the progressive ambitions and teleology that explicitly or implicitly undergird and inspire so much leftist thought. The most notable contemporary exception on the left are some relatively rare Marxist deployments of the term as a basis for declaring that late capitalism is no longer vital, but is instead on its last legs, decayed and thus barely able to sustain or defend itself.

Decadence, of course, can be given a leftist twist if the focus of attention is shifted away from the condition itself (decay) to the question of its root causes. In this regard, it would not be difficult to show that neoliberalism is a driver of (or simply is) the decadence that has taken root. And decadence need not imply that the solution is a return to the status quo ante. That is just a non sequitur.

As a generalized diagnosis, however, the concept of decadence seems unsatisfying. The diagnostic seems shallow, even as it aims to describe something very deep. In part, this shallowness might be attributable to its character as a derivative concept: decadence is always only relative to some baseline state of affairs. It is that baseline that effectively defines the substance—the identity of the decadence in question. The remainder of the diagnosis is form. And as form goes, decadence is not terribly complex. Viewed as an *organic* metaphor, decadence is about decay and stagnation—ultimately, a slouch toward a literal or figurative corruption of something already dead. Viewed as *historical movement*, decadence indicates a kind a loss of direction or goals, a stall or a regression. None of this precludes movement (though not the desired one). Regression is movement, but almost by definition, in the wrong direction. As for the stall, what is key is the sense of not going anywhere. And there are many ways of not going anywhere: Arrest counts, but so does oscillation, arrested dialectics, circularity, or simply fevered excitation. The latter, when combined with artificial attempts to induce vitality by exciting the senses, helps connect the frivolous kind of decadence to the more serious kind: A society or a life that doesn't go anywhere often yields a desperate search for artificial stimulants and contrived distractions—anything to feel alive, to escape the sense of stasis. As decadence becomes normalized, the new baselines become the new floors. Everything needs to be amped up: decadence begets more decadence.

What has just been said is not useless in understanding the concept of decadence, but nonetheless, the diagnosis of decadence still seems lacking in depth. Indeed, the diagnosis of decadence often seems itself decadent— the charge is all too easy to deploy, as if the one issuing the charge of decadence can only barely muster the will or vitality to do serious analysis and thus settles for the delivery of a mere insult. As diagnosis decadence is a bit of a tautology. "And the explanation for our fallen condition is . . . wait for it . . . decadence (our fallen condition). Voila."

It is easy then for the diagnosis of decadence to seem unserious. Still . . .

Look around at America. We are a dissociative state that has lost track of its ideals. We are an infrastructure composed of judges, lawyers, and law professors who have but the thinnest account of their own law and who can barely identify its organizing logic. We are a socioeconomic system riddled with precarity and unconscionable wealth disparity. We are an oversized and incontinent mass culture given over to the vulgar, the vapid, and the violent. The list goes on: we are led by a class of cosmopolitan leaders who are culturally clueless, fatuously self-contented, and politically anemic. We are a people exhausted by needless trillion dollar wars. And all of this is soaked in a turgid mix of nihilism and cynicism.

So, yes, decadence is a plausible diagnosis. But before adopting this diagnosis (and calling it a day) consider that it is pretty much the end of the road. When a society suffers *from a culture-wide decadence*, there is no reason to believe that the very cultural processes typically relied upon to correct this state of affairs will not themselves be compromised by the very same condition—to wit, decadence.[5] In other words, with decadence there is no reason to suppose that the processes of replenishment, education, evaluation, selection, initiative, creativity, and revolution will not themselves be decadent. And, again, if we look around it is not hard to see that this has already happened.

Just one example: in the university, the triumph of administration over faculty is nearly complete. Accordingly, the standard administrative m.o. for deciding on how to evaluate programs, centers, and faculty follows something like this formula:

"We are all here in favor of providing the *highest quality* X."

"And, of course, to produce the highest quality X, *we need accountability.*"

"Good point, but accountability to what? I think we should *specify our objectives.* Perhaps a list then?"

"Yes, and the objectives should be *prioritized.*"

"Absolutely—and afterwards we *can establish benchmarks* so as to measure our success. . . ."

". . . So as to *enable longitudinal studies.*"

"Of course, but in that case, we need some method to ascertain whether we have reached our benchmarks. I suppose *what we need is some sort of scale?*"

"Yes. But doesn't that *depend on a metric?*"

Succinctly, summarized, the logic of institutional degeneration—the administration of mediocrity—is as follows:

Quality→Accountability→Objectives→Prioritization→Benchmarks→Scaling→Metrics→Mediocrity

This chain displays the inexorable logic of serial reductionism from the qualitative to the quantitative. It achieves its zenith when metrics become valued as ends in themselves (and quality drops out of view altogether).

If all this is correct, then, apart from fortuitous or exogenous shocks, decadence is destiny. An end of the line diagnosis. There is nothing to be done—because there is nothing to do it with, no one to do it, and no one to do it for.

If usefulness is the relevant criterion for a diagnosis, then decadence doesn't work very well unless it is aimed at selective targets. That is to say, decadence works best as a diagnosis to tag one's enemies, while affirming some logic to exempt oneself and one's friends. As a *total diagnosis,* by contrast, decadence is ultimately disabling because it strips everyone of agency. Everyone is a carrier and all are contagious. All of us are prone to reproduce decadence, even as we say and claim to do otherwise. This is an instance of the *agency problem,* to which we will return. In addition to the agency problem, decadence implies a *resource problem*: a culture-wide decadence implies we are lacking in the cultural and psychic resources to climb out of the holes we are busily digging. With both an agency problem and a resource problem, it is not clear at all how we could get out of this predicament.

Indeed, the decadence diagnosis is so devastating that even for conservatives or reactionaries who typically advocate some kind of return to the status quo ante, it is unclear, even in their narratives, who or what would be poised to return us to their preferred golden age. Nor is it clear, even if return were plausible, why we should not expect, upon a hypothetically successful return, a repetition of the same devolutionary story.[6]

Of course, just because the diagnosis of decadence is devastating does not make it untrue.

Macro Blockage—Micro Proliferation

The establishment of a constitution is a macro moment par excellence. Broad outlines are sketched out.[7] Jural concepts are laid down. Modes of interpretation are intimated. To be sure, a constitution is not all macro and not entirely revolutionary because a constitution, even if it claims to be constitutive and supreme, unavoidably relies upon, incorporates, and reenacts antecedent laws, legal institutions, and practices. Accordingly, it is to be anticipated that a constitution's "broad outlines" will be an internalization of the conceptual architectures and aesthetics of the extant micro-law (property, contracts, and so forth). Put differently, the "broad outlines" will often be a projection, largely through aesthetics, of concrete micro-law to the plane of constitutional abstraction.

As a constitution ages, the lawyers will fill out the micro-details of its macro-outlines. In turn the macro-outlines with their micro-details become sedimented in habitual forms of practice, institutional organization, architectural layouts, demographic dispersions—in short, in all aspects of material life. In turn, this materiality will reflexively accord a sense of reality, of plausibility to the status quo. The idea that "things could be otherwise" thus has to fight not only against a contrary political-legal idea (and the ostensible virtues of the status quo), but also against the considerable support that status quo ideas gain by their resonance with this sedimented materiality.

At some point, as a constitution ages, its once seemingly boundless possibilities reduce to small changes in *this* micro-detail or *that* one. The idea of changing the macro, by contrast, is experienced as impossible because so many micro-details (all of them materially sedimented) hang in the balance. The possibility of effecting change at the macro level thus diminishes. And all the action seems to be referred and channeled to the micro level.

This channeling and its narrowing effects are by no means limited to law or to the political-legal. In general, broad-ranging contestation of the character of the ontological, the theological, the political, and the intellectual are increasingly channeled into much more specialized, limited, constrained, and narrow activities. The channeling in place at both the intellectual and the material level is designed somewhat like this:

Macro→meso→micro

God→theology→religion→denominations→priests

The ontological→epistemic→normative→technical[8]

The political→ideological politics→program politics→interest-group politics

The intellectual→academia→discipline→expertise

Reason→reasonableness→ratiocination→calculation

Values→goals→norms→benchmarks→rankings

Politics→law→juridification→judicialization→constitutionalization→court watching[9]

Why does the tendency toward the micro prevail? One answer is that, should ever trouble arise, a "system" is likely to be more resilient and enduring if the trouble can be referred to the domains, institutions, or personnel located toward the micro end (not the macro end) of the spectrum. Why? Well, making adjustments or modifications to the micro is relatively easy and, the butterfly effect notwithstanding, disturbances tend to remain localized. By contrast, adjusting or modifying the macro is a much more consequential, less easily controlled, and definitely more disturbing affair. Consider an example from theology: to discover that your priest, rabbi, or imam is fallen and needs to be replaced is bad news. No doubt, it is upsetting. But whatever local discomfort might arise as a result, finding a replacement will be a relatively mundane problem. By contrast, discovering that your scriptures are erroneous poses difficulties of a different magnitude. As for finding out that your god is a fraud—that is pretty much a game-ender. This helps explain why successful theologies (religious or secular) tend to shuffle challenges away from their gods (the macro end) toward their humble priests (the micro end).

This sort of institutionalized, one-way channeling is thus wholly understandable. At the same time, it's important to recognize that few systems exhibit an *absolute* one-way channeling. Rather, it is a question of procedures, burdens, defaults, and inclinations. These are all organized to route or refer problems toward the micro. Meanwhile, movement toward the macro end is rendered more difficult. It is thus possible to move toward the macro end, but the entire ethos of the system is to move everyone and everything toward the micro end.

This is part of the reason those who are dispossessed or disfavored by the "system" must use particularly intense means (e.g., violence, mass protests, general strikes) to induce radical change. So long as it is clear that they will "stay within the system," their claims will be referred to the micro end where radical change is inhibited and deemed non-cognizable. In law, for instance, the insistence on obeisance to legal authority, the injunction to decide cases narrowly, and the common law insistence on analogy play huge roles in inhibiting change in legally cognizable entitlements and disablements.

All this being said, serious problems can arise if a system channels only in this narrowing and reductive way (i.e., an absolute one-way channeling). At that point, the system becomes blocked. Absolute one-way channeling becomes a recipe for authoritarianism in politics, hierarchy in social life, control and command in institutions, and domination in general. Indeed, in a sufficiently powerful one-way channeling, the possible human or institutional agents of change have been physically, socially, or intellectually neutralized or eliminated from the scene.

Blockage is arguably what the various iterations of the American state have produced: the political-legal has been narrowed such that conscious or deliberative efforts to reorganize or modify the state are increasingly blocked. This does not necessarily forestall change, but it does imply that change would require some sort of forceful disruption of the micro-channels in place. And, of course, change is not necessarily benign.

The Dark Specters

In recent work, Stephen Griffin describes two major dysfunctions that threaten to derail constitutional democracy: policy disasters and loss of trust.[10] Jack Balkin adds two more: increasing inequality and polarization.[11] Additions of similar stature could be offered (no doubt a short-lived interim measure to be supplemented by someone else). Still, we have at this moment:

   policy disasters
   loss of trust
   increasing inequality
   political polarization

We could add:

structural corruption

cultural nihilism

permanent war

These dark specters describe overlapping conditions. They are also interactive—often reinforcing each other in disquieting positive feedback loops.

One important thing to recognize is that these disturbances should not automatically be considered exogenous. They do not come out of nowhere. The state typically plays a role here. The state is not simply called upon to "respond" to emergencies or disasters. Its role is also to anticipate and prepare for major disturbances, and, most of all, to refrain from preparing the grounds for the dark specters that will be its undoing.

The dark specters are disturbing enough all on their own. But they are also disruptive because a state caught in the throes of macro blockage and micro proliferation is not equipped to address what turn out to be "macro-disturbances." Putting it more strongly, sometimes the state is poised to avoid addressing the macro-disturbances.

Misapprehending Social Coordination Systems

The Current Disorder could be seen as an unhappy situation resulting in part from the failure to recognize the ways in which our various modes of social coordination (e.g., law, morality, technology, police) interact. The separation of institutions and specialization of personnel leads us to think of these as arranged in the tidy form of the grid aesthetic (distinct domains) or some coherent form of the energy aesthetic (separation of functions). But the kind of ordering established by these two aesthetics seems out of time. Too much order, not enough flexibility. Not only do our modes of social coordination— for example, law and technology—compete with and contest each other, but in a more advanced logic they appropriate and colonize each other.

Recognition of this point would be a first step in exercising awareness and reconnaissance of the situation, the challenges posed, and possible responses. What makes the current situation so challenging is precisely that those who might be counted upon to provide understandings of how our various modes of social coordination are working (or not) do not stand outside these modes of social coordination. Not only are we living amid these various modes, but they are in us and, at the limit, they are us. Hence it is that the putatively reflective and self-critical aspects of various modes of social coordination (to wit, academia, journalism, education, various professional formations, and so forth) are derailed from playing their reflective and self-critical roles. The risk is that all of these institutions and professional formations are at risk of reproducing symptoms *rather than* reflection—or perhaps more accurately, reproducing symptoms *as* reflection.

Consider a possibility: What if one of the things that has helped produce the Current Disorder is a failure—in this case, a meta failure—to apprehend the character and actions of the various modes of social coordination and how they relate to each other? What if we, as the specialized carriers and progenitors of one or more modes of social coordination, were nonetheless (and within the limitations of our own blinders) momentarily able to perceive these difficulties? What would we do?

Here is a description of what the situation might look like.

Consider that the state is but one mode of social and economic coordination in competition with others, including markets, architecture, technology, morality, religion, and all manner of professions and knowledges, such as public health, social welfare, and administrative science. In our unreflective mode, we tend to think of these modes, knowledges, and professions as having their own *discrete domains or functions*. In this unreflective mode, we acknowledge a certain degree of overlap and contestation around the edges, but, when viewed unreflectively, these modes of social coordination are apprehended and represented as relatively discrete and linked to particular domains or functions that are relatively well defined. Notice that the university is still very much organized along these lines: the law school, the business school, the economics department, the political science department, the *whatever* department. Against this, of course, is the decades-old effort to create "interdisciplinary centers." It was certainly an inspired idea—though many of these centers hit the wall upon the recognition that reconciling *discrete knowledges* built over centuries on different, often incompatible assumptions is pretty much a deal breaker.

Once we start thinking about the various modes of social coordination explicitly, it is possible to imagine different *overarching social arrangements* in which the state, markets, policing, social welfare, architecture, technology, professions, and so forth might each play a much greater or much lesser role vis-à-vis the others. Though the image offered here is too quantitative and too simple, we could imagine arrangements with different ratios. Thus, with regard to any given social problem—poverty, drug addiction, whatever—it is possible to think of a social response that would involve different allocations of responsibility to the state, markets, social welfare, and so on.[12] Indeed, a "social problem" (whatever it might be) can be apprehended in any number of ways. Drug addiction, for instance, could be apprehended as a health/medical issue (requiring medical facilities and resources), a social welfare problem (requiring community-building and social assistance), an economic problem (requiring job creation and wealth redistribution), or even a military problem (hence, the figurative and literal "war on drugs").[13] The different framings motivate different kinds of responses, as well as enable the deployment of different kinds of knowledges and personnel wielding different analyses, tools, and responses.

The various modes of social coordination compete to achieve supremacy in addressing the problems—problems that, of course, they conceptualize differently. Indeed, as part of this competition, the modes also compete to apprehend and conceptualize social problems *in their own idioms*. This allows the various modes of social coordination to offer their analytical modes, tools, and responses, and their own personnel as crucial to the development of possible solutions.

If this is right, then we must abandon the conventional rationalist or analytical tendency to presuppose that the various modes of social coordination are themselves self-contained and distinct. (This conceit is in part a legacy of the grid aesthetic and professional guilds.) Instead, we can imagine that each of the modes of coordination might be, at times, more or less colonized by the others. One can imagine, by way of example, a police force that is juridified just as one can imagine a juridical system that is infused with policing. One can imagine an economy in which market and state actors are ostensibly kept separate (e.g., liberal democracy) or one in which market and state actors are conjoined (neoliberalism, industrial policy, dirigisme, cooperative governance, corporatism, fascism).

Beyond this, we might go a step further and recognize that each of the modes of social coordination, knowledges, and professions advance their power, not just by apprehending, but by constructing social realities (social artifacts and social agents) in their own image. So it's not merely a question of how modes of social coordination apprehend, frame, and define social phenomena (as mentioned above); there is also, for good or ill, a creative, constructive, performative aspect to the activities of the various modes of social coordination. The more successful (and law traditionally has been very successful) a mode of social coordination is in constructing social realities, the more easily it can then re-uptake those very same social realities as amenable to treatment according to its own methods, protocols, and personnel. Modes of social coordination construct and embed mode-specific "social handles" that are then used later as "the levers" or "footholds" to further expand domain and function. In addition, we might recognize that the various social coordination mechanisms (e.g., market, law, morals) advance their modes of social coordination by constructing social realities through means in which they enjoy comparative advantages. The market *commodifies, quantifies, and calculates.* The law *structures, decides, and enforces.* Morality *guilts and shames.* Architecture *objectifies and metonymizes.* The various social coordination mechanisms will create or construct (real or fictional) events, facts, texts, rituals, spaces, dramas that predispose parties to adopt their methods, follow their protocols, and heed their personnel. At some point, the modes become vigorously self-reflexive—observing themselves to the nth degree as they reference or analyze an object—a trial, a campaign, an election. Today, the algorithms of social media do that silently, invisibly for, in, and against us.

Importantly, the various modes of coordination advance their claims to supremacy or dominance by cultivating and communicating their ostensible normative, political, aesthetic, or instrumental virtues. Law, for instance, is portrayed as *careful, rational, orderly, fair, just, neutral, and deliberative.* Markets are portrayed as *flexible, adaptive, innovative, entrepreneurial, responsive, and decentralized.* Morals are portrayed as *virtuous, imperative, fundamental, and redemptive.* Technology is portrayed as … (and so on.) The crucial rhetorical maneuver—and in law, it is acutely manifested in judicial opinions—lies in *construing and constructing* the situation or the issue as one that calls for the virtues and capacities of the particular mode of social coordination to be deployed. The character of this "construing and constructing" ranges from the solicitous to the brutal, from the dialogical to the monological.

In the United States, law and politics have for a long time been widely understood among the populace as the dominant forms of deliberative self-governance. In other words, law and politics were viewed as the formations that constitute and organize the social and economic order. Americans turned almost instinctively to law and politics as these were understood to be the discourses, practices, and institutions of deliberative governance. Law and politics were understood to be *the* coordination mechanisms primus inter pares. None of this evident any longer.

Coda

Not everything that is faced can be changed, but nothing can be changed until it is faced.
—JAMES BALDWIN[1]

According to the story told here, the American state confronts a series of set pieces, all with attitude—all seemingly poised to produce bad outcomes. Not only has the American state developed into some highly destructive iterations (the neoliberal and dissociative states) but it confronts the possibility of some dark futures: political paralysis, structural corruption, nihilism, permanent war, the politics of spectacle, and authoritarianism. Whether and to what degree any of these dark futures materialize is a different question—decidedly not pursued here.

Set aside as well are the more positive aspects of our political-legal condition. And clearly there are some. Clearly things could be worse and in many parts of the world they certainly are. Far worse. But we do not need more self-celebration—and particularly not in law. It is, of course, easy to say, as some have, that an optimistic outlook is important because a pessimistic one is likely to become a self-fulfilling prophecy—helping to bring about precisely the conditions feared. This dictum is correct . . . as far as it goes, which is not very far given that any thinking person will soon encounter its opposite: optimism tends to breed problems because it leads people to ignore precisely the conditions that will precipitate their downfall.

Pessimism and optimism are relative terms—each referring to a baseline that does not exist independently of either orientation. When the two conflicting cautions in the paragraph above are brought together, they yield a dilemma where no one is guaranteed to be right in advance absent some untenable invocation of metaphysics or teleology. But invocation of either, at this late date, is implausible.

One possible evolution described in this book—the rise of the authoritarian state—is relevant not just in the U.S. but throughout the world. As many

have noted, the nascent authoritarian states do not dispense with the invocation of law (e.g., "law and order"). Rather, they honor law in its thinnest senses
and make it do the most brutal work. In the U.S., it could be that the rise of
the authoritarian state is an odd amplification of, as well as reaction to, the
dissociative state and its failing political-legal architecture.

It's not clear where the forces of reversal would come from. American
exceptionalism, untutored optimism, decades of inattention to the political-
legal infrastructure, and a bumptious legal outlook can only sustain so much.
At some point, despite the display of confidence, some reckoning with actualities seems unavoidable.

There is an economy of thought that suggests that insofar as the big problems escape resolution, we would do well to devote ourselves to addressing the small ones. Yes, that too is surely right . . . except to the degree that
devoting attention to solving the small problems doesn't make the big ones
go away. One wonders, looking around, whether inattention to the big problems has not produced a malign macro feedback: climate change, precarity,
inequality, environmental degradation, right-wing political lunacy, and post-
truth governance. These macro-issues render fixation on the micro somewhat unserious—akin to the proverbial rearrangement of deck chairs on the
Titanic.

I realize, of course, that to many readers, this book will seem nihilistic, the
counsel of despair, or some such thing.

I reject that flat out.

In moments when we acknowledge that a "system" suffers from radical
failures, these failures often have to do with the core assumptions, commitments, and institutions of a system that cannot fix itself. The system cannot
fix itself because it is grounded in those core assumptions, commitments,
and institutions, and thus lacks the intellectual, political, legal, and cultural
resources required to address the flaws. The system literally cannot "get over"
itself. To be sure, reflexivity in thought and action continue to happen—it
is just that it happens to be too narrow, too shallow, too weak—reaffirming
blithely what ought to be questioned. The idea that law has embraced mechanisms of denial now seems obvious. That this law then exports this infrastructure of denial throughout the body politic, the culture, and the individual seems clear. That much of this infrastructure is devoted to devising ways
of bypassing, working around, and circumventing law (producing the law of
nonlaw) is evident. That a great deal of the law of business transactions is an
oddly "privatized" version of the "state of exception" now seems thinkable.

As stated in the foreword, there is no conclusion here, no recommendation, no prescription, no fix. But this I do know: this is what we should be talking about. So, no, there's nothing nihilistic here. Nihilism, rather, is the attitude of turning away, averting the gaze, not wanting to see, not wanting to know. As if everything were all right. It's not.

NOTES ON METHOD

Relative to our social and intellectual conditions, we are not on the nearly finished edge of understanding and explanation. Indeed, while advances have been made in the human and social sciences, the political, economic, and social orders we have constructed (in part with the aid of those very same advances) have vastly outpaced and outdistanced our intellectual and academic efforts at integration. The most relevant criterion in terms of knowledge production at any given moment is not a time line in which *present* knowledge production is compared to *past* knowledge production. The relevant criterion is how does present knowledge production stand *relative* to its society by comparison to where past knowledge production stood *relative* to its society. Using this criterion, it may be doubted that this moment represents an apex.

Moreover, law as it has been thought and institutionalized is in the main a reactive endeavor: something new happens and at best law responds. Of course, it responds by tapping into its own traditions and conserving practices (which themselves, offer only so much latitude for creativity.) The art of law, so to speak, is securely grounded in the notion that if something has worked before, it will work again. Given such built-in time lags, law is constantly belated, and particularly so when history is unfolding at an accelerating rate.

The State

The idea of setting out various iterations of the state calls both for explanation and caution. As the text notes, with Foucault's highly influential bracketing of "the state" in favor of an *analytics of governmentality* "the state" became for a while a disfavored topic in academia. And not without reason. "The state" has been a sort of fatal attractant for all sorts of reifying as well as animistic formulations—investing the state with an ontology, essences, and capacities that fail to take into account the wide varieties of states and the radicality and speed of their transformations in extending and contracting the state/nonstate, the state/failing state, or the state of law/state of exception divides. It's all more fuzzy, pluralistic, and mutable than we have typically made it out to be. There is something powerfully right in Pierre Bourdieu's announcement that "the state is unthinkable."

In terms of American law, the state as such has not been the subject of much theoretical attention recently. One reason is that, from a legal perspective, the theoretical identity of the state is almost always referred to and then derived from the U.S. Constitution. That is to say that the Constitution, in establishing the United States (and in recognizing the several states), is, from a legal perspective, widely viewed as the ultimate authority on the identity of the state—its powers and limitations. In one sense, this cannot surprise: what the Constitution might mean or effectively do in its establishment of the state matters to courts, judges, and lawyers. Constitutional scholars oblige by playing a significant role in analyzing what the Constitution may say about the state. Despite their efforts and their internecine struggles (often very sophisticated) it's not clear that "the Constitution" can bear the weight of such attention. In any event, one thing that should probably not be expected from this work of constitutional exegesis are deep insights into the identity or character of the American state.

Why not? Well, because there is absolutely no reason to think that the authoritative juridical creators and interpreters of the U.S. Constitution have much of anything to say of theoretical interest about the identity of the state. Theoretical edification has not been their job, their forte, or their predilection. Instead, they are in many ways disabled in these regards.

Certainly jurists are not to be trusted on this score. They are the state—or rather they are the juridical facet of the state. They are "interested parties," and while their extrapolations matter (and need to be taken into account), according them authority so far as analytical or intellectual inquiry is concerned is a category mistake.

A huge one it turns out because the mistake is made often, broadly and apparently without much notice by legal scholars. Indeed, so far as American constitutional scholars are concerned, one might say that the mistake is baseline. Not to be mean or anything, but most of them are involved in the exegesis of a juridical theology by means of the theology itself.[1]

State as government. One referent for the state is basically what is often considered to be government. This idea of the state excludes all aspects of social life that are not readily identifiable as aspects of government. In a liberal democratic state, these are thought to include aspects of civil society such as the market, family, religion, and the like. This is a problematic conception of the state, however, because on further analysis, it turns out that pretty much all the institutions of civil society (including market, family, and religion) are regulated and constituted in part by the state. In modern societies, the market, family, and religion are shaped by the state. Once this is accepted it is not at all clear how the state conceived as government could somehow designate and segment some off its own actions and effects as external to itself. The attempt to do so is what in the U.S. is called "state action doctrine." It is an incoherent mess that, for understandable reasons, the U.S. Supreme Court tries to visit as little as possible.

The state as political-legal genre. A second referent for the state (one that is more interesting) is the idea of the state as a genre—one that encompasses the political and legal order of a given society. In this sense, we can speak of states as liberal democratic, monarchical, feudal, authoritarian, corporatist, and totalitarian. Viewing the state in this way, we abandon a government/ nongovernment distinction *except to the degree* that a particular state (e.g., the liberal democratic state) attempts to establish and enforce such a distinction. In these latter cases, the distinction becomes a characteristic, perhaps even a definitive feature of that state—even if the distinction is conceptually incoherent. The notion of political-legal genre is at work in this book. One might consider the four iterations of the state as political-legal genres—albeit genres that are in practice routinely conflated, hybridized, decomposed, recomposed, and so on. Whatever objectionable intimation of literary or discursive character is elicited by the term "genre" is hopefully dispelled by the qualification "political-legal"—implying coercion, realization, and legitimation as necessary aspects.

The form of the genre. What we still need to understand is the form of the state (or, to follow through on the above, the form of the genre). The state presents in many different guises. Sometimes it appears as an *agent*—and is thus easily personified (e.g., the state as police action). At other times, the state appears more as a *condition*, a state of affairs (e.g., the so-called *facilitative law* such as contracts that affords a system of rituals enabling certain kinds of transactions). At other times, the state appears more as a *set of relations* among various constitutional institutions (e.g., the state as separation of powers, federalism). At other times, the state appears more as a kind of *political-legal ontology*—an establishment of fundamental identities that enable relations to be established (e.g., the state as defined by identities such as persons, citizens, courts, and Congress). At other times, the state appears a kind of *political-legal logic*—an internal structure, langue, mode of thought, and so forth that effectively defines, organizes, and distributes political-legal actions. We could probably go on here to describe other possibilities. Let's not. Let's simply recognize that the state both as conception and as material social reality morphs into various forms—among them the state as . . .

Agent

Condition

Set of Relations

Political-legal ontology

Political-legal logic

And more

For purposes of this book, there is no attempt to nail down the form of the American state or its iterations to any one of these—neither as starting point nor as conclusion. There is thus no forthcoming "theory of the state" here. Instead, there is an *exploration* at the level of the four iterations of the state. In the same way that one would not want to prejudge the exploration of specific genres by an overly exigent or restrictive theory of genre, the same goes for the state. The point is to address the specific aspects of the four iterations of the state.

The need to avoid prejudging the political-legal identity of the state was made particularly clear during the writing of this book in the case of the neoliberal state. With only a bit of exaggeration, that particular iteration might be called a state of work-arounds, bypasses, circumventions, dispensations, and so forth. A legalized state of sundry exceptions from legality—akin to a "state of exception," but without resort to or invocation of emergencies, national necessities, or the like. The insidious growth of this neoliberal "nonstate state" is what paves the way for transition to the extremis of the dissociative state.

As a general matter, each iteration may well exhibit or transition from one or more of the forms mentioned above (agent, condition, and so on). In turn, the determination in any instance of whether it is more appropriate to represent the state in *this* form or *that* one will often be elusive and contestable. The idea of describing the state *apart from all* images, metaphors, and so forth is not an option. (Philosophers may have destroyed metaphysics, but not its language—a point that was made explicitly clear by Derrida in his attacks on logocentrism.)

The state as derivative. One of the enduring discussions about the state lies in its relations to aspects of society that are sometimes cognized as distinct: the economic, the social, and so forth. Is the state autonomous? Is it relatively autonomous? Or is it intertwined? Or dedifferentiating? Or what? We will not address these questions. Once temporality is considered, there is no reason to believe that the state might not morph from one of these relations to another.

One important point to note is that, even if state or law is derivative, it does not mean that the state is without effect or implication. The translation of the economic or the social into statal or legal terms can have effects such as coercion, entrenchment, and legitimation.[2] Moreover the state might be considered the Rome of the illocutionary.

Iterations

The idea of multiple iterations of the state requires caution that *these not be reified or thingified into four integrated entities—with discernible boundaries and essential characteristics—that are somehow animated to take turns occupying a mystical space called statehood.* At the same time, the state, as an actualization of governance mechanisms[3] and legitimation forms, is performed and achieved through the state's self-representation and self-actualization as "a presence in the world." The state creates its own self-illusions, which then serve to bring about the state's own presence in the world. The state may be an illusion, but if so, it is an illusion made real and indeed entrenched—and not just as a mode of thought, but as performance, relations, entailments, practices, and institutions.[4] The description of the four iterations are attempts to articulate the "logic" of each (with due attention to the fact that "logic" will itself have different meanings and identities in the four iterations). Again, as suggested above, it is not at all my goal to have the four iterations pass through some compulsory unitary theoretical archetypal template (e.g., "the ideal type"), but instead to allow each to emerge in part through its own idioms and self-conception.

It is also not my aim to suggest that these four iterations are frequently instanced in "pure" form. To the contrary, the iterations are often hybridized, fused, combined, and reciprocally referenced. They are routinely reified/dereified, formalized/deformalized, differentiated/dedifferentiated, and not just by academic observers, but more importantly by the people (e.g., administrators, judges, lawyers, citizens, parties, persons) who act them out.

At this point, it could very reasonably be asked: How can anyone possibly hope to identify a "logic" for each iteration given all the tumult and motion adverted to above? How can there be a "logic"? In fact, how can there be iterations at all? Good questions.

Two things.

First Thing: each of the four iterations operates a bit the way genres operate in fiction. Genres are like *fatal attractants*—they will draw both author and reader into a particular organization of the work of fiction (e.g., mystery, satire) to produce a certain literary effect. One doesn't write (or read) fiction any which way. And even if one wants to "break form" one can't successfully do it any which way. The iterations of the state are akin to genres. The iterations are fatal attractants—constellations of governance mechanisms and legitimation forms that tend to congeal into one of the four iterations. Again it might be objected that I will be describing the logics of illusions (again, four of them—no less). But it is important to appreciate that the ascription of illusion or fiction to the state is unlikely to make the latter go away.

Second Thing: sometimes the fatal attractants are no longer on the scene—that is to say, they are no longer attractants or they are no longer fatal, or both. This will be close to what is described in the latter part of the book as the dissociative state—something within reaching distance of the proverbial failing state.

Much of the discussion here aims to lead away from the idea that the U.S. is a liberal democratic state. The aim is not to deny the importance of liberal democratic aspects of the American state. But it is to get away from the presumption (so prevalent) that liberal democracy is the fundamental, essential, overarching, or the grounding aspect of the American state. That presumption institutes a further assumption—to wit, that the American state is somehow fully or mainly integrated. To call the American state a liberal democracy—as so many historians, legal thinkers, philosophers, politicians, and commentators routinely do—hides matters very important about the contemporary character of the American state. What this singular appellation, liberal democratic state, often affirms is a degree of integration of the American state into a singular unity ("the liberal democratic state") that is simply not helpful to analysis or understanding. This is a species of integration by designation or identity by nomenclature. Here the argument is instead that the U.S. is composed of several different iterations of the state that conflict and that continually vie for dominance. It is these conflicts that will help us understand the continuity and the metamorphosis of the American state. It will also help us understand the staggered drift of the U.S. toward the failing state.

Among American jurists and legal scholars (though not just) *integration by designation* is often prompted by a sequence of misguided reductionist moves. Jurists and legal scholars, for instance, typically seek a legal conception of the state (as opposed, for instance, to a sociological one). In turn, that prompts a turn to legal authority. That leads then almost immediately to consultation of the paramount self-declared authority—the U.S. Constitution. That crucial three-step move leads readily to designating the American state as a liberal democracy. The three-step move is suspect and would require what is virtually never forthcoming: a three-step justification.

This widespread mistake often yields an important concluding error. Once the heterogenous aspects of the American state are subsumed under the unifying heading of liberal democracy, the identity and character of liberal democracy must be loosened so that the heterogeneous aspects can indeed be seen as integrated. This is not just a matter of semantics or semantic creativity: the loosening of the identity and character of liberal democracy leads away from a full realization of the extent to which liberal democracy has already been partially abandoned and is currently challenged. The *integration by designation* also tends to obfuscate the degree to which the loosening hides sharp conflicts and contradictions.

This analytical shortfall is an instance of a more generalized mistake in American legal thought. Presuming a degree of coherence and integration at the outset, American legal thought typically tries to make sense of law. To that observation, one almost wants to reply, "Well, of course, it does! What would you have it do—try to make nonsense of law?" Right—except that the response misses something important. While it seems gratuitous and hugely unhelpful to try to make nonsense of law, that is not the issue. The issue is whether the legal scholar starts out with a project of making sense of law, setting aside *ab initio* the possibility that the object of inquiry (law) does not make sense. Not only is this priestly orientation problematic in itself, but it often leads to a truncation of analysis where the legal scholar allows his or her rationalizing project to establish precisely the kind of vision of law that will render his or her efforts at rationalization possible. This is circularity and there is nothing quite as good for self-validation.

I am more of an agnostic. Legal scholars should not be trying to make nonsense of law (a useless task), but they should try to detach themselves from the kind of theological predilection that rules out the possibility of nonsense from the beginning. The claim is often made in disciplines (law is not alone here) that we need to posit X (e.g., rational utility maximizer, sentence meaning,) in order for our research agendas to get anywhere. Maybe so, but that sort of begs the question—doesn't it? There is after all another obvious possible course of action. (We just need someone to turn off the lights.)

As I see it, assuming integration as a starting point and then looking for yet more integration (Ronald Dworkin?) is not helpful to analysis or understanding. There is a very real sense in which thinking can only begin after things have fallen apart for the thinker. No falling apart? Well, then, not much to explain, not much to understand—is there? Moreover, there is not much intellectual honor in understanding how things cohere if you have already presumed (1) that they do indeed cohere and (2) have also presumed the grounds therefor. Much of analytical jurisprudence comes to mind here.

A few more words now about the American state. I am trying to place emphasis on the four iterations of the American state. The interactions among the four iterations are pervaded by conflicts and contradictions. These in turn are variously defused, diffused, denied, or evaded by the particular iteration at stake, bringing about the compromise of each iteration and thus paving the way to the next one. By the time we reach the dissociative state, we have quite a mess on our hands. From there, one can glimpse the political-legal possibility of the *authoritarian temptation*.

Back?

In the first few pages of *The Political Concept of Law*, Schmitt famously showed that any attempt to identify "the political" would fail if the political were conceptualized by reference to the state. The reason Schmitt so concluded is that he perceived in the advent of the "total state" that the state could take all sorts of different forms and control any and all aspects of life. This argument was a predicate for Schmitt's articulation of "the political" (his true interest in "The Concept of the Political"). Nonetheless, it's clear that in the course of making this argument, Schmitt left the idea of "the state" and the project of theorizing the state decisively weakened.

Michel Foucault bracketed "the state" in favor of "a multiplicity of force relations." From Foucault:

> The analysis, made in terms of power, must not assume that the sovereignty of
> the state, the form of the law, or the over-all unity of a domination are given at
> the outset; rather, these are only the terminal forms power takes. . . . It seems
> to me that power must be understood in the first instance as the multiplicity
> of force relations immanent in the sphere in which they operate . . . and lastly,
> as the strategies in which they take effect, whose general design or institu-
> tional crystallization is embodied in the state apparatus, in the formulation of
> the law, in the various social hegemonies. Power's conditions of possibility . . .
> must not be sought in a central point, in a unique source of sovereignty from

which secondary and descendent forms would emanate; it is the moving substrate of force relations. . . . It is in this sphere of force relations that we must try to analyze the mechanisms of power. In this way we will escape from the system of Law-and-Sovereign which has captivated political thought for such a long time.[5]

Yes again. Or, more accurately, yes to the aspiration of freeing inquiry from unreflective positings of the state or sovereignty as a starting point for the analysis of power. Analysis of the power of "the state" cannot start by presuming the state's existence (and then tracing how "it" achieves that status and political-legal realization). That would illegitimately pack the subject (here, "the state") with the potentialities to effectuate precisely what needs to be understood or explained. Friedrich Nietzsche had a few devastating things to say about this sort of reasoning—one which takes a happening and then divides it into a subject (e.g., the thunder) and its action (e.g., the roar). This division comports with daily parlance: we typically say that the thunder roars. Nietzsche sharply corrects this usage, noting that the thunder *is* the roar. Now, if the notion of thunder as a subject that roars ought to give us pause, then treating "the state" as a subject ought to give us vertigo.

As against all this, the perceptive Foucauldian focus on "the relation of forces" can only be a part of the story. Another part lies in going in the other direction—namely, showing how the state (even as fiction or illusion) produces effects, implications, and scripts repeatedly acted out by jurists, legal scholars, officials, parties, firms, citizens, and so on.[6] Again, it's one thing to try to avoid the dead-ends and the false paths encountered as the result of an ontological positing of the existence of the state. But the identification of dead-ends and false paths does not mean that the state goes away or that the state has no effect. The state may be a fiction or an illusion, but even if so, that does not mean that the fiction, the illusion isn't real.[7] Nor does it mean that the state is not entrenched—as practices, as institutions, as materiality.[8] Nor does it mean that the state is not lived out in the everyday. The same can certainly be said about law: in many ways, law is an elaborate network of fictions. At the same time, no one should forget that law is among the most compelling and efficacious of fictions—collectively lived out in the everyday and often very convincingly enforced when actors deviate too far from the scripts.

To push the point a bit further it seems, from the admittedly limited and highly contestable perspective of a jurist or a legal scholar, that Foucault effectively eliminates the juridical object of inquiry and its possible effects. It's true, of course, that in light of the "paradox of inquiry",[9] one needs to take sufficient detachment from the object of inquiry to avoid merely repeating its moves or actions. At the same time, however, one needs to avoid taking up an approach that eliminates the object of inquiry *ab initio*.

Taking all this into account, the idea here is to discuss the iterations of the state in terms of various *modes of governance and legitimation schemes*. These modes rarely appear in practice as pure or unmodified instantiations of the various iterations. Instead, they are fused, merged, hybridized, aggregated, and internalized in all sorts of ways. At the same time, they are also in competition, conflict, contradiction, and antagonism.

This prompts the question: How could the modes of governance possibly be both (e.g., fused and conflicted) at once? Don't the iterations have to have a distinctive identity in order for them to conflict . . . but if they have a distinctive identity how then can they possibly be fused? Right—exactly. The way to think about it is that the various iterations are in contests of differentiation and dedifferentiation, of formalization and deformalization and the like. The iterations are not "things" with fixed object-like identities, but rather mutable modes of organizing *and* disorganizing political-legal practices. The idea in political-legal analysis is to try to retain allegiance to this insight while at the same time using whatever intellectual resources are available to reveal the various patterns (or at least their possibility).

The Political-Legal Register

One of the things that this expression, *the political-legal register*, is designed to do is avoid the partiality and reductionism of conceptions that would distinguish the political and the legal. That too would engage disputes that are not terribly helpful here.

More specifically, the expression "political-legal" is meant to sidestep a long-standing point, initially raised by Schmitt and later U.S. critical legal studies, that law is political. Much of the work of U.S. critical legal studies was designed to show in a variety of ways that law is politics. The expression *political-legal register* is designed deliberately to move beyond those claims by bracketing the question out of existence: law here is assumed to be political. How and in what ways is left unresolved. But the virtue of the political-legal as an expression is that it reprieves us from having to determine the relations of law to politics and to allocate between the two.

The identity and character of the political-legal is thus itself politically legally contestable. Viewing things this way comes at some cost: the political-legal remains somewhat vague, not fully nailed down. That is to say that this expression accommodates a wide array of different conceptions of what is and what is not political-legal.

Here to close off is a relatively uncontroversial idea: the state is not composed solely of the political-legal. There are aspects of the state that are typically viewed as not *distinctly and solely* political-legal and that are nonetheless crucial to form a state's identity and character:

> the composition of the leadership class
> the training and capacities of functionaries
> the links between the state and its supporters, enemies, clients
> the state's role in international and transnational economic and cultural affairs
> the state's economic and financial status
> the degree of institutionalization
> and more[10]

These, of course, are not impermeable, exclusive, or exhaustive aspects. At different moments these aspects will be activated and invoked to varying degrees, in varying ratios to perform different tasks. Law has something to say about the relative power of all these aspects just as they have something to say about the power of law.

NOTES

Chapter 1

1. José Ortega y Gasset, *Man and Crisis* (1958).

2. Matthew C. MacWilliams, *On Fascism: 12 Lessons from American History* (2020).

3. *Supra*, note 2. https://www.theatlantic.com/magazine/archive/2020/06/underlying-conditions/610261/

4. Victor Davis Hanson, *The Case for Trump* (2020).

5. This tracks Duncan Kennedy's "gaps, conflicts and ambiguities." Duncan Kennedy, *A Critique of Adjudication (fin de siècle)* (2001).

6. *See* Ivan Illich, *Deschooling Society* (1995).

7. This egalitarian aspect manifests itself first in limited ways as in formal equality, which becomes over time more substantive. Equality before the law requires some degree of social equality. This move from formal to substantive equality, even though limited, yields a displacement (not extinction) of the state/civil society distinction. In the United States, a great deal of movement occurs under legal headings of the equal protection clause of the Fourteenth Amendment and civil rights legislation. The great limitation of this expansion of equality is that the rights that get equalized remain themselves steeped in inequality. And, of course, is advanced all that much if the rights to be equalized are effectively rights to midlevel misery.

8. This usage may be unusual among U.S. jurists and legal scholars, but in other domains it is not so clearly unconventional. For instance, Max Weber, in addition to his institutional conceptualization of the formal rationality of bureaucracy, also treated it as a mode of reasoning—to wit, means-ends rationality. Max Weber, *Economy and Society* 215–16 (Guenther Roth & Claus Wittich eds., Ephraim Fischoff et al. trans., 1978).

9. This all goes back to Karl Marx, Carl Schmitt, Franz Neumann, and Friedrich Hayek.

10. Jon D. Michaels, *Constitutional Coup* (2017); Duncan Kennedy, *Three Globalizations of Law and Legal Thought 1850–2000* in *The New Law and Economic Development, A Critical Appraisal* 22 (David Trubek and Alvaro Santos, eds., 2006); Ed Rubin, *Beyond Camelot: Rethinking Politics and Law for the Modern State* (2005); Bruce Ackerman, *We the People (Foundations)*, vol. 1 (1993).

11. Indeed, one could note by way of example that John Rawls's legendary 1971 work, *A Theory of Justice*, self-consciously enshrines precisely this problematic. Indeed, what Rawls offers in his two principles of justice (the "first principle" about

maximum liberty and the "second principle" stating the "difference principle" for the allocation of basic goods) is precisely a restatement of this conflict articulated as a solution—at an Olympian level of abstraction. I mention Rawls's 1971 work here for the express purpose of illustrating that this conflict has been with us in unresolved form for some time. John Rawls, *A Theory of Justice* (1971). The conflict, of course, preceded Rawls. For an early effort in the critical legal studies literature to capture both the conflict and its erasure, *see*, Karl E. Klare, *The Judicial Deradicalization of the Wagner Act and the Origins of Modern Legal Consciousness, 1937–1941*, 62 Minn. L. Rev. 265, 280 (1978) (describing the absorption of legal realism by liberal thought as a kind of "social conceptualism").

12. In part, it is because they have de facto taken to heart William James's endorsement of the scholastic's advice: "When you encounter a contradiction, make a distinction." William James, *Essays In Pragmatism* 141 (1948).

13. No doubt the accretion of many William Jamesian distinctions in the effort to avoid contradictions plays a part in the production of this intricacy. *Id.*

14. See Chapter 4.

15. I am grateful to Andrew Coan for pointing this out.

16. For an exploration of this trend in the administrative (not the administered) state, *see* Michaels, *supra* note 21.

17. The arresting and historic 2016 election of Trump stands out as an indicator of a serious legitimation crisis. His election may be interpreted, *inter alia*, as a repudiation of the Establishment. Trump's election also signals a governance crisis—the loss of capacity or competency to govern. The election of Trump can also be seen as a response to failed governance—namely, the failure of the state to address the economic and social displacement wrought by globalization of markets and technological advance.

18. F. R. Ankersmit, *Political Representation* 91–92 (2002).

19. David Singh Grewal & Jedediah Purdy, *The Original Theory of Constitutionalism*, 127 Yale L. J. 664 (2018).

20. Herbert Marcuse, *One-Dimensional Man* (1964).

21. I am adopting a lesser known aspect of Schmitt's conceptualization of the political ("forms of life"), not the more widely known friend/enemy distinction.

22. We could go from here to a "death of law narrative." Here is what it would look like: it could be, though there is no way to tell, that the "state ruled by law" is an exhausted genre. More specifically, the idea that thought, encoded into texts, can effectively regulate action by virtue of the authority of legal norms may well be over. Although, again, there is no way to tell, we may well have gone through the available iterations. Just to be clear, I am not adopting this view. But the view can't just be ruled out.

Chapter 2

1. G. W. Hegel, *Phenomenology of Mind* (2003).

2. For a succinct historical account of this normative triumphalism, *see* Goncalo de Almeida Ribeiro, *The Decline of Private Law A Philosophical History of Liberal Legalism* 290–91 (2019).

3. F. R. Ankersmit, *Political Representation* 92 (2002).

4. Despite this critical caution, what follows in this chapter is a much more charitable account of liberal democracy than my earlier effort aimed at the practice of "liberal justification" by contemporary legal thinkers. Pierre Schlag, *The Empty Circles of Liberal Justification*, 96 Mich. L. Rev. 1 (1997) (hereinafter, Schlag, *Empty Circles*). The reason for the divergence is simple: what might be viewed as acceptable in an *actual* political-legal regime might well fall far short of what is acceptable in an *intellectual* effort at its justification.

5. This seems like a useful heuristic, but as most heuristics go, it is not necessarily universally applicable. While it may apply to the liberal democratic state and the administered state, it is less obvious that it applies readily to the neoliberal or the dissociative state. We will confront that problem later on. All of this is to say that it seems plausible to ascribe a degree of conscious construction-by-design to the liberal democratic and administered states that would be hard to ascribe to the later states.

6. Theodor Adorno, *Negative Dialectics* (1990).

7. Astra Taylor, *Democracy May Not Exist, But We'll Miss It When It's Gone* 11 (2020).

8. The point that other states—fascist, communist, theocratic, and the like—are even more deficient in this regard is neither here nor there.

9. The "rights" that Hobbes accorded the sovereign are extensive—indeed, by contemporary standards, remarkable. Thomas Hobbes, *The Leviathan*, Chapter XVIII (1651), https://www.gutenberg.org/files/3207/3207-h/3207-h.htm#link2H_4_0225

10. Kant was not a partisan of democracy, but he was a liberal.

11. Immanuel Kant, *An Answer to the Question: What Is Enlightenment?* in *What Is Enlightenment: Eighteenth Century Answers and Twentieth Century Questions* 58 (ed. James Schmidt 1996).

12. Alexander Somek captures the ethos succinctly:

[T]here has been a core of liberalism's association with law, namely freedom from interference or, *pace* "neo|Republicans," freedom from domination. Whatever end a liberal society is supposed to serve primarily, it uses parliaments and courts of law in order to erect bulwarks against state interference and to make sure that the rule of law is observed so that people can stand a fair chance to conduct their life in anticipation of how the state may react to their conduct.

Alexander Somek, *Liberalism and the Reason of Law*, 10 *Modern Law Review* 394, 395 (2020).

13. Frank Michelman, *Between Facts and Norms by Jurgen Habermas*, 93 J. Phil. 307, 309 (1996) (book review).

14. Frank Michelman, *Law's Republic*, 97 *Yale L. J.* 1493, 1500 (1988).

15. *Id.*

16. As David Dyzenhaus wrote, "it seems clear that once Hitler had come to power, Schmitt and the other conservatives had no philosophical resources to do anything but welcome him." David Dyzenhaus, *Legality and Legitimacy: Carl Schmitt, Hans Kelsen, and Hermann Heller in Weimar* 83 (1997).

17. Robert M. Cover, *Violence and the Word*, 95 *Yale L. J.* 1601, 1607 (1986).

18. David Singh Grewal & Jedediah Purdy, *The Original Theory of Constitutionalism*, 127 *Yale L. J.* 664 (2018).

19. Paul Kahn, *Political Theology: Four New Chapters on the Concept of Sovereignty* (Columbia Studies in Political Thought/Political History) 27 (2011).

20. It is true, of course, that all other political systems—theocracy, communism, fascism, and even anarchism—face the same kind of dilemma. Hence, the noted anarchist Mikhail Bakunin's endorsement of a secret police. Mikhail Bakunin, Rebuke of Nechayev, Mikhail Bakunin Archive at https://www.marxists.org/refere nce/archive/bakunin/works/1870/rebuke.html

21. For discussion in the U.S. context, *see* Stephen M. Griffin, *Constituent Power and Constitutional Change in American Constitutionalism*, in *The Paradox of Constitutionalism Constituent Power and Constitutional Form* 51 (eds. Martin Loughlin & Neil Walker 2007). Among the big breakthroughs was Bruce Ackerman's differentiation of ordinary from extraordinary politics in *We the People: Foundations* (Cambridge, MA: Belknap Press of Harvard University Press, 1991).

22. Or, in Rousseau's words:

> So he who draws up the laws doesn't or shouldn't have any right to legislate; and the populace can't deprive itself of this non-transferable right, even if it wants to, because according to the basic compact the only thing that can bind individuals is the general will, and the only way to be sure that a particular will is in conformity with the general will is to put it to a free vote of the people. I have already said this, but it's worth repeating it. *Thus in the task of law-giving we find two things together that seem incompatible: an enterprise that surpasses human powers, and for its execution an authority that isn't anything.*

Jean-Jacques Rousseau, *The Social Contract*, Book 2, Section 7 (1762) (The Law-Maker) (emphasis added).

23. Carl Schmitt considered "the people" politically inert, and taking a page from Lenin and his vanguard party, catastrophically determined that the people were in need of a "movement" to be provided by a political party—to wit, National Socialism. The argument is found in an understandably less often cited work of Carl Schmitt, "State, Movement, People"—which was his full-on theoretical embrace of National Socialism. Carl Schmitt, *State, Movement and People* (1933).

24. Jacques Derrida, *Force of Law: "The Mystical Foundations of Authority,"* 11 *Cardozo L. Rev.* 92, 923 (1990). Derrida describes this here as a circle though for him it is also an *epoché*—and accordingly, the foundations of authority remain shrouded in the mystical.

25. *Id.*

26. This is a dangerous line of argument as evidenced by the actions of the German National Socialists who in the interwar years glorified the "volk," and used this glorification to institute a politics of the worst kind.

27. Schmitt, *supra* note 23.

28. As for Marx's proletariat, it has been deskilled, deschooled, *embourgeoisé*, and plunged into the precarity of an atomizing gig dependency. To exaggerate only

a little, much of Marx's proletariat has been lumpenized. Moreover, even if it was once possible to believe in the proletariat as the universal class, confidence has been largely shattered by repeated working class reactionary tendencies throughout the twentieth century.

29. Carl Schmitt, *Constitutional Theory* 181 (2008).

30. Schmitt, *supra* note 29 at 181.

31. *Id.* at 187.

32. *Id.* at 187.

33. *See*, J. L. Austin, *How to Do Things with Words* (Oxford: Clarendon Press, 1962) (on the locutionary, illocutionary, and perlocutionary).

34. Schmitt, *supra* note 29_at 187.

35. For discussions of the role of bad faith in law (Sartrean and otherwise), *see*, Duncan Kennedy, *A Critique of Adjudication (fin de siècle)* 202-05 (1997); Duncan Kennedy, *The Hermeneutic of Suspicion in Contemporary American Legal Thought*, 25 *Law & Critique* 91, 125–27 (2014); David E. Pozen, *Constitutional Bad Faith*, 129 *Harv. L. Rev.* 885 (2016). For discussions of the rule of law and dirty hands, *see* Meir Dan-Cohen, *Decision Rules and Conduct Rules: On Acoustic Separation in Criminal Law*, 97 *Harv. L. Rev.* 625, 665–76 (1984).

36. Schmitt, *supra* note 29 at 187.

37. Franz Kafka, *The Trial* (1925).

38. Schmitt, *supra* note 29 at 204 (emphasis added).

39. David Dyzenhaus, *Legality and Legitimacy Carl Schmitt, Hans Kelsen and Hermann Heller in Weimar* 60–61(1997).

40. Schmitt, *supra* note 23 at 26-27.

41. A familiar and acute instance of this problem lies in how the liberal democrat should deal with those illiberal individuals or groups committed to its overthrow. As Alexander Somek succinctly puts it:

> As is well known, such insistence is the Achilles heel of "militant democracy" that is, the use of the coercive force of the state against anti|democratic political groups, which is both unavoidable and at odds with liberal democracy. It is unavoidable because it would be deleterious for a democratic polity if it tolerated its intolerant enemies; it is, however, also inconsistent with it since a liberal democracy is supposed to rest on free support by its citizenry not least for the reason that it leaves room for disagreement. Such support, however, can be reasonable only if it is uncoerced. Any use of threat of violence in order to sustain liberal democracy asphyxiates its free endorsement by reason and hence puts into question whether it is indeed worthy of support.

Alexander Somek, *Liberalism and the Reason of Law*, 84 *Modern L. Rev.* 394 (2020) (citing, *see* K. R. Popper, *The Open Society and Its Enemies: New One Volume Edition* 581 (Princeton: Princeton University Press, 1994).

42. Alexander Bickel, *The Least Dangerous Branch* 16–17 (1962).

43. Barry Friedman, *The Counter-Majoritarian Problem and the Pathology of Constitutional Scholarship*, 95 *N.W.U. L. Rev.* 933, 936 (2001).

44. Bruce Ackerman, *We the People (Foundations)*, vol. 1 (1993).

45. Steven Winter, *An Upside/Down View of the Countermajoritarian Difficulty*, 69 *Tex. L. Rev.* 119, 1921–23 (1991). As Winter puts it:

What begins as a problem concerning the legitimacy of judicial review in a democracy invariably and inexplicably turns into a debate about judicial method. Routinely, discussions of the countermajoritarian difficulty undergo a stunningly swift metamorphosis from a question of institutional legitimacy (what justifies judicial review?), to one of institutional relations (how should the Court coordinate with the "political" branches?), to one of institutional competence (what is it that courts do better than legislatures?), to one about institutional role performance (has the Court acted in a properly constrained manner?).

Id. at 1922–23.

46. This is a bit unfair to Chief Justice Marshall: he was a bit more nuanced given his recognition of constitutional "political questions" as beyond the reach of the Court. 5 U.S (Cranch) 134, 167 (1803).

47. For Arthur Leff,

[The] ultimate normative power is divided between two fundamentally different conceptions of personhood: person as fundamental moral building block of "people," and person as mere constituent cell of the fundamental moral entity known as "the people." In short, the Constitution simultaneously establishes rights and democracy. It may by now be obvious why it could not be otherwise. As we have seen, if total, final normative authority were assigned to each biological individual, and he were made morally autonomous, no rules to govern the interaction between those individuals—the Godlets, as I have called them—could be justified under the assumption of moral autonomy. There would be nothing but rights. If, on the other extreme, moral finality were lodged in "the people" as a class, then no claim for moral breathing space could be upheld for any atom out of which the class was constituted. If "the people" decided, by whatever process it validated, what was right, it would be unchallengeably right for each person: there could be no rights.

Arthur Leff, *Unspeakable Ethics, Unnatural Law*, 1979 *Duke L. J.* 1229, 1246 (1979).

48. Schlag, *Empty Circles, supra* note 4.

49. For an interesting comparison and contrast of the U.S. Constitution to the British royal family, see Duncan Kennedy, *American Constitutionalism as Civil Religion: Notes of an Atheist*, 19 *Nova L. Rev.* 910, 911 (1995).

50. Karl Marx's description remains one of the most lucid (and one keyed to the United States). Karl Marx, *On the Jewish Question*, in *Karl Marx & Frederick Engels: Collected Works 1843–44*, 3:146 (Jack Cohen et al. trans., 1975). For a recent overview of rule of law conceptions, *see* Frank Lovett, *A Republic of Law* (2016). In discussing the rule of law, I will generally follow Franz Neumann's insistence on *the generality of norms* (and the separation of state and civil society) as crucial. Franz Neumann, *The Rule of Law: Political Theory and the Legal System in Modern Society* 185–86, 212–65 (1986). In the U.S., the more well-known variant of rule of law was articulated by

Lon Fuller in his list of formal virtues (e.g., publicity, notice, generality) Lon Fuller, *The Morality of Law* (1969). As Neumann noted prior to Fuller's work, such formal criteria (which, of course, preexisted Fuller) are implicit in the idea of following the generality of norms. As for the ideas that governance should depend upon "the rule of law, not men," and especially that law should not be "arbitrary," these variants are also relevant and important, but, for obvious reasons, somewhat lacking in analytical and critical bite. For a good general introduction on U.S. conceptions of the rule of law, *see* Richard H. Fallon Jr., *"The Rule of Law" as a Concept in Constitutional Discourse*, 97 *Colum. L. Rev.* 1 (1997).

51. For the sake of clarity, at no point is the term "liberal" used here in its contemporary colloquial sense.

52. In a slightly different vein, it might be noted that the nearly sacred reverence in which the U.S. Constitution is held in the U.S. by both citizens and legal professionals (including academics) goes a long way toward explaining the archaic particularities of American political-legal culture.

53. *But see* Shelley v. Kraemer, 334 U.S. 1 (1948).

54. Typically, in liberal thought, state and civil society are apprehended as separate and distinct "spheres," "realms," "zones," "sectors," "areas," and "regions"—in short, territorialized spatial areas. I treat this prefiguration as an aesthetic determination—specifically, an aspect of the grid aesthetic. On the latter, *see* Pierre Schlag, *The Aesthetics of American Law*, 115 *Harv. L. Rev.* 1047, 1055–70 (2002) (the "grid aesthetic"). Such a spatial separation is not self-evidently possible at this historical juncture: the various social coordination systems (e.g., the legal, the technological, the economic) have already imposed their logics, idioms, and grammars on, within, and through each other. The aesthetic (or it is metaphysical?) spatialization move that posits them as distinct and then seeks an account of their relation is itself suspect: there is, *at the conceptual and theoretical level*, no economics that is not legal, no legal that is not technological, no technological that is not . . . and so forth. Pierre Schlag, *The Dedifferentiation Problem*, 42 (1) *Cont. Phil. Rev.* 35 (special issue on Continental Philosophy of Law) (2009). Note that this does not mean that life or reality is all monochromatic (that would be silly—I do not know anyone who experiences things that way). It does mean, however, that our conventional theoretical constructs and our classic conceptual strategies for constructing theories may need some work.

55. Pierre Schlag, *Hohfeldian Analysis, Liberalism and Adjudication* in *The Legacy of Wesley Hohfeld: Edited Major Works, Select Personal Papers, and Original Commentaries* (Shyam Balganesh, Ted Sichelmnan, & Henry Smith, eds., Cambridge University Press 2022) (explaining the difference between the horizontal and vertical dimensions).

56. Public notions appear in various doctrinal areas in a variety of different doctrinal formulations: public realm, public law, public rights, public interest, public policy, public figure, public utility, open to the public, public accommodation, and so on.

57. Private notions appear in various doctrinal areas in a variety of different doctrinal formulations: private realm, private law, private rights, private property, private right of action, right of privacy, invasion of privacy, private information, private association, private place of business, private figure.

58. In the United States, these notions are spelled out in (though not necessarily exhausted by) many constitutional provisions.

59. It is irrelevant in this context whether the sovereignty of the individual liberal subject is grounded in and circumscribed by the "will theory" or instead the "interest theory." That is an old and important dispute, but it is not implicated *at this point*. For an introduction to the dispute, *see* Leif Weinar, *Rights, Stanford Encyclopedia of Philosophy* (2020), https://plato.stanford.edu/entries/rights/#FuncRighWillTheoInte Theo

60. John Rawls, *A Theory of Justice* (1971).

61. Pierre Schlag, *The Knowledge Bubble—Something Amiss in Expertopia* in *In Search of Contemporary Legal Thought* (Justin Desautels-Stein and Christopher Tomlins eds., Cambridge University Press 2017).

62. Franz Neumann provides an apt summary. Neumann, *supra* note 50 at 187–98 (1986) (referencing Smith, Bolingbroke, and Sidgwick).

63. *The Federalist No. 51*, at 347 (Alexander Hamilton) (Jacob E. Cooke, ed., 1961).

64. Marx, *supra* note 45 at 154.

65. Robin West, *Reconstructing Liberty*, 59 *Tenn. L. Rev.* 446–53 (1992).

66. Joseph William Singer, *The Legal Rights Debate in Analytical Jurisprudence from Bentham to Hohfeld*, 1982 *Wis. L. Rev.* 975 (1982); Duncan Kennedy, *The Stakes of Law or Hale and Foucault!*, 15 *Leg. Stud. F.* 327, 328–41 (1991); Pierre Schlag, *How to Do Things with Hohfeld*, 78 *Law & Contemp. P.* 185 (2015).

67. The liberal democratic state, from its own perspective, *lacks the political-legal conceptual feedback mechanisms* through which to register the problems and conflicts of civil society. This is not some sort of *contingent or accidental deficit*. On the contrary, this is deficit by design: it is the negative consequence of what liberal democracy views as its beneficent "hands-off" civil society. But, this design means that the state cannot have it both ways. Viewed from the other side, the political-legal structures and mechanisms designed to leave civil society alone are also and simultaneously the political-legal structures and mechanisms that preclude learning what is happening in civil society. There are political-legal costs and vices of not knowing what is happening in civil society.

68. As Kennedy & Michelman have aptly put it, "law abhors a vacuum." Once an entitlement or a disablement is created in law, it can be changed or reallocated, but it is damned hard to extinguish it. Duncan Kennedy & Frank Michelman, *Are Property and Contract Efficient?*, 8 *Hofstra L. Rev.* 711, 760 (1980).

69. J. L. Austin, *How to Do Things with Words* (1962).

70. Frank Michelman & Duncan Kennedy, *Are Property and Contract Efficient?*, 8 *Hofstra L. Rev.* 711, 760 (1980).

71. *Id.*

72. For elaboration, *see* Schlag, *Hohfeldian Analysis*, *supra* note 55.

73. For an extended discussion, *see* Kennedy, *supra*, note 66; Singer, *supra*, note 66.

74. Schlag, *The Aesthetics*, *supra* note 54 at 1055–70.

75. George Lakoff & Mark Johnson, *Metaphors We Live By* 29–32 (1980) ("the container metaphor").

76. To all this we can add a more materialist origin story: in the 1800s, few things

were more important than land and thus its legal status. Land, of course, is already spatialized. It becomes territorialized through the legal establishment of borders and boundaries. Because of its economic importance, land thus arguably becomes the model for property and the legal incidents of property. Thus the characteristics of land are projected onto property rights and from there onto other rights. The form of property law is thus abstracted (in the manner described) and accordingly this form acquires a near universal character expressed in the aesthetic of the grid. Thus it is, as Jennifer Nedeslsky showed, property (in the sense of both law and its object) played a huge role as inspirational and formative metaphors and images for the construction of many other very different rights—privacy, freedom of speech, and so on. Jennifer Nedelsky, *Private Property and the Limits of American Constitutionalism: The Madisonian Framework and Its Legacy* 167 (1990).

77. Langdell (at great length) by way of demonstration:

> Equity jurisdiction is a branch of the law of remedies; and as it affects, or is affected by, nearly the whole of that law, it is impossible to obtain an intelligent view of it as a whole without first taking a brief view of the law of remedies as a whole. Moreover, as all remedies are founded upon rights, and have for their objects the enforcement and protection of rights, it is impossible to obtain an intelligent view of remedies as a whole, without first considering the rights upon which they are founded.
>
> Rights are either absolute or relative. Absolute rights are such as do not imply any correlative duties. Relative rights are such as do imply correlative duties.
>
> Absolute rights are of two kinds or classes: First, those rights of property which constitute ownership or dominion, as distinguished from rights in the property of another,—*jura in re aliena*; secondly, personal rights; *i.e.*, those rights which belong to every person as such.
>
> Relative rights, as well as their correlative duties, are called obligations; *i.e.*, we have but one word for both the right and its correlative duty. The creation of every obligation, therefore, is the creation of both a right and a duty, the right being vested in the obligee, and the duty being imposed upon the obligor. Undoubtedly the word "obligation" properly expresses the duty, and the use of the same word to express the right is a defect of nomenclature which is unfortunate, as it has given rise to much confusion of ideas. [etc. etc. etc.]

Christopher Columbus Langdell, *A Brief Survey of Equity Jurisdiction*, 1 *Harv. L. Rev.* 55, 56 (1887).

78. Lawrence M. Friedman, *A History of American Law* 535 (1973).

79. Nedelsky, *supra* note 76.

80. One classic exposition here is Felix Cohen, *Transcendental Nonsense and the Functional Approach*, 35 *Colum. L. Rev.* 809 (1935).

81. On vexations peculiar to the grid aesthetic, *see* Schlag, *The Aesthetics*, *supra* note 49 at 1062–70.

82. Singer, *supra* note 66; Kennedy *supra* note 66; Schlag, *supra* note 66.

83. *Id.*

84. For a succinct discussion of this aspect of the history, see Morton Horwitz,

The History of the Public/Private Distinction, 130 *U. Pa. L. Rev.* 1423 (1982) and particularly at 1424–27.

85. I am referring to the empirical social science ambitions of the legal realists. Beyond parking studies and the like, these did not fare well. John Henry Schlegel, *American Legal Realism and Empirical Social Science* (1995).

86. Joseph William Singer & Isaac Saidel-Goley, *Things Invisible to See: State Action and Private Property* 5 *Tex. A&M L. Rev.* 445 (2018).

87. 334 U.S. 1 (1948).

88. Thurman W. Arnold, *Criminal Attempts: The Rise and Fall of an Abstraction*, 40 *Yale L. J.* 53, 58 (1930) (quoting Thomas Reed Powell).

89. Richard L. Abel, *Why Does the ABA Promulgate Ethical Rules*, 59 *Tex. L. Rev.* 639 (1981).

90. The not infrequent sense that the solutions offered are coherent, is achieved in virtue of careful *framing, scaling, temporizing, and scoping.* (Once the *framing, scaling, temporizing, and scoping* vanish, the sense of coherence has a tendency to vanish.)

91. Abel, *supra* note 89.

92. Arthur Leff, *Injury, Ignorance and Spite—The Dynamics of Coercive Collection*, 80 *Yale L. J.* 1, 25–26 (1970).

Chapter 3

1. As quoted in Dwight Waldo, *The Administrative State: A Study of the Political Theory of American Administration* 69 (2007).

2. Today, most commentators (rightly) differentiate sharply between fascist and administrative states, but in the 1930s, the character of these various regimes was emerging and their directions were not entirely clear. Commentators in law as well as economics at the time were watching the rise of fascist states and, in some senses, not having yet experienced in the 1930s the full horror of fascism, saw considerable similarities between the evolution of administrative states and fascist states. Thus, some commentators, politicos, and academics at the time viewed FDR's New Deal as a kind of economic fascism. *See generally*, Wolfgang Schivelbusch, *Three New Deals: Reflections on Roosevelt's America, Mussolini's Italy, and Hitler's Germany, 1933–1939* (2007). One commentator who opined that the distinguishing factor in fascism was its economic program (not dictatorship) described FDR's programs as fascist—aimed at securing welfare for the middle class. Francis E. Brown, *The American Road to Fascism*, 38 *Current History* 392, 396 (1933) (fascism as "an adaptation of the fundamentals of capitalism, but under government control.") Interestingly, Julius Stone, the noted jurisprudential thinker, believed that the intense planning of civil society in fascist Italy was actually something that democratic states had already accomplished. Julius Stone, *Theory of Law and Justice of Fascist Italy*, 1 *Modern L. Rev.* 200 (1937).

3. Duncan Kennedy, *Two Globalizations of Law & Legal Thought: 1850–1968*, 36 *Suffolk L. R.* 63, 649–50 (2003).

4. Bruce A. Ackerman, *Foreword: Law in an Activist State*, 92 Yale L. J. 1083, 1084 (1983).

5. Theodor Adorno, *Negative Dialectics* (1990) (first published in German 1966) 96; Herbert Marcuse, *One-Dimensional Man* (1966).

6. *See*, e.g., Jerry L. Mashaw, *The American Model of Federal Administrative Law: Remembering the First 100 Years*, 78 Geo Wash. L. Rev. 975–76 (2010) (noting that the rise of the administrative state is ascribed to this moment, but documenting that administrative law was in existence throughout the nineteenth century); Jerry L. Mashaw, *Creating the Administrative Constitution: The Lost One Hundred Years of American Administrative Law* 1–13 (2012).

7. Reuel Schiller, *The Era of Deference: Courts, Expertise, and the Emergence of New Deal Administrative Law*, 106, Mich. L. Rev. 399, 421–25 (2007) (describing the 1938 ABA annual report). The gist of the argument was that the agencies were not sufficiently like courts. Since they were not like courts—or so the argument went— the 1938 ABA Annual Report concluded that the work of the agencies ought to be submitted to exacting judicial review. *Id.*

8. Richard Pildes captures the ethos of this "institutional formalism":

When courts engage in reviewing the actions of other governmental institutions, such as Congress, they nominally apply, or purport to apply, what I call "institutional formalism." This formalism consists of treating the governmental institution involved as more or less a formal black box to which the Constitution (or other source of law) allocates specific legal powers and functions. Legal doctrine, that is, assimilates the institution—"the Congress," or "the President"—at a high level of abstraction and generality. By design, this institutional formalism blinds courts to any more contingent, specific features of institutional behavior, or to the particular persons who happen to occupy the relevant offices, or to the ways in which the institution actually functions in particular eras in which the institution is embedded within distinct political, historical, and cultural contexts.

Richard Pildes, *Institutional Formalism and Realism in Constitutional and Public Law*, 2013 Sup. Ct. Rev. 1, 2 (2013). Pildes contrasts this institutional formalism with institutional realism (also a prevalent genre).

9. Duncan Kennedy, *Three Globalizations of Law and Legal Thought 1850–2000* in *The New Law and Economic Development: A Critical Appraisal* 22 (David Trubek and Alvaro Santos, eds., 2006) (hereinafter, *"Three Globalizations"*); Pierre Schlag, *The Aesthetics of American Law*, 115 Harv. L. Rev. 1047, 1070–80 (2002) (hereinafter, *"Aesthetics"*); Pierre Schlag, *Rights in the Postmodern Condition*, Austin Sarat & Thomas R. Kearns, eds. *Legal Rights Historical and Philosophical Perspectives* 284–300 (1996).

10. The description of the administered state that follows will differ from all three descriptions as well. It's a question of perspective as well as choice of different topics and materials.

11. Schlag, *Aesthetics*, *supra* note 9.

12. Schlag, *Aesthetics*, *supra* note 9 at 1071.

13. This is, depending upon one's politics (left/right, statist/anti-statist), anywhere from perfectly fine to absolutely horrible. Mostly, it is the libertarian right (Friedrich Hayek, Ludwig von Mises, James Buchanan, Richard Epstein, Randy Barnett, and more) who have been most vocal and visible in their objections.

14. Lauren B. Edelman & Mark C. Suchman, *When the "Haves" Hold Court: Speculations on the Organizational Internalization of Law*, 33 *Law & Soc. Rev.* 941, 943 (1999); *See also* Tehila Sagy, *What's So Private about Private Ordering?*, 45 *Law & Soc. Rev.* 923 (2011).

15. This, by the way, is one reason the recent opinions of the Supreme Court are so ghastly to read—it's layers upon layers upon layers of bureaucratic form—literary and institutional. As aesthetically off-putting as this style may be, consider that this is not entirely the fault of the justices and judges: the cases arrive in their chambers already dressed up in this bureaucratic aesthetic. The justices have few options but to plunge into and take up the highly bureaucratized schemes and facts that happen to be the subject under constitutional review. Off the cuff opinions are not really an option (they would produce their own legalist disturbances and complexity!). Hence, the Court uploads law as administration into constitutional law and then downloads more of the same. The predictable result (want it or not) is a bureaucratic constitution.

16. (Until it turns to mud).

17. This is arguably one of the drivers of the Weberian nightmare. Max Weber, *Politics as a Vocation*, in *From Max Weber, Essays in Sociology* 77, 128 (Hans Gerth & Charles Mills eds. & trans., Galaxy Books 2009).

18. Caroline Levine, *Forms Whole, Rhythm, Hierarch, Network* 141 (2015).

19. Duncan Kennedy aptly describes these as exemplary of a mode of legal consciousness he calls "the social," and which he details at length. Kennedy, *Three Globalizations, supra* note 9 at 22.

20. John Henry Schlegel, *American Legal Realism and Empirical Social Science* (1995) (showing *inter alia* how and why the projects of the legal realists for empirical social science research on the effects of law came to naught).

21. For example, Annelise Riles provides a sophisticated account of the realist conception of law as a tool and, most interestingly, develops the idea that the tool metaphor became ontologized into an object. Annelise Riles, *A New Agenda for the Cultural Study of Law: Taking on the Technicalities*, 53 *Buff. L. Rev.* 973, 1001–18 (2005) ("In the hands of mid-century Conflicts scholars, I argue, the metaphor—the idea that law was a tool—became, quite literally, a tool of legal knowledge").

22. To appreciate the often underrecognized complexity of (and problems with) the instrumentalist mode of legal reasoning, *see* Robert S. Summers, *Pragmatic Instrumentalism in Twentieth Century American Legal Thought—a Synthesis and Critique of Our Dominant General Theory about Law and Its Use*, 66 *Cornell L. Rev.* 861 (1981).

23. Michael C. Dorf & Charles F. Sabel, *A Constitution of Democratic Experimentalism*, 98 *Colum L. Rev.* 267, 284–85 (1998).

24. On the latter, *see* Pierre Schlag, *Rights in the Postmodern Condition* in Austin Sarat & Thomas R. Kearns, *Legal Rights—Historical and Philosophical Perspectives* (1997) (hereinafter "Rights.")

25. Kennedy, *Three Globalizations, supra* note 9 at 21.

26. *But see*, Kennedy, *Three Globalizations, supra* note 9. There is a parallel process with regard to the *administrative state* and liberal democracy. That is to say that most jurists and legal thinkers, with few exceptions, view the liberal democratic state

and administrative state as compatible insofar as the latter was the legitimate and constitutional creation of the former. This view sometimes occasions what appears to be a non sequitur—that because one state legitimately begotten the other, the two are compatible as a matter of legitimation schemes and governance mechanisms. That simply doesn't follow.

27. Roe v. Wade, 410 U.S. 113 (1973).

28. Griswold v. Connecticut, 381 U.S. 479 (1965).

29. Roe v. Wade, 410 U.S. 113 (1973).

30. Such medical technical issues have reached the Supreme Court a number of times. *See* Madsen v. Women's Health Center, Inc., 512 U.S. 753 (1994); Schenck v. Pro-Choice Network of Western New York, 519 U.S. 357 (1997); Hill v. Colorado, 530 U.S. 703 (2000).

31. Price v. Chicago, 18–1516 (cert. denied) (July 2, 2020).

32. Price v. Chicago, 18–1516 (cert. denied) (July 2, 2020).

33. Morton Horwitz, *The History of the Public/Private Distinction*, 130 *U. Pa. L. Rev.* 1423, 1427 (1982).

34. Just to be clear: the law and economics people would say that it is the concept of "opportunity costs," not "accounting costs," that does the bulk of the work in economic analysis. OK. However, the use of the term "accounting" here is designed to draw attention to a particular aspect of economic analysis: the "willingness to pay" calculations, which are not only crucial to efficiency determinations, but involve a lot of counting and calculation of costs and benefits. Hence the reference to accounting.

35. Ronald J. Pestritto, *The Progressive Origins of the Administrative State: Wilson, Goodnow, and Landis*, 24 *Social Philosophy and Policy* 16 (2007). It would not be until 1984 that Jack Schlegel would announce what would become the slogan of critical legal studies: "Law is Politics." John Henry Schlegel, *Notes Towards an Intimate, Opinionated, and Affectionate History of the Conference on Critical Legal Studies*, 36 *Stan. L. Rev.* 391, 410–11 (1984) (noting that policy is a Trojan horse for politics).

36. Ronald Coase, *The Problem of Social Cost*, 3 *J. L. & Econ*, 1, 2 (1960).

37. For elaboration, *see* Pierre Schlag, *The Problem of Transaction Costs*, 62 *So. Cal. L. Rev.* 1661, 1684 (1989).

38. OIRA requires Cost-Benefit Analysis of administrative regulations. Executive Order 12866 *Regulatory Planning and Review* (58 FR 51735; October 4, 1993). While these analyses are not nothing, they are performed *ceteris paribus* with metrics that are either controversial (e.g., "willingness to pay") or rather vague (e.g., nonquantitative). As for common law courts and constitutional courts, they perform versions of such analyses in ways that are frequently speculative or conjectural.

39. As for efficiency analysis per se, the method was applied with great frequency by legal scholars. It was, however, analytically bereft in a number of ways. Most decisive perhaps was the absence of any method through which to translate the quantitative (generally nonmarginal/indivisible) economic effects of laws into the (marginal) measures of economic costs and benefits—to wit, dollars. For elaboration on the "non-marginal/indivisible" aspects of law, *see* Pierre Schlag, *supra* note 37 at 1669–1671; Pierre Schlag, *Coase Minus the Coase Theorem—Some Problems with Chicago Transaction Cost Analysis*, 99 *Iowa L. Rev.* 175, 202–04 (2013) (hereinafter, Schlag, *Coase Minus*).

40. Richard H. Thaler & Cass R. Sunstein, *Nudge: Improving Decisions about Health, Wealth and Happiness* (2008).

41. "Cognitive infiltration" is a policy proposal propounded by Cass Sunstein and Adrien Vermeule that government infiltrate conspiracy groups to challenge their "crippled epistemology." The infiltrators would either front honestly about their real identities or dissemble. Cass R. Sunstein & Adrian Vermeule, *Conspiracy Theories* 21 (January 15, 2008). Harvard Public Law Working Paper No. 08-03; U. of Chicago, Public Law Working Paper No. 199; University of Chicago Law & Economics, Olin Working Paper No. 387. https://ssrn.com/abstract=1084585 or http://dx.doi.org/10.21 39/ssrn.1084585

42. Of course, if compared to education and empowerment, nudges can easily seem more intrusive and more manipulative. Peter Huang, *Empowering People to Choose Wisely by Democratizing Mindfulness and Thinking Tools* (November 1, 2015). https://ssrn.com/abstract=2639953 or http://dx.doi.org/10.2139/ssrn.2639953

43. *Id.* By this stage, we are deep into the assessment of the desiderata, wants, and needs of private groups in civil society. The administrative state is still run by lawyers but increasingly the latter think and process decisions not just as accountants, but as cognitive therapists. In the book *Nudge* by Richard Thaler and Cass Sunstein, citizens are treated as consumers and government is often cast as a kind of provider. The civil society metaphor of market—of producer and consumer—where it is the interest of the latter that is supposed to be sovereign ("consumer sovereignty") has fully infiltrated analysis. Thaler and Sunstein's vehicle for introducing the concept of nudge is a high school cafeteria with students picking out food. Descriptively—that is, as a description of our polis—Thaler and Sunstein are dead on. Politically, it is of concern: Thaler and Sunstein seem unaware of the implications of the totalizing reach of their own "consumer welfare" approach. That is not to say that nudge is a bad idea (in a welfarist society, nudge is arguably *ceteris paribus*, a good idea.) But notice here the two qualifications: a welfarist society and *ceteris paribus*. For elaboration of these points, *see* Pierre Schlag, *Nudge, Choice Architecture, and Libertarian Paternalism (Review-Essay of Sunstein & Thaler, "Nudge")*, 108 *Mich. L. Rev.* 913 (2010).

44. Ironically, and very much against orthodox Chicago economic analysis of law, this was a crucial point made by Coase in his pathbreaking essay, *The Problem of Social Cost.* Schlag, *Coase Minus, supra* note 39.

45. Pierre Schlag, *The Knowledge Bubble—Something Amiss in Expertopia* in *In Search of Contemporary Legal Thought* (Justin Desautels-Stein and Christopher Tomlins eds., Cambridge University Press 2017); Schlag, *Coase Minus, supra* note 53. Schlag, *supra* note 39.

46. Pierre Schlag, *How to do Things with Hohfeld*, 78 *Law & Contemp. Probs.* 185, 221–22 (on the unbundling of the state by the right).

47. David Foster Wallace, *This is Water* (commencement speech, Kenyon College [2005]), https://www.youtube.com/watch?v=8CrOL-ydFMI

48. Herbert Wechsler, *Towards Neutral Principles of Constitutional Law*, 73 *Harv. L. Rev.* 1 (1959).

49. Felix Cohen, *Transcendental Nonsense and the Functional Approach*, 35 *Colum. L. Rev.* 809 (1935); or, to Posner's Kaldor-Hick's analysis, Richard Posner, *Economic Analysis of Law* (9th ed. 2014).

50. Schlag, *Aesthetics supra* note 9.

51. Ronald Dworkin, *Law's Empire* (1986).

52. Daniel Farber, *Legal Pragmatism and the Constitution*, 72 *Minn. L. Rev.* 1331 (1988).

53. Cass Sunstein, *Incompletely Theorized Agreements*, 108 *Harv. L. Rev.* 1733 (1995).

54. Jack M. Balkin, *Living Originalism* (2011) (living originalism); Richard H. Thaler & Cass R. Sunstein, *Nudge: Improving Decisions about Health, Wealth and Happiness* (2008) (libertarian paternalism).

55. For a prior diagnosis of this state of affairs (i.e., the symbiosis of opposites), see Pierre Schlag, *Normativity and the Politics of Form*, 139 *U. Pa. L. Rev.* 801, 908–09 (1991).

Chapter 4

1. Mark Meckler, *Mick Mulvaney's Handy Guide to Exploiting the Trump Swamp*, New York Times (April 27, 2018).

2. *Compare* David Harvey, *A Brief History of Neoliberalism* (2007) with Wendy Brown, *Undoing the Demos: Neoliberalism's Stealth Revolution* (2015) with Philip Mirowski & Dieter Plewhe, eds., *The Road from Mont Pèlerin: The Making of the Neoliberal Thought Collective* (2015) with Kean Birch, *A Research Agenda for Neoliberalism (2017)*. In an engaging call for papers, Kean Birch and Simon Springer describe aptly the many flavors of neoliberalism:

> Neoliberalism is a ubiquitous concept nowadays, used across numerous disciplines and in the analysis of diverse and varied phenomena. It is conceptualized in different ways as, for example, a geographical process; a form of governmentality; the restoration of elite class power; a political project of institutional change; a set of transformative ideas; a development policy paradigm; an epistemic community or thought collective; and an economic ideology or doctrine.

Kean Birch and Simon Springer, *Peak Neoliberalism? Revisiting and Rethinking the Concept of Neoliberalism*, Ephemera Theory & Politics in Organization (call for papers 2016).

3. A helpful introduction to the different origins and meanings of the term is Daniel Rogers, *The Uses and Abuses of "Neoliberalism,"* Dissent (Winter 2018) https://www.dissentmagazine.org/article/uses-and-abuses-neoliberalism-debate

4. For discussion of this idea and a retort, see Philip Mirowski, *Institute for New Economic Thinking* (2014), https://www.ineteconomics.org/uploads/papers/WP23-Mirowski.pdf

5. Pierre Schlag, *Cannibal Moves: The Metamorphosis of the Legal Distinction* 429, 971–72 (1988).

6. Among some of the best book-length treatments in law we have so far Katerina Pistor, *The Code of Capital: How the Law Creates Wealth and Inequality* (2019): *The Politics of Legality in a Neoliberal Age* (2018); Astra Taylor, *Democracy May Not Exist, but We'll Miss It When It's Gone* (2019); *Neoliberal Legality: Understanding the Role of Law in the Neoliberal Project* (Honor Brabazon, ed.) (2017).

7. Philip Mirowski, *The Neo-liberal Thought Collective*, 17 Renewal: A Journal of Social Democracy, 26–36 (2009).

8. *Nine Lives of Neoliberalism*, Philip Mirowski, Dieter Plehwe and Quinn Slobodian, eds. (2020).

9. *Mutant Neoliberalism Market Rule and Political Rupture*, William Callison and Zachary Manfredi eds. (2019).

10. This point struck me when I read the preface to *the second edition* of the pathbreaking book—and Plehwe and Mirowski's "The Road from Mont Pèlerin: The Making of the Neoliberal Thought Collective," *supra* note 2. In the second preface, the authors write looking back: "A remarkable number of disciplines, notably modern intellectual history, history of economic thought, political science, cultural studies, sociology, and geography, have featured [our] work in their discussions." And in this grouping of disciplines, what is the one discipline that had nothing to contribute?

11. Brabazon, *supra* note 6.

12. Jamie Peck, *Constructions of Neoliberal Reason* (2010) Kindle edition (Loc. 98).

13. Cary Coglianese, Gabriel Scheffler, & Daniel Walters, *Unrules* 73 Stan. L. Rev. 885, 896–903 (2021) (describing how informal *categorical* exceptions from existing regulations serve to negate or reduce regulatory obligations.)

14. *Id.* at 896–908 (describing how informal *case-by-case* exemptions from existing regulations reduce regulatory obligations).

15. Peter Thiel, "Competition Is for Losers" (lecture at Stanford University 2014) https://www.youtube.com/watch?v=3Fx5Q8xGU8k at around 45 seconds.

16. That too is something to be avoided.

17. Robert Knox, *Law, Neoliberalism and the Constitution of Political Subjectivity: The Case of Organised Labour* in *Neoliberal Legality supra* note 6 at 109.

18. On the transnational scene, Quinn Slobodian states:

The core of twentieth-century neoliberal theorizing involves what they called the meta-economic or extra-economic conditions for safeguarding capitalism at the scale of the entire world. I show that the neoliberal project focused on designing institutions—not to liberate markets but to encase them, to inoculate capitalism against the threat of democracy, to create a framework to contain often-irrational human behavior, and to reorder the world after empire as a space of competing states in which borders fulfill a necessary function.

Quinn Slobodian, *Globalists: The End of Empire and the Birth of Neoliberalism* (2020).

19. The failure to appreciate that neoliberalism is not liberalism 2.0 has been long-standing and difficult to set aside.

20. Brabazon, *supra* note 6 at 1.

21. *Id.*

22. Angela P. Harris, Amy Kapczynski, & Noah Katz, "Where Is the Political Economy?" LPE, June 21, 2021, https://lpeproject.org/blog/where-is-the-political-ec onomy/

23. Friedrich Hayek *Law, Legislation and Liberty* (1998) (passim).

24. Michel Foucault, *The Birth of Biopolitics Lectures at the Collège de France 1978–1979* 119–21 (2008) (emphasis added).

25. S. M. Amadae, *Prisoner of Reason Game Theory and the Neoliberal Economy* 17 (2015).

26. *Id.*

27. Marshall Phelps, *How Uber Built Up Its Patent Strength Quickly*, chief executive, April 24, 2018, https://chiefexecutive.net/how-uber-built-up-its-patent-strength-quickly/

28. Hence, by way of example consider a 2015 UK agreement between Uber and its "customers" (customer = driver).

Customer acknowledges and agrees that Customer's provision of Transportation Services to Users creates a legal and direct business relationship between Customer and the User, to which neither Uber nor any of its Affiliates in the Territory is a party. Neither Uber nor any of its Affiliates in the Territory is responsible or liable for the actions or inactions of a User in relation to the activities of Customer, a Driver or any Vehicle. Customer shall have the sole responsibility for any obligations or liabilities to Users or third parties that arise from its provision of Transportation Services. Customer acknowledges and agrees that it and each Driver are solely responsible for taking such precautions as may be reasonable and proper (including maintaining adequate insurance that meets the requirements of all applicable laws) regarding any acts or omissions of a User or third party.

UBER B.V. SERVICES AGREEMENT (Last updated: October 20, 2015), https://s3.amazonaws.com/uber-regulatory-documents/country/united_kingdom/Uber+BV+Driver+Terms+-+UK+Preview.pdf

29. Brown *supra* note 2.

30. Amadae, *supra* note 25.

31. As Philip Mirowski puts it:

Our major theme will be: what holds neoliberals together first and foremost is a set of epistemic commitments, however much it might be ultimately rooted in economics, or politics, or even science. It didn't start out like that; but a half-century of hard work by the neoliberal thought collective has wrought a program that rallies round a specific vision of the role of knowledge in human affairs.

Philip Mirowski, *The Road from Mont Pèlerin: The Making of the Neoliberal Thought Collective*, 417 (2015). *See also*, Philip Mirowski, *Hell Is the Truth Seen Too Late*, 46 boundary 2, 1 (2019).

32. Brown, *supra*, note 2.

33. Pierre Schlag, *The Faculty Workshop*, 60 *Buff. L. Rev.* 807 (2012).

34. For one illuminating empirical exploration, see Cary Coglianese, Gabriel Scheffler, & Daniel E. Walters, *Unrules*, 73 *Stan. L. Rev.* 885 (2021).

35. UBER B.V. SERVICES AGREEMENT Last update: October 20, 2015. https://s3.amazonaws.com/uber-regulatory-documents/country/united_kingdom/Uber+BV+Driver+Terms+-+UK+Preview.pdf

36. As many have recognized, the French expression *"dispositif"* does not translate well into English. Possibilities include "apparatus," "device" "assemblage," and the one used here, "mechanism." None do justice to the French expression.

37. J.L. Austin, *How to Do Things with Words* (2d ed. 1975).

38. This is an economically perverse ideal and like all ideals it is only partially realizeable. Indeed, in an adverse-cooperative relation it is impossible to structure legal *entitlements or disablements* so that they work *only* to the benefit of one party. But this is neither here nor there: even feudalism extends some benefit to the serf. Adverse-cooperative relations implicitly involve some degree of reciprocal dependency.

39. A brilliant exploration of this kind of introjection can be found in Lauren B. Edelman & Mark C. Suchman, *When the "Haves" Hold Court: Speculations on the Organizational Internalization of Law,* 33 *Law & Society Rev.* 941 (1999).

40. As Will Davies puts it, "[T]he central defining characteristic of all neoliberal critique is its hostility to the ambiguity of political discourse, and a commitment to the explicitness and transparency of quantitative, economic indicators, of which the market price system is the model." Davies, *supra* note 26 at 5–6.

41. That drive toward dissipation is a fatal flaw: *the market universalism* of neoliberalism is self-cannibalizing. It destroys the nonmarket institutions, norms, practices, selves, upon which the successful maintenance of markets depend.

42. *See,* e.g., Lawrence Lessig, *America, Compromised* (2018); *See also,* Zephyr Teachout, *Corruption in America: From Benjamin Franklin's Snuff Box to Citizens United* (2014). There is a whole literature that differentiates between structural corruption, institutional corruption, dependence corruption, and so on. For an excellent introduction, see Irma Sandoval-Ballesteros, *From 'Institutional' to 'Structural' Corruption: Rethinking Accountability in a World of Public-Private Partnerships* (December 20, 2013). Available at SSRN, https://ssrn.com/abstract=2370576

43. As Nicolas Perrone aptly summarizes, "Neoliberal reform, in short, redefined the state in market terms ensuring that the remaining public functions are exercised in manners compatible with investor expectations." Nicolas M. Perrone, *Neoliberalism and Economic Sovereignty: Property, Contracts, and Foreign Investment Relations,* in *Neoliberal Legality: Understanding the Role of Law in the Neoliberal Project* 47 (2017).

44. *See* Theodor Adorno & Max Horkheimer, *The Dialectic of Enlightenment* (1947) (for the incipient Frankfurt School critique of the foreboding culture industry).

45. Justice Lewis Powell, "The Powell Memorandum," (1971), http://reclaimdemocracy.org/powell_memo_lewis/

46. It is worth pondering Hayek's words by way of comparison:

The rules of just conduct are thus not concerned with the protection of particular interests, and all pursuit of particular interests must be subject to them. This applies as much to the tasks of government in its capacity as administrator of common means destined for the satisfaction of particular purpose, as to the actions of private persons.

Friedrich Hayek, *Law, Legislation and Liberty* 184 (1993).

47. *See* Brown, *supra* note 2 (*passim*).

48. Pierre Schlag, *The Problem of the Subject*, 69 *Tex. L. Rev.* 1627, 1701 (1991).

49. For an early description of the opportunistic though already successful appropriation of normative language, *see* Pierre Schlag, *Normative and Nowhere to Go*, 43 *Stan L. Rev.* 167 (1990); Pierre Schlag, *Normativity and the Politics of Form*, 139 *U Pa. L. Rev.* 801 (1991); Pierre Schlag, *Values*, 6 *Yale J. L. & Hum.* 219 (1994).

50. *Id.*

51. Michel Foucault, *The Birth of Biopolitics: Lectures at the Collège de France, 1978–79*, 131 (2008).

52. White House, fact sheet, Putting the Public First: Improving Customer Experience and Service Delivery for the American People, https://www.whitehouse.gov /briefing-room/statements-releases/2021/12/13/fact-sheet-putting-the-public-first -improving-customer-experience-and-service-delivery-for-the-american-people/ (December 13, 2021).

53. Amadae *supra* note 25 at 146–47.

54. *Id.*

55. Ronald Coase, *The Problem of Social Cost*, 3 *J. L & Econ* 1 (1960).

56. Moreover, in the complex world of sophisticated business ventures, these "negotiations and renegotiations" occur in a highly segmented and bureaucratized network of lawyers, bankers, investment bankers, accountants, certifying agencies, consultants, and the like. This sort of dispersed decision-making has two major effects: (1) it makes it hard to coordinate; (2) it makes it easy for responsibility to be partitioned and thus avoid accountability.

57. At the extreme, Trump's demotion of policy to transactional dealing seems to be enacting a particularly extreme form of neoliberalism. In its extremism, such a neoliberalism eviscerates the structures of the liberal democratic state in favor of oligarchy and transactional government—rent-seeking unbound. *See*, Lawrence Summers, *Trump's Carrier Deal Could Permanently Damage American Capitalism, Washington Post* (December 2, 2016), https://www.washingtonpost.com/news/wonk /wp/2016/12/02/why-trumps-carrier-deal-is-bad-for-america/?utm_term=.381dace b7550

58. Michel Foucault, *The Birth of Biopolitics: Lectures at the Collège de France 1978–1979*, 243–60 (2008) (discussing Gary Becker's work as emblematic of American neoliberalism).

59. Pierre Schlag, *The Problem of Transaction Costs*, 62 *S. Cal. L. Rev.* 1661 (1989).

60. Pierre Schlag, *An Appreciative Comment on the Problem of Social Cost—a View from the Left* [1986] *Wis. L. Rev.* 919, 949.

61. Nicholas Kaldor, *Welfare Propositions of Economics and Interpersonal Comparisons of Utility*, 49 *Econ J.* 549 (1939).

62. Philip Mirowski, *supra* note 31.

63. William Davies, *The Limits of Neoliberalism: Authority, Sovereignty and the Logic of Competition (Theory, Culture & Society)* (xiv). London: SAGE. Kindle Edition.

64. Michael Taylor, *Rationality and the Ideology of Disconnection* (2006).

65. Karl Marx & Friedrich Engels, *Capital: A Critique of Political Economy* (1887)

(volume 1 outlines his early conceptualization of the commodity and commodity fetishism, expanded upon throughout the text).

66. Pierre Schlag, *Normativity and the Politics of Form*, 139 *U. Pa. L. Rev.* 801, 906–8 (1991).

67. Schlag, *supra* note 49 at 184–86.

68. Eric Schmitt, *Iraq-Bound Troops Confront Rumsfeld over Lack of Armor*, New *York Times* (December 8, 2004) https://www.nytimes.com/2004/12/08/international /middleeast/iraqbound-troops-confront-rumsfeld-over-lack-of.html

69. Oliver Wendell Holmes, *The Path of the Law*, 10 *Harv. L. Rev.* 457 (1897).

70. Franz Neumann, *Behemoth: The Structure and Practice of National Socialism, 1933–1944* (2009).

71. Wolfgang Streeck, *How Will Capitalism End?* 34 (2017).

72. *See*, e.g., Brown, *supra* note 2 at 122–36.

73. Dep't. of Justice, *Investigation of the Ferguson Police Department* 2–4 (March 4, 2015) (police and municipal court practices of revenue generation) https://www.just ice.gov/sites/default/files/opa/press-releases/attachments/2015/03/04/ferguson_pol ice_department_report_1.pdf

Chapter 5

1. Notice that in one sense, this challenge is no more insuperable than the idea of separation of powers (where we also have uncertainty). The great difference, of course, is that we know about and are accustomed to the separation of powers, whereas the identity and dissonant interactions of the three conflicting iterations described here are still largely under the radar.

2. Pierre Schlag, *The Enchantment of Reason* (1998).

3. *See* Chapters Two and Three, *supra*.

4. The kind of mind described here has more in common with Steven D. Smith's insightful essay, "Law without Mind," than the more conventional "theory of mind" elaborated in psychology. Steven D. Smith, *Law without Mind*, 88 *Mich. L. Rev.* 104 (1989).

5. Some commentators have observed, and correctly so, that for all of Trump's extra- or unconstitutional excesses and possible criminal activity, there has been a serious "rule of law" pushback. As well as some heroes. True. But, without in any way trivializing this pushback, and the heroism and sacrifice involved, it is nonetheless all too easy (too journalistic?) for third parties to declare (from a safe distance) that these efforts have a generalized determinative significance.

6. As Robert Cover noted, there is "a persistent chasm between thought and action." Robert M. Cover, *Violence and the Word*, 95 *Yale L. J.* 1601, 1610–11 (1986).

7. Richard A. Posner, *The State of Legal Scholarship Today: A Comment on Schlag*, 97 *Geo. L. J.* 845, 851–52 (2008).

8. For *three different* accounts of legal mind, *see* Steven D. Smith, *Law without Mind*, 88 *Mich. L. Rev.* 104 (1989), and Pierre Schlag, *The Problem of the Subject*, 69 *Tex. L. Rev.*1627 (1991); Christopher Tomlins, *The Presence and Absence of Legal Mind: A Commentary on Duncan Kennedy's "Three Globalizations of Law and Legal Thought, 1850–2000"* 78 *Law & Cont. Probs.* 1 (2015).

9. Robin West, *Teaching Law: Justice, Politics, and the Demands of Professionalism* 29–30 (2014).

10. Pierre Schlag, *Normative and Nowhere to Go*, 43 *Stan. L. Rev.* 167, 185 (1990).

11. In this condition, values have been stripped of their moral and political content. Pierre Schlag, *Values*, 6 *Yale J. L. & Hum.* 219 (1994).

12. Pierre Schlag, *Normativity and the Politics of Form*, 139 *U. Pa. L. Rev.* 801, 931–32 (1991).

13. Robin West, *Normative Jurisprudence—An Introduction* (2011).

14. Pierre Schlag, *A Brief Survey of Deconstruction* 27 *Cardozo L. Rev.* 741 (2005).

15. Judith N. Shklar, *Legalism: Law, Morals, and Political Trials* 9–10 (2012).

16. The legalism Shklar described was one that accorded well with liberal democracy—as indeed a number of critical legal studies thinkers pointed out in their accounts of liberal legalism. Karl E. Klare, *Judicial Deradicalization of the Wagner Act and the Origins of Modern Legal Consciousness* 1937–1941, 62 *Minn. L. Rev.* 265, 276–77 (1978).

17. *See* John Gardner, *The Twilight of Legality*, Oxford Legal Studies Research Paper No. 4/2018 (2017), *available at* SSRN: https://ssrn.com/abstract=3109517 or http://dx .doi.org/10.2139/ssrn.3109517

18. It might seem that there is a powerful counter-example to this point and that is "the oral argument" where judges question the appellate advocates on what effect a ruling along these lines will have on these other (earlier or later) cases over here. The U.S. Supreme Court justices do this routinely. The irony (and this is what falsifies the counter-example) is that they are not at all looking at the micro-issues before them in terms of macro implications or consequences. They are instead looking at how this micro will have effects and implications for these other selected micros. It's still micro all the way across.

19. Felix Cohen, *Transcendental Nonsense and the Functional Approach*, 35 *Colum. L. Rev.* 809, 811–12 (1935).

20. *Tauza v. Susquehanna Coal Co.*, 115 N.E. 915, 91 (N.Y. 1917) 8 (emphasis added).

21. Pierre Schlag, *How to Do Things with Hohfeld*, 78 *Law & Contemp. Probs.* 185 (2015).

22. Pierre Schlag, *The Aesthetics of American Law*, 115 *Harvard L. Rev.* 1047 (2002).

23. This is a radicalization of Arthur Corbin's earlier insights into the polysemy of the term "contract." Arthur Corbin, *Book Review*, 29 *Yale L. J.* 942, 943 (1920) (noting that the popular notion of contracts is broad enough to include the acts of the parties, the paper document, and the legal relations brought into being).

24. For reasons similar to those articulated in Walter Benjamin, *The Critique of Violence* in *On Violence* (Bruce B. Lawrence & Aisha Karim, eds. 2020).

Chapter 6

1. The classic work is Theodor Adorno et al., *The Authoritarian Personality* (2019).

2. Daniel Ziblatt & Steven Levitsky, *How Democracies Die* (2018).

3. The selective appropriation of leftist agendas is classic fascist fare. For instance, the fascist Italian Labour Charter provided as follows:

> The fascist state has the following aims: first, the perfection of accident insurance; second, the improvement and extension of maternity insurance; third, insurance against occupational illness and tuberculosis as an introduction to a system of general health insurance; fourth, the improvement of insurance against involuntary unemployment, and, fifth, the adoption of special forms of endowment insurance for young workers.

Italian Labour Charter of April 27, 1927, Art. 27 (as quoted in Julius Stone, *Theories of Law and Justice in Fascist Italy*, 1 *Mod. L. Rev.* 177, 183 [1937]).

Interwar fascists and Nazis were quite unabashed about their appropriation of leftist and socialist programs: By way of example, Robert Brassilach, a French fascist and collaborator, notes with approval the Belgian Rexist Leon Degrelle rejoicing in his party's appropriation of the communist's thunder and support. Robert Brassilach, *Je Suis Partout 1936: Recueil de textes de Robert Brasillach* 123–127 (2015).

4. Matthew Nussbaum, *Trump at Debate: Minorities in Cities Are "Living in Hell,"* *Politico* (September 26, 2016), http://www.politico.com/story/2016/09/trump-minorities-living-in-hell-228726; *see also* Abby Phillip & Mike DeBonis, *Without Evidence, Trump Tells Lawmakers 3 million to 5 million Illegal Ballots Cost Him the Popular Vote,* *Washington Post* (June 23, 2017), https://www.washingtonpost.com/news/post-politics/wp/2017/01/23/at-white-house-trump-tells-congressional-leaders-3-5-million-illegal-ballots-cost-him-the-popular-vote/

5. Umberto Eco, *Ur-Fascism*, *New York Review of Books* (1995).

6. Eco's succinct description of Italian fascism is worth the read:

> [Italian] Fascism was a fuzzy totalitarianism, a collage of different philosophical and political ideas, a beehive of contradictions. Can one conceive of a truly totalitarian movement that was able to combine monarchy with revolution, the Royal Army with Mussolini's personal milizia, the grant of privileges to the Church with state education extolling violence, absolute state control with a free market? The Fascist Party was born boasting that it brought a revolutionary new order; but it was financed by the most conservative among the landowners who expected from it a counter-revolution. At its beginning fascism was republican. Yet it survived for twenty years proclaiming its loyalty to the royal family, while the Duce (the unchallenged Maximal Leader) was arm-in-arm with the King, to whom he also offered the title of Emperor. But when the King fired Mussolini in 1943, the party reappeared two months later, with German support, under the standard of a "social" republic, recycling its old revolutionary script, now enriched with almost Jacobin overtones.

7. Eco, *supra* note 6.

8. This view also echoes Roger Griffin's account of fascism as myth:

[I]t is just as misguided to seek to establish that there is a common denominator between all forms of fascism at the level of articulated ideas as to deny fascism any coherent ideological content. The coherence exists not at the surface level of specific, verbalized "ideas," but at the structural level of the core myth which underlies them, serving as a matrix which determines which types of thought are selected in national cultures and how they are arranged into a political ideology, whether at the level of theory, policies, propaganda, culture, or of semiotic "behaviour," such as the use of symbols or the enactment of ritual. The term myth here draws attention, . . . to its power to unleash strong affective energies through the evocative force of the image or vision of reality it contains for those susceptible to it. This generic mythic image laden with potential mobilizing, and even mass-mobilizing, force, may, like any psychological matrix or archetype (such as the Hero or Paradise), take on a wide variety of surface formulations according to the particular cultural and historical context in which it is expressed.

See also Roger Griffin, *the Nature of Fascism* 3 (2009).

9. *Id.* at 1–12; E. Eugen Weber, *Varieties of Fascism* 13–43 (1982).

10. Jason Stanley, *How Fascism Works—The Politics of Us and Them* (2018).

11. Corey Robin, *The Reactionary Mind: Conservatism from Edmund Burke to Donald Trump* (2017).

12. This is a virtually standard manifestation of scapegoat theory applied to the level of national politics. Rene Girard, *The Scapegoat* (1989).

13. Roger Griffin, *Fascism* 4 (2009).

14. Eco, *supra*, note 6. For Eco, the traditionalism of fascism extends across national borders to the embrace of ancient traditions from foreign civilizations. For Eco, this eclecticism is linked to the syncretic character of fascism.

15. Alexander Reid Ross, *Against the Fascist Creep* 5 (2017).

16. Eco, *supra* note 6. As Eco notes, fascists view the Age of Reason, the Enlightenment, "as the beginning of modern depravity."

17. As the proto-fascist Julius Evola put it:

From the point of view of principle, every socialist and democratic ideology was surpassed in Fascist political doctrine. The state was recognised as possessing pre-eminence in respect to people and nation, that is, the dignity of a single superior power through which the nation acquires a real self-awareness, possesses a form and a will, and participates in a supernatural order. Mussolini could affirm (1924): "Without the State there is no nation. There are merely human aggregations subject to all the disintegrations which history may inflict upon them', and 'The nation does not beget the State [. . .] On the contrary, the nation is created by the State, which gives the people [. . .] the will, and thereby an effective existence." The formula "The people is the body of the state and the state is the spirit of the people" (1934), if adequately interpreted, brings us back to the Classical idea of a dynamic and creative relationship between "form" and "matter" (body).

See also Julius Evola, *Fascism Viewed from the Right* 32 (2013) (footnotes omitted).

18. Carl Schmitt, *Political Theology* (2006).

19. Eco, *supra* note 6.

20. Leon Degrelle as quoted in Weber, *supra* note 9 at 29.

21. William E. Connolly, *Aspirational Fascism: The Struggle for Multifaceted Democracy under Trumpism* 14 (2017) (for a perceptive linking of the "weak" intellectual tendencies against the "strong" physical tendencies in Trump-speak).

22. Weber, *supra*, note 9 at 29.

23. Eco, *supra* note 6.

24. Girard, *supra* note 12.

25. According to Julius Evola, the proto-fascist, fascism aspired to "an existence that was anti-bourgeois, combative and even dangerous. Julius Evola, *Fascism Viewed from the Right* 36 (2013).

26. Julius Evola, *Revolt against the Modern World* (1995).

27. Eco, *supra* note 6.

28. Susan Sontag, *Fascinating Fascism, New York Review of Books* (1975).

29. William E. Connolly, *Aspirational Fascism: The Struggle for Multifaceted Democracy under Trumpism* 48–55 (2017).

30. *Final Entries, 1945: The Diaries of Joseph Goebbels* (Hugh Trevor-Roper, ed., 1978).

31. Walter Benjamin's famous description of fascism as the aestheticization of politics:

> The growing proletarianization of modern man and the increasing formation of masses are two aspects of the same process. Fascism attempts to organize the newly created proletarian masses without affecting the property structure which the masses strive to eliminate. Fascism sees its salvation in giving these masses not their right, but instead a chance to express themselves. The masses have a right to change property relations; Fascism seeks to give them an expression while preserving property. The logical result of Fascism is the introduction of aesthetics into political life. The violation of the masses, whom Fascism, with its Führer cult, forces to their knees, has its counterpart in the violation of an apparatus which is pressed into the production of ritual values.

Walter Benjamin, *The Work of Art in the Age of Mechanical Reproduction* (1936).

32. Sontag, *supra* note 28.

Chapter 7

1. Pierre Schlag, *Coase Minus the Coase Theorem—Some Problems with Chicago Transaction Cost Analysis* 99 *Iowa L. J.* 175 (2013).

2. Immanuel Kant, *An Answer to the Question: What Is Enlightenment?* in *What Is Enlightenment? Eighteenth-Century Answers and Twentieth-Century Questions* 58 (ed. James Schmidt 1996).

3. H. L. A. Hart, in following Kelsen, provides perhaps the most well-known *formalization* of this point in the idea of "secondary rules." H. L. A. Hart, *The Concept of Law* 109–14 (1961).

4. It is taken from Pierre Schlag, *Normativity and the Politics of Form*, 139 *U. Pa L. Rev.* 801, 805–806 (1991).

5. Pierre Schlag, *America the Young? (Full-On Decadence), Brazen and Tenured— Law, Politics, Nature, and Culture* (October 3, 2011), https://brazenandtenured.com /2011/10/03/america-the-young/. *See also* Jack Balkin, *Constitutional Crisis and Constitutional Rot* 77 *Md. L. Rev.* 147 (2017).

6. One answer: Perhaps we have learned our lesson?

7. McCulloch v. Maryland, 17 U.S. (4 Wheat.) 316 (1819).

8. McCulloch v. Maryland, 17 U.S. (4 Wheat.) 316 (1819).

9. Duncan Kennedy, *The Hermeneutics of Suspicion*, 25 *Law & Critique* 109–124 (2014).

10. Stephen M. Griffin, *Broken Trust: Dysfunctional Government and Constitutional Reform* (2015).

11. Balkin, *supra* note 6.

12. *See* Donald A. Schon, *Generative Metaphor: A Perspective on Problem-Setting in Social Policy*, in Andrew Ortony, *Metaphor and Thoughts* 149 (1993).

13. *Id.*

Coda

1. James Baldwin, *As Much Truth as One Can Bear*, *N. Y. Times Book Review*, January 14, 1962 at 1.

Notes on Method

1. This is a challenge for anyone who wishes to "think" the state. As Pierre Bourdieu says, "I insisted on the fact that our thinking, the very structures of consciousness by which we construct the social world and the particular object that is the state, are very likely the product of the state." Pierre Bourdieu, *On the State* (3). Hoboken, N.J.: Wiley & Sons. Kindle edition.

2. *Id.* At 9.

3. I mean "governance mechanisms" in a sense very different from the association of "governance" with neoliberalism. *See*, e.g., Wendy Brown, *Undoing the Demos: Neoliberalism's Stealth Revolution* 126–31 (2015). My use is much more capacious— and owes much to the law world, where "governance" arguably serves as a generously ecumenical term. "Governance mechanisms" could thus be likened to "*dispositifs*" or "apparatus" or "technique." In law, the challenge is to articulate what law does and means independently of what the law says it does and means.

4. Bourdieu, *supra* note 1 at 357–58.

5. Michel Foucault, *The History of Sexuality, Volume I: An Introduction* 92–93 (1978).

6. As Duncan Kennedy states, "What is problematic here is that Foucault's critique of the fetishizing of sovereignty has led him to picture law as 'only the terminal form' or 'crystallization' of processes of power that take place at a distance from legal institutions." Duncan Kennedy, *The Stakes of Law, or Hale and Foucault*, 15 *Legal Studies Forum* 358 (1991).

7. Bourdieu, *supra* note 1.

8. As Duncan Kennedy puts it:

Foucault doesn't seem to see lawmaking (or judging) as a "praxis" in its own right. Because it is a praxis in its own right, it adds or subtracts something. This happens in part through the deployment of power inside lawmaking institutions. We need to bring Foucault's methodology into the courthouse, so to speak, rather than checking it before we go through the metal-detector. . . . Again, in fairness to Foucault, his purpose in speaking of "formulation," "crystallization," "instruments," and "agents" of solutions worked out elsewhere is to combat the notion that the content of law flows in a necessary way from the combination of regime-defining abstract premises and technical legal reasoning. But in rejecting this notion (easier to do in the United States than in Europe), there is no need to go to the opposite extreme of reducing law to a reflection.

Id. at 359–60.

9. Pierre Schlag, *The Knowledge Bubble: Something Amiss in Expertopia* in Justin Desautels-Stein & Chris Tomlins, *Searching for Contemporary Legal Thought* 438 (2017).

10. Max Weber, *Economy and Society Vol. II* 956–58 (1978).

INDEX